Mysticism and Social Change

Martin Luther King, Jr. Memorial Studies in Religion, Culture, and Social Development

Mozella G. Mitchell
General Editor

Vol. 2

PETER LANG
New York • San Francisco • Bern
Frankfurt am Main • Berlin • Wien • Paris

Alton B. Pollard, III

Mysticism and Social Change

The Social Witness of Howard Thurman

PETER LANG
New York • San Francisco • Bern
Frankfurt am Main • Berlin • Wien • Paris

Library of Congress Cataloging-in-Publication Data

Pollard, Alton B.
    Mysticism and social change : the social witness
of Howard Thurman / Alton B. Pollard III.
      p. cm. — (Martin Luther King, Jr. memorial
studies in religion, culture, and social development ;
vol. 2)
    Includes bibliographical references.
    1. Thurman, Howard, 1900-1981—Contributions
in mysticism.   2. Mysticism—History—20th century.
3. Sociology, Christian—History—20th century.
I. Title. II. Series.
BV5075.P65 1992 248.2'2'092—dc20   91-35655
ISBN 0-8204-1612-6   CIP
ISBN 0-8204-1981-8 (paperback)
ISSN 1052-181X

Die Deutsche Bibliothek-CIP-Einheitsaufnahme

Pollard, Alton B.:
Mysticism and social change : the social witness of
Howard Thurman / Alton B. Pollard, III.—New York;
Berlin; Bern; Frankfurt/M.; Paris; Wien: Lang, 1992
    (Martin Luther King, Jr. memorial studies in
religion, culture, and social development ; Vol. 2)
    ISBN 0-8204-1612-6
NE: GT

Cover Design by Geraldine Spellissy.

The paper in this book meets the guidelines for permanence and
durability of the Committee on Production Guidelines for
Book Longevity of the Council on Library Resources.

© Peter Lang Publishing, Inc., New York 1992

Printed in the United States of America.

TO JESSICA, BROOKS, AND ASHA

Table of Contents

Acknowledgments

The year was 1975, and I was a student at Fisk University in Nashville, Tennessee, when my life was fatefully and dramatically changed. C. Eric Lincoln, professor, mentor and friend, who was then chairman of the department of religious and philosophical studies excited my intellectual curiosity, and has since continued to challenge me in a way that few others have. Edwin Sanders, another outstanding member of the faculty, introduced me to Howard Thurman — and a galaxy of brilliant African American minds — through *Jesus and the Disinherited*. So, too, was I challenged by Roosevelt Hughes, whose commitment to engaging the deeper matters of life proved contagious. I am most grateful, however, to one Jessica Juana Bryant, whose love and spirit entranced me and has since sustained me.

There are others to whom I owe a debt of thanks. During the years this study was in progress Mary R. Sawyer of Iowa State University, Joel Martin of Franklin and Marshall College, Cheryl J. Sanders of Howard University School of Divinity, and Jon Michael Spencer of Bowling Green State University proved to be "friends indeed" through their constant encouragement and support. Charlotte Carlton of Worcester, Massachusetts, Paula J. Waters of Boston, Massachusetts, and Lulu and Prezell Robinson of Raleigh, North Carolina always opened their hearts and homes. Fruitful beyond measure were the hours spent with my good friend and comrade John Mendez of the Emmanuel Baptist Church here in Winston-Salem, North Carolina.

I especially wish to express my indebtedness to Mrs. Sue Bailey Thurman, the Howard Thurman Educational Trust, and the members of the Fellowship Church without whose cooperation this work could not have been completed. Appreciation is also due to series editor Mozella Mitchell and Peter Lang Publishing for their enthusiastic embracing of my manuscript. A note of thanks must also go to my colleagues in the religion department at Wake Forest

University, who have extended me every courtesy while completing the manuscript.

There have been many people, Charles H. Long of Syracuse University, Edward Tiryakian of Duke University, the growing cadre of Thurman scholars, and others too numerous to mention, who provided me with insightful commentary during the writing of this book. My parents have always been there for me: Alton B. Pollard, Jr. and Lena L. Pollard, and also my mother-in-law Jessie M. Bryant. Finally, I record the words of my son who some years ago, at the discerning age of three, was heard to tell his grandfather that he loved "God and Howard Thurman!" Through it all, my family has patiently and faithfully persevered.

Search me, O God, and know my heart;
Test me and know my thoughts.
See if there is any wicked way in me,
And lead me in the way everlasting

Psalm 139:23-24

While there is a lower class I am in it.
While there is a criminal element I am of it.
While there is a man in jail I am not free.

Eugene Debs

We have lost our fear of our brothers and are
no longer ashamed of ourselves, of who and what
we are — Let us now go forth to save the land
of our birth from the plague that first drove
us into the "will to quarantine" and to separate
ourselves behind self-imposed walls. For this is
why we were born...

Howard Thurman

Howard Thurman 1900-1981

Introduction

Mysticism as Activism

This work grew out of a deeply felt need to examine religion from the "underside" of American society and culture, focusing on the life and work of the gifted African American mystic, Howard Thurman. Thurman, a grandson of slaves, has long been recognized as a profound and sensitive interpreter of the religious journey.[1] Considerably less attention has been given, however, to his thinking about and, indeed, involvement in social change activity. The intent here is to explore and delineate Thurman's role as an actor and agent for change in twentieth century America. This process will be guided in part by the conviction that mystic verities — for Thurman as well as others — can make a radical and enabling difference in behalf of human community.

Mystic-Activism

As a point of departure, I am employing the phrase "mystic-activism" as descriptive of Thurman's involvements. Such a designation, it will be argued, more accurately focuses attention on the real potential of mysticism as a discomforting yet compelling and principled call to action. Briefly defined, the mystic is one who believes that she or he has experienced a special angle of perception or encounter with ultimacy (however construed), which encounter departs from normative social constructions of what is "real."[2] Mystic-activism, therefore, is a praxis-orientation to the world which relies but in part — albeit considerable part — on the political and intellectual arguments and dictates of society; the more demanding motive is located in the obligation engendered by spiritual experience. From our purview, Thurman is an exemplary representative of that form of modern mysticism which builds on and goes beyond social activism as conventionally understood.

As a sociologist of religion, I am especially interested to know how the social-sciences have understood the relation between vital religious experience and social change.[3] Popular in the literature are examinations of the so-called "new religious movements" of anti-colonial Africa, Oceania, Asia and elsewhere.[4] Many if not most of these movements have benefited, at least in their early history, from a modicum of messianic or prophetic leadership. In the United States, one need but recall the names of Malcolm X, Fannie Lou Hamer, and Martin Luther King, Jr. as prominent recent examples of social transformation issuing from the religious experiences and ideas of an exploited people.

The notion of interplay between religious experience and social change is thus not uncommon. In many ways, however, Thurman as a mystic actor represents an unfamiliar type in the topography of activism. He does not readily adhere to established academic assessments of mystical activity or to models of religiously-promoted social change. A mystic, he actively engages the world and effects an impact; nonetheless, he does not (ambitiously) endeavor to lead the masses. As Thurman scholar Luther Smith has accurately observed, "Thurman's primary identity was that of a mystic; a mystic who recognized the necessity of social activism for enabling and responding to religious experience."[5]

My analysis takes seriously Thurman's radical understanding of mysticism as personally transforming and socially transformative. First, presenting a descriptive and interpretive profile of Thurman, I will situate his work in the religious and social dynamics of early to mid-twentieth century America, and then move on to more specifically investigate both the configuration and implications of his activity as change agent.

The Question of Significance

As has already been stated, the significant objective of this study is to make explicit the role of Thurman as mystic-activist. Accordingly, for those unacquainted with his life and work, some brief introductory remarks are in order.

Thurman was born and raised at the turn of the century (1900) in segregated Daytona, Florida. His ministerial career formally began in Oberlin, Ohio, where from 1926-28 he pastored a small

African American baptist congregation. He lost little time in attracting attention with expansive sermons which were given to socially unitive and theologically universal themes. From 1932-44, as the Dean of Rankin Chapel and Professor of Theology at Howard University, he disturbed ecclesiastical traditionalists by utilizing what were then considered radical liturgical forms (such as interpretive dance and drama) to enhance worship. In 1953, he became the first African American dean at a major white university, the Dean of Marsh Chapel and Professor of Spiritual Resources and Disciplines at Boston University. During this same period (1961) he formed the Howard Thurman Educational Trust, which disburses funds for various humanitarian endeavors, most notably scholarships to African American college students in the South. Prominent among his many involvements, however, was the San Francisco based church which he cofounded and copastored from 1944-53 — The Church for the Fellowship of all Peoples (Fellowship Church) — heralded as the first authentically inclusive model of institutional religion in the United States.

Thurman's message and activity has been gaining in interest among scholars as of late, particularly in the African American community. Yet and still, it remains commonplace to hear that his stance has little or no real application as concerns social activism. Thurman is credited with having impacted disparate lives, to be sure, but seldom viewed as a focal force serving to promote creative and effective means to societal transformation. Unfortunately, less than critical support for this sentiment is also found in the social sciences, particularly the sociology of religion. An overview of the literature there not only reveals a dearth of investigation but strong disinterest in the relationship between modern forms of mysticism and social change among America's marginalized. Under these less than favorable conditions, the total absence of reference to Thurman hardly comes as a surprise.

The bypassing of mysticism as socially/sociologically significant is attributable to a complex of largely unscrutinized factors. To begin with, there exists in American sociological circles a considerable intellectual parochialism and prejudice toward anything resembling "mysticism," if the preponderance of reductionist studies is to be taken seriously. By reductionism, I am referring of course to the pan-scientific tendency to define religion and its cognates, mysticism included, as something other than itself. So stated, to dismiss mysticism *a priori* as little more than a reaction to social phenomena — and a most unproductive reaction at that — is to synonymously waive the possibility, however serendipitous, of investigating mysticism as a subject meritorious in its own right. It goes without saying that such a stereotypical view impedes any effort to study Thurman.

The unwillingness of the academic community to take seriously mystic-material conjunctions is exacerbated by the almost complete lack of exposure that students in both religious studies and the social sciences have had to Thurman. Interestingly, academic interests and preparation seldom seem to warrant acquiring familiarity with his thought and praxis. In my view, this failure to consider the contributions of Thurman to American society and culture consistently coalesces with the broader dismissal — conscious and/or otherwise — of African America's rich contributions to the national life.

Not surprisingly, one of the most persistent obstacles to inquiry into Thurman has been the over-mystification of his personality, especially his oratorical abilities. Over the years, he has been the deliberate inspirational focus of studies by myriad individuals seeking to understand his message and ministry. As vital and beneficial as these investigations are, however, they have been limited to select areas of inquiry — primarily homiletics, theology, and biography. Only now are more diversified, interdisciplinary approaches emerging in the effort to more adequately assess Thurman's contributions to the social sphere.

The Methods of Inquiry

Thurman never provided a systematic statement on his method of social transformation; such was not his intent. The main of my considerations, therefore, will be based upon a vigorous conceptualization of his major motifs and involvements. Three mutually beneficial modes of analysis are employed in this effort. These include perspectives taken for the most part from sociology, phenomenology, and history.

Even though the concerns of Thurman were universal in thrust, his work cannot be understood in isolation from those social experiences that help account for his choices and his thoughts. In order to more accurately assess his import, therefore, elucidation of the socio-historical context in which he lived and moved is necessary. The method of contextualization adopted in these pages basically adheres to what sociologist Lewis A. Coser has described as the "social ecology of sociological ideas."[6] This thematic appropriation from the sociology of knowledge focuses upon the historical "background" of sociological masters and their respective theories, and also discloses the social and historical source of their ideas. The distinctive appeal of this approach, in my estimation, is its recognition of the multi-faceted influence of social environment on the sociological thinker. In terms of our investigation of Thurman, one need but substitute the phrase "religious thinker" for that of "sociological thinker."

Situating Thurman in this manner will go a long way toward explaining the focus of his attentions, especially his social change activity. Let us take, as an example, the racial discrimination and depreciation Thurman was subjected to as an African American youth growing up in segregated turn-of-the-century Florida. One learns from his autobiography that these conditions were mitigated against by the steadying and self-respectful examples of both mother and grandmother. As a result of the intimate influence of family, the reality of Thurman's marginality in the larger social structure was largely negated, providing a particular texture consistently mirrored in his life work.

Similarly, Thurman's cofounding of the Fellowship Church in San Francisco during the 1940's, when viewed against the backdrop of World War II democracy, portentous civil rights stirrings, and the demographic pluralism of the Bay area, can scarcely be called fortuitous. Let it be noted, however, that these illustrations should not be construed to mean there is a simple or direct one to one correlation between the thought and work of Thurman and the social climate in which he lived. The task of elucidating the specific cast of Thurman's work is far too involved to make such a facile claim.

I have already remarked on the refusal of American sociology to consider the possibility of a salient and searching social component to mysticism. The shortcomings of this stance are rather obvious, say, when viewed against the backdrop of Thurman's specific organizational activities. In particular, the work of Fellowship Church merits examination. The church's founding and expressed purpose, as well as its membership demographics, organizational structure, and relation to the larger ecclesiastical and social community serve as a potent institutional paradigm for Thurman's efforts in behalf of social change.

As of this writing, no study has attempted to situate Thurman's work in the larger sphere of African American activism. As one grounded in and shaped by the vicissitudinous struggles of African America, Thurman offers a perspective on the global phenomenon of religiously-related social change among oppressed and exploited peoples that is at once accordant and distinctive. The capacity of African Americans to decry the debasements of larger society through a plethora of means — often discernibly religious in promotion, both violent and non-violent in expression — is historic, deep-rooted and not without considerable documenta-tion.[7]

So, too, it is a well-known fact that the condition of struggle is not restricted to the North American context, but has numerous counterparts wherever situations of cross-cultural contact — that is, Western forms of conquest and domination — have occurred in the modern world. A canvassing of the literature in this area reveals a strong bond of commonality among these seemingly disparate movements, not infrequently reflected in their mystic-like envisagement or cognition of a regenerate and reordered society, where the value of all human life and the actualizing of human potential are ascendent. Thus, at least in their initial stages, a holistic sense of recreation and affirmation with respect to self, community, and culture is often found to inform and permeate movements in the "Two-Thirds World."[8]

Of course, few of the leaders of these movements qualify as mystics in conventional Western terms. Indeed, strictly speaking, it appears to be the case that scarce are the number of mystics identi-fiable at any level of social reform. And yet, despite the seeming contradiction presented by mystic forms of activism in the modern (and not simply modernizing) world, the ideal-typical characteriza-tions of the prophetic or charismatic leader and the mystic do in fact intersect.[9] Sociologist Andrew Greeley, in a somewhat uneven but inviting discussion of what he identifies as "political mysticism," describes the social potential of the modern mystic in the following manner:

> It is but one step from seeing a vision of unity and love to reaching the conclusion that unity and love ought to be realized in the everyday world. If the everyday world is disorganized and evil enough, one can take the next short step and conclude that indeed the unity and love one has perceived in a mystical interlude *will* be realized. And it is yet another short step to decide that if the world will not cooperate in the implementation of one's mystical vision, then one will rally a band of saints to impose that vision on the world whether it wants to or not. The [mystic] ... can be an extremely dangerous fellow...[10]

Greeley's analysis poses a number of problems, not least of which is his weighty reliance upon examples from the 16th century — to wit, mystics Thomas Muntzer and John of Leyden both of whom, we might add, he refers to as "madmen." Neither can rightfully be compared to Thurman in terms of outlook, temperament, geography or periodicity. Yet Greeley's discussion, which follows the significant historical studies of Norman Cohn[11] and Steven Ozment,[12] does serve as a springboard to further exploration. As I hope to make clear, Thurman more than verifies Greeley's thesis, albeit his mysticism is doubtless of the more rational variety.

I not only seek to define Thurman's involvement in the social arena but to retain its spirit as well. For this reason, I have adopted the phrase "social regeneration," which type of mystic action discloses an ethical program working on three levels — synchronizing intra-individual (personal), inter-individual (communal) and inter-group (societal) orderliness. In Thurman's case, social regeneration denotes a holistic process that is generally critical of church and society, but not in a fundamentally hostile or negating sense. The disturbing upshot is this: the impetus (if not onus) for social regeneration lies not so much in social structures as the transformation of individuals, who alone are capable of generating a force fully vibrant and sufficient to break through oppressive structures. Social regeneration is increasingly effected as enough individuals experience this transforming "sense of wholeness" or ethical orderliness and will to implement its verity in society. The aim of social regeneration, in other words, is not to perpetuate conflict in society simply because or whenever there is no abiding evidence of hope, but in order to facilitate and increase rapprochement between individuals and social groupings. This is the *sine qua non* for Thurman's advancement of the concept of "community."

Thus far, the preponderance of my attention has been devoted to sociological and historical parameters. Clearly, these are not the only factors that account for the specific cast of Thurman's work. In particular, there is the determinant which counts as the distinctively religious/spiritual aspect of existence, both in terms of the practical and institutional, and the beliefs which provide the focus of such ritual. As a mystic, Thurman placed great importance on the meaning and comprehension gained from what he termed variously as the "experience of encounter" and the "creative encounter."[13] In his estimation, an unqualifiedly important and qualitatively different sort of knowledge could be grasped from the heightened perspective of the experienced Other. The insistence was not so much that a vague "something" invade the life of the individual from without, but that the person finally becomes conscious of what is at the core of individual being already.[14] Thurman thus understood social regeneration to be shaped not only by social influences, but predicated even more profoundly upon the individual's own encounter with ultimacy — God.

Of course, from a strictly empirical point of view no one can easily or confidently concur with Thurman that that which is socially enabling and transforming is somehow also associated with the supernal or transcendent.[15] Fortunately, help is available in attempting to illuminate and explain the explicitly mystic in the form of phenomenology. William V. Spanos supplies a semblance of terminological sensibility to this most evasive of methods, defining it as

> ...the unmethodological mode of knowing developed especially by Husserl, Martin Heidegger, and Maurice Merleau-Ponty, that has as its essential goal to bring the perceiver into a more immediate, or better, original relationship to the living world (*die Lebenswelt*) than the traditional methodological epistemologies, whether empirical or idealistic.[16]

Considered in this way, the application of phenomenology to religious experiencing is part of that movement which sympathetically yet critically evaluates positivist methods in the social sciences. Fundamentally, it recognizes that even empiricity is shaped by a socially constructed and historically defined universe. Phenomenology seeks as much as possible, therefore, to adopt a stance of "methodological agnosticism" when investigating objects of religious attitudes.[17] Familiar applications of the method include Mircea Eliade's use of "hierophany,"[18] Rudolf Otto's idea of the *sensus numinus*,[19] and Ninian Smart's distinction between objects which are "real" and objects which "exist."[20] These formulae address, however partially, the issue of heightened interiority via discussion of numinous and mystical perceptions *qua* perceived. This is the task here as well, to delineate the inner dynamics of religious experience as recognized by a particular mystic — namely, Thurman, but always relating to the significance of his external social influences.

Phenomenology thus provides a useful methodological orientation for eliciting an understanding of the self - sacred interaction, particularly where it concerns the promotion of social change vis-a-vis social regeneration. By returning, in Edmund Husserl's terms, "back to the data," an appreciable description and delineation of the way in which the inner structure and motivation of the "creative encounter" is real to Thurman may be undertaken without, I hope, ignoring questions of manifest truth or falsity. The latter issue is important albeit not pivotal to the purpose of establishing the currency of mystic materiality.

Let us look for just a moment at Thurman's interpretation of the radical imperative as it relates to the promotion of social activism. Principally, he averred that the unconditional seriousness of the religious experience itself impels social corroboration, causing one to engage "the powers of this world" with a strident social dimension. The knowledge accrued in this encounter is relational and transactional in character, ushering in a personally transformative system of values and a new, or at the very least, revitalized mode of interaction with others (community and society) and God. To be more specific, the impetus for social regeneration occurs when an individual's ultimate allegiances — race, creed, gender, nationality, socio-economic standing and the like — are transvalued to a less defensive, penultimate status.[21] As shall be seen, this understanding has a most important bearing on Thurman's work, especially as it concerns his incessant struggles against that expression of being so endemic to American civilizing culture — racial sacrality.

Thurman's own description of the mystic (or religious) actor's movement into the social arena clearly coalesces with my earlier synopsis of his means to social change, namely, social regeneration. It is his insistence that the manner and means of such activity is affected by the power of vital religious cognition, dissimilar from most conventional means to social change or protest. This in part explains why the actions of Thurman have been so difficult to assess because, accurately or not, they take into account a vision broader than the particular and often short-lived *cause celebre'* which motivates most. What is required, perforce, to rightly understand Thurman's activism is an expanded conception of the "social change agent."

Taken together, then, the primary methods of investigation to be considered — sociology, history, and phenomenology — will provide a rich accounting of Thurman's involvement in social change. As we shall see, these multiple determinants will be particularly helpful in examining the dual qualities so integral to his mystic-activism, the structuring of community and the more or less fluid aspects of *communitas.* Structurally, Thurman's sympathies and actions will be fairly easy to identify: revitalization efforts in the institutional church; participation in extra-religious organizations such as the Congress of Racial Equality (C.O.R.E.) and the Fellowship of Reconciliation (F.O.R.); and the establishment of resource centers for inner renewal which have invariably attracted social activists of every hue.

The *communitas* dimension of Thurman's activity will be more difficult but not impossible to distinguish. For now, we simply note that the radical imperative disclosed in Thurman's religious experience was never implemented under the auspices of what has been so felicitously phrased the "official model of religiosity."[22] Nor, for that matter, did he ever take such imperative as justification for establishing his own social action organization. The exposition of Thurman's model of social change as "social regeneration" takes seriously this Protean element, which is bound neither to religious denominations, nor for that matter, to political and economic institutions. In Thurman's thinking — and we are in substantial agreement — organizations given solely to social change while critical and instrumental are also vulnerable, and subject to abdicate long-range responsibilities for the particular issue. Even more inexcusable, from his purview, is the example set by the institutional church in North America; one of shameful, historic and repeated acquiescence before maleficent social forces, and a concomitant deferral to the icons of factionalism.

To summarize, my search for a way to study the mutual relations between the internal and external, fluid and structured dynamics of Thurman's mystic role in society has taken the form of symbiotic inquiry. I realize, of course, the "tower of Babel-like" risk involved in bringing to bear differing disciplines and, in particular, the difficulty which resides in knowing how far to appeal to each in my treatment of Thurman. Adding to our dilemma, of course, is the fact that there are no absolutely sharp or unambiguous boundaries to distinguish religion from the non-religious. Still, there is much to warrant this approach, insofar as a vigilant and healthy respect for each of the factors shaping and influencing Thurman's role as mystic-activist is maintained.

Finally, it is my hope that this attempt to treat Thurman in the round will initiate further discussion among both social scientists and religionists on other mystic-activist movements in the United States (the work of Thomas Merton comes to mind). Analogously, may this study prove of some benefit to those scholars and activists (occasionally one and the same) engaged in the task of constructing a contemporaneous approach to the study of African American (and other marginated groups) religious experiences.

The Sources

Source materials for this book are both primary and secondary. I have drawn selectively upon the vast corpus of Thurman publications for this study, which includes some twenty-two books, and a plethora of articles and other extant literature. On occasion those taped sermons and lectures disclosing his general approach to our subject are also utilized.

In addition, a number of important secondary sources are consulted, including contributions by several Thurman scholars.[23] To date, research on Thurman has failed to incorporate any appreciable material from his social involvements, therefore, the precise benefit of much of this literature is attributable to the particular "for instances" cited.

These materials are augmented by data collected from taped personal interviews and various symposia. On-site research was conducted in Daytona Beach, Florida, the birthplace of Thurman; Fellowship Church and the Howard Thurman Educational Trust, both in San Francisco; and at Boston University's Mugar Library (repository of the Howard Thurman Archives) and Howard Thurman Foundation (formerly the Howard Thurman Center).

Synopsis

This work examines a fundamental question: What is the relationship between mysticism as vital religious experience and social change in contemporaneity? To my mind, there is little question but that the involvements of Howard Thurman offer insights critical to the future of African American and broader American activism.

Chapter One examines the social and historical foundations of Thurman's work in social transformation. First of all, a historical sketch of Thurman's life is given that takes into account among other things his social origins and developing outlooks, and significant others. Secondly, I locate Thurman and his work in the broader texture of the times, thus drawing attention to the social milieu as one of two major referencing points for his deliberations.

Chapter Two explores the inner dynamics of Thurman's mysticism. Specifically, I employ perspectives drawn from phenomenology, articulating Thurman's experience of mystic realities while exposing the key meanings, motivations, and conceptualizations. For it is this, the expressly mystical/religious dimension which serves as the second and, more importantly to Thurman, major referencing point of his involvements.

Chapter Three essentially integrates the findings of the two previous chapters. Here I study a historic but neglected model of social interaction, The Church for the Fellowship of All Peoples. First, a theoretical analysis of *communitas*, community, and worship as paradigms for change is undertaken. Based largely on the work of anthropologist Victor Turner, this assessment is followed by an exploration of the social efficacy of the Fellowship Church community. In the third and final place, I refine my working definition of "social regeneration" in light of the chapter's conclusions.

Chapter Four continues where the previous chapter left off, analyzing Thurman's regenerative approach to social change by focusing on the specifically individual aspect of his witness. Here some effort is made, for one, to delineate his charismatic impact on others. Attention is then given to the moral-ethical underpinnings of Thurman's profound sense of relatedness, linking him to the impersonal social order, on the one hand, and social movements and organizations on the other. An important case study follows, detailing Thurman's relationship to the Civil Rights-Black Consciousness Movement. This section of the book, perhaps more than any other, discusses departures which I consider critical to establishing broader and deeper parameters for social activism.

Chapter Five provides a summary of findings on Thurman, mysticism, and social movements, particularly as relates to African Americans. Here is presented a cornucopia of sorts that, it is hoped, will both instruct and inspire further inquiry.

Finally, as an appendix I examine the historic role of sociology in fostering prevailing anti-social and/or asocial understandings of mysticism and, by definition, Thurman. Here the major concern is to present the leading perspectives on Western mysticism, classic and contemporary, critiquing their viability in light of the North American context and, finally, their significance for the ongoing study of mysticism and social change.

PART ONE:

THE MAKING OF A MYSTIC

Chapter One

Social Passages:
Marginality and Destiny

"The way of the pioneer is a lonely journey."
—Howard Thurman—

Life and Work

Social commentator, historian, and journalist Lerone Bennett is one of the most prominent African American voices of our time. In a speech delivered a few years ago he declared Thurman to be a modern day prophet, saying "he was uniquely qualified, first of all, because he was a *social outsider*.... Nor was it an accident that the historical Thurman was black."[1] (emphasis added)   Indeed, grounds for such a viewpoint are well substantiated. The words of Robert Young describe for us in concise fashion the texture of experiences which impressed Thurman's life:

> He was a man who grew up knowing first-hand the blatant racism of Jim Crow laws: who knew the painful ostracism of a class-ordered society in the Old South; who knew the factionalism of a Christian Church that was divided, not only into black and white, but into scores of splintered denominations and sects; who knew the elitism of the academic world as a student and as a faculty member; who came to know intimately the separatism and nationalism of various peoples and races of the world.[2]

The Early Years

Thurman was born on November 18, 1900, in Daytona, Florida, into the constricted way of life of the old American South.[3] He was the middle of three children, the only son from the union of Alice Ambrose and Saul Solomon Thurman. His father, a railroad crewman who held little regard for churches and preachers, died when Thurman was still young. His mother, a sensitive and devoutly religious person, imparted a sense of sureness and inner quietness to her children. But the death of her husband necessitated the spending of long hours away from home "downtown" where she cooked for white families in order to provide for her own. Many of the household responsibilities subsequently were shouldered by grandmother Nancy Ambrose, a former slave whose deep and uncompromising sense of personal dignity proved an inestimable influence on young Howard's development.

Thurman grew up experiencing in its fullness the suffering exacted by racial discrimination and injustice. As a youth he could not navigate the Halifax River (which separated the African American community in Daytona from the white resort area of Daytona Beach) after dark without special authorization from a white person. The public school program was carefully structured to abort the education of African Americans at the seventh grade. Only the intercession of Thurman's principal, who taught him the eighth grade on his own time, enabled him to secure the diploma necessary to attend high school.[4] This achievement notwithstanding, Thurman shared in the common knowledge that the white community would continually find ways to deny his dignity on other levels, resorting to the use of such insidious and anonymous terms as "boy" or "nigger" for instance, and when he got older, "Jack" or "uncle." Thus, young Thurman's freedom of movement was carefully circumscribed in Daytona; the worlds of Black and White defined and separated by the uncrossable chasm of race.

The first years of Thurman's life were bounded by more than just the strictures of racial prejudice. He also had to come to terms with what was at times a parochial and even hypocritical church. When his father died, in Thurman's seventh year, the pastor disallowed the burial of anyone living outside the formal communion of the church. There ensued a confrontation between the chairman of the board of deacons and Thurman's grandmother and, as was often the case, she prevailed. Authorization was finally given for the church funeral but a traveling evangelist had to be called in to preside. To the dismay of young Howard and all who were in attendance, the preacher took the opportunity to remonstrate against the likes of "sinner" Saul Thurman, supremely self-vindicated in his efforts to condemn a man he had never met to hell. After this mortifying ordeal Thurman resolved to disassociate himself from formal religion.[5]

Although Thurman's youthful decision faded with time, the pain of his father's funeral did not. This experience certainly helps to explain why Thurman, who came out of such a traditional religious environment, later eschewed all barriers of religious formalism and sectarianism.[6] Five years later young Howard came up against the rigidity of institutional religion once more, this time while endeavoring to establish formal ties with his home (Baptist) church. The officers, disturbed by the unorthodoxy of his statements, refused him candidacy to baptism. Within minutes, however, Howard's ever forceful and resourceful grandmother had the verdict reversed. Later, as a struggling young minister, Thurman would be frustrated repeatedly by the seeming irrelevancies of organized religion.

All this does not mean that the institutional church and young Thurman were hopelessly or continually at odds. To the contrary, in the African American sections of Daytona and in every aspect of life the church fostered a sense of self-worth and an experience of shared communal responsibility. The same held true for Thurman's life. But Howard was also decidedly different as a child, described by those who knew him as intense, a loner, a sensitive and creative spirit. In fact, he tended to find more companionship in nature than he did among people. The natural boundaries of his world did not affront — the oak tree in the backyard and the woods, the river and the ocean's surf; these were the undergirdings that articulated for him a certain overriding freedom.

The peculiar temperament Thurman displayed embraced as well the endless reaches of nightfall and the boundless energies of the storm. At the age of ten he witnessed the fascination and terror of Halley's comet. Thurman felt that the dynamic forces of nature were consonant with his own nascent perceptions of religious experience. He found therein a confident affirmation and enduring evidence of expansive possibilities for his world, however terrifying and harsh the social context. It was in the early childhood years that the encapsulated young Thurman thus established a lifelong participation in transcendent and cohesive energies, and equilibrium between himself and his social milieu. There also began to emerge during this time a dim but growing sense of his personal destiny.

The Academic Preparation

There was the stirring confidence of religion, but strong hope also in the enrichment of education, and during the next few years Thurman's attention was especially given to the latter. His grandmother, who could neither read nor write, and his mother alike impressed upon him the emancipating effect of knowledge. After becoming the first child of African descent to receive an eighth grade certificate in Daytona, he attended the Florida Baptist Academy in Jacksonville, overcoming financial and physical hardship to graduate as valedictorian of his class. In 1919 Thurman entered Morehouse College in Atlanta, Georgia. His insatiable appetite to learn was fed there by African American men of sober scholarship and inspiring example: President John Hope and Dean Samuel Archer, economist Lorimer Milton, english professor and social historian Benjamin Brawley, logic and ethics professor Benjamin E. Mays, and sociologists E. Franklin Frazier and Gary Moore. Four years later he graduated with a Bachelor of Arts degree and academic honors, acquiring numerous prizes and recognitions along the way. Economics had been his major but he was consumed by a longing to further assess and articulate his experience of religion (he was licensed to preach while in college). He had experienced the vicissitudes of African American life in Daytona and student life in segregated Jacksonville and Atlanta. He would now meet the challenges of seminary.

In 1923 Rochester Theological Seminary in Rochester, New York (now Colgate-Rochester Divinity School), had a policy of enrolling no more than two African American students in any given year and Thurman was one of them. For the first time he was exposed to a totally different social climate — the northern white world. "I had the most horrendous and lacerating experience of my total life," he stated nearly fifty years later, "nothing has touched it since quite like it..."[7] Gradually, Thurman overcame a lifetime of social conditioning, exhuming his own and others fixed racial prejudices by breaking the long-established segregated housing policy of the seminary and often speaking before white church groups. Encounters with the Ku Klux Klan and other hostile elements were not unknown to him during this period; even white friends were liable to lapses of obscene insensitivity. But none of these tests diminished his growing convictions about the value of racial interaction. The Rochester years radically transformed the somewhat reticent young man into an active participant in matters racial and religious, and a disciplined and progressive thinker.

Thurman tended to identify more and more fully with liberal religious thought during this period. Three professors in particular left their mark. Conrad Moehlman introduced him to the impact of cultural influences on the historic movements and creeds of the Christian Church, and the struggle for survival of the essential religion of Jesus. He attended Henry Burke Robins' lectures in the history of religion, which opened up for him new vistas beyond the sphere of Christianity. But it was the theologian George Cross who influenced Thurman most with his scrupulous dismantling of orthodoxies and creative scholarship in contemporary religious thought. Thurman had so close a relation with this teacher that at the end of his senior year (he graduated class valedictorian) Cross told him that he had superior talents and would be able to make an original contribution to American spiritual life. Warning him against becoming absorbed by temporary social issues, including the race question, Cross urged Thurman instead to apply himself to facing "the timeless issues of the human spirit." Thurman accepted the *prima facie* truth of this statement; however, he also deemed it neither wise nor desirable to revel in the serenity of pristine thought. His reflective response was that "a man and his black skin must face the 'timeless issues of the human spirit' together."[8]

In the Rochester days, Thurman increasingly freed himself from inherited orthodoxies. Nonetheless, he continued his involvement with the church and entered the ordained ministry. It was also during this time, while attending a student retreat in Pawling, New York that Thurman would be introduced to the works of a writer who resonated deeply with his own thought, the white South African feminist, pacifist, and visionary Olive Schreiner.

The Oberlin and Haverford Years

Following graduation from seminary in the summer of 1926, Thurman married Kate Kelley and assumed his first pastorate, the Mt. Zion Baptist Church in Oberlin, Ohio. It was here that his germinal ideas concerning religious inclusiveness first became translated into modes of action. Mt. Zion was a well-established church in the African American community, conventional both in terms of its theological understanding and its segregated role in the city. After a brief tenure of two years, the congregation's religious interpretations had considerably broadened. Likewise, the deleterious effect of socially inherited predispositions were slowly remedied. Black and white students and faculty from neighboring colleges became regular and integral participants in Sunday morning services. A Chinese worshiper expressed his deep appreciation for the experience: "When I close my eyes and listen with my spirit I am in my Buddhist temple experiencing the renewing of my own spirit."9

Thurman's endeavors led onward in January 1929 to Haverford College and an endowed independent study with Rufus Jones. The next six months were a seminal period in his life as Jones, a Quaker mystic-activist, exposed him to the wide-ranging field of mysticism and mystical religion. For the first time, much of what Thurman had already sensed and experienced as mystical was given formal expression — inner illumination, meditation, and the validity of religious experience in the quest for personal and social change.

The Morehouse and Howard Years

Thurman's first teaching position was a joint appointment at Morehouse and Spelman Colleges, where he taught a variety of religion and philosophy courses as well as counselled students. During his second year in Atlanta, his wife Kate died. The emotional scars of this tragedy were finally overcome in 1932, when he married former college friend Sue Bailey, a national Y.W.C.A. secretary and writer.

During this time, Thurman moved on to Howard University, where for the next twelve years he committed himself to President Mordecai Johnson's vision of establishing the school as a center of academic excellence for African Americans. As the Dean of Rankin Memorial Chapel and Professor of Theology at Howard University, he became the first chapel dean at a Black college and only the third such person designated on any American university campus. His unconventional sermons and experimental liturgical forms were on the radical edge of worship, and brought him to the attention of a vaster religious and scholarly community than he had been able to previously reach. The wide array of persons invited to speak for Chapel events likewise reflected his still evolving concern for the dissolution of determinations based on race and faith. Thurman's impact on the chapel congregation was telling: allegiances rooted in "race, sex, culture, material belongings, and earlier religious orientation" were for many transvalued in importance, at least temporarily.[10]

India

Other significant events occupied Thurman's attention during the Howard years. Apart from his teaching, he addressed numerous gatherings nationwide, continuing his longtime work with the Student Christian Movement of the Y.M.C.A. and Y.W.C.A.[11] It was in association with this group that he embarked on the most important journey of his life, as the leader of a delegation of four African Americans including his wife Sue, invited to Burma, Ceylon (Sri Lanka), and India. They departed from the United States in September 1935 and remained in South Asia until the following Spring, lecturing and sharing their experience as African Americans while in turn learning from Indian culture and society.

In a sense, the trip to South Asia provided a crucial global context and catalyst for Thurman's understanding of the relationship between what was for him authentic religion and human suffering. Here he was confronted with the tension of political and social patterns of exclusiveness that rivaled racial discrimination in America. He discovered that the Hindu Untouchable and the African American alike were bound in their subordinate status. Equally unsettling was the fact that religion and culture had conjoined to legitimate and encourage this sordid quarantine. Penetrating discussions with many people, prominent among them Mahatma Gandhi and poet laureate Rabindranath Tagore, proved pivotal. A few days later Thurman's reflections culminated with a mystical experience in the Khyber Pass overlooking Afghanistan, a religious invasion which he attested to be of life-changing proportion. He returned to Howard University with the conviction that, all evidence to the contrary, a religious fellowship in America had to be conceived which would unite persons across social and creedal divisions. The litmus test came within the next few years.

The Fellowship Church Years

In 1943 Thurman moved to California's polyglot San Francisco Bay area to devote himself to establishing and copastoring with Alfred G. Fisk (a Presbyterian minister and professor of philosophy at San Francisco State College) The Church for the Fellowship of All Peoples.[12] For Thurman, this was the chance to conclusively determine whether institutional religion could develop a model which annealed separations rooted in socio-economic standing, gender, age, denomination, and faith. He was particularly hopeful for the dissolution of barriers of race and culture within Fellowship church, thereby serving as a decisive conduit for societal change.

Fellowship Church was racially, culturally and religiously diverse during the Thurman years from 1944-53. In fact, the degree of cooperation realized within the congregation caused it to often be singled out as an unusual, unique and even "peculiar" church. And yet this was precisely what caused Thurman so much anguish, because in his estimation it was not Fellowship Church but American Christianity which was the "peculiar insitution." By precept he had sounded the premonitory chord: The church in America, reeking of segregation, hierarchy, and exclusivity, constituted its own greatest moral and ethical dilemma.

Thurman added writing to his other efforts on behalf of human coexistence, witnessing to the wider possibilities while brooding over the ineptitude of the church in the face of wholesale inequalities. Among the earliest of his writings was the 1945 publication of *Deep River: An Interpretation of Negro Spirituals*, followed two years later by *The Negro Spiritual Speaks of Life and Death*.[13] These consequential works were originally lectures presented at Spelman College and Harvard Divinity School. In 1949 he published his seminal work on religion and social change from the underside of history, *Jesus and the Disinherited*.[14] This slender volume bears all the marks of Thurman's attempt to define a vital and viable socio-religious orientation from the perspective of the historical Jesus, whose subordinate social position he regarded as kindred to the great majority of humankind. There followed numerous books, many of which were meditative and poetic in intent, others more immersed in issues of direct social concern. Among the latter are two important works written against the volatile backdrop of the sixties, entitled *The Luminous Darkness* and *The Search for Common Ground.*[15] In both volumes Thurman addresses the role of religion in dispelling "the will to quarantine" in social relations, advocating the unpopular merits of a justice-endowed reconciliation in a time of profound global upheaval.

Boston and Beyond

After nearly a decade in San Francisco, Thurman accepted a call in 1953 to become the first African American Dean of Boston University's Marsh Chapel and Professor of Spiritual Disciplines. By this time he had become such a major figure in the worlds of both preaching and religious scholarship that his exceptional social witness went largely unnoticed. Boston University's restricted environment — a large and impersonal, diverse but predominantly white urban academic community — presented a unique and pioneering forum for his understanding of the nexus between life and religious experience. By the time he left Boston, his ability to impact a broad cross-section of lives was again substantiated. As had been the case in his previous ministries, he exposed people to broader and deeper frames of reference in religious and human encounters. In that year before the Supreme Court ruling on *Brown* vs. *Topeka Board of Education*, the considerable contributions of Thurman to intergroup relations seemed especially portentous.

Thurman's retirement from Boston University in 1965 marked the end of his formal academic and pastoral career. From there he engaged in what he described as the "wider ministry," subsequently traveling to Hawaii, Israel, Japan, the Phillipines, Egypt, and Hong Kong. His most moving experience occurred in Nigeria, however, where he was nourished by the genius of what he said were perhaps "the oldest religious memories of mankind."[16] In an enigmatic way, he understood that the ancient heritage of Africa was indissolubly tied to his own being.

Upon his return to the United States, Thurman embarked on a new phase of his career, returning to San Francisco to work under the aegis of the Howard Thurman Educational Trust. This nonprofit charitable organization became the nucleus of his "wider ministry," dedicated to interracial and intercultural efforts which would "multiply experiences of unity between peoples."[17] The

Trust was to be Thurman's last major endeavor. He died on April 10, 1981.

An Exemplary Mystic-Activist

Thurman was indeed a person in the tradition of Luther's "Here I stand, I can do no other," even though many of his contemporaries were ambivalent about his actual commitment to social change. To critics he appeared to be out of tempo with the times, either conservatively or liberally so, depending on the purview. Many African Americans were prone to dismiss his contributions to the Civil Rights-Black Consciousness Movement (dating from the early 1950's to early 1970's) as at best negligible. On the other hand, his course of action at times seemed overly daring if not outright impossible to some of his friends — the organizing of Fellowship Church for example. Always and everywhere he remained characteristically independent in his religious activism, refusing to be bridled by either the expectations or prejudices of others.

As integral as mysticism was to the life of Thurman, he never advocated an introverted mysticism or privatistic approach to human transformation. For in valuing the vitality derived from spiritual experience, he believed that moral obligation was mandated on the collective level. He affirmed non-violent mass direct-action, fostering this approach through his own mystic-activism. He engaged in individual challenges to social wrongs, whether in white-owned hotels, hospitals or mortuaries. He demonstrated his active interest in social change through long-time participation in organizations such as the Fellowship of Reconciliation (F.O.R.) and the Congress of Racial Equality (C.O.R.E.). Without reservation he quoted the ancient dictum of Petrarch, "If those whom it behooves to speak are silent in the presence of evil, then let any man speak that the truth may be heard and that righteousness prevail."[18] In remaining true to the mystical source in his own life, Thurman struggled against myriad inequities with a consistently vigorous and unorthodox social activism. In so doing he provided a challenging, effective witness for activists of every hue over several generations.

How could Thurman, the grandson of slaves and a product of the Deep South at the turn of the century become a prominent exponent of mysticism? What is the locus for his insights and efforts on behalf of religion and social change? Further clues to these questions can be derived from examining the seminal intellectual influences.

Intellectual Influences

Thurman's mind was amazingly free and the influences on his thought were many and diverse. He was not a philosopher in the formal sense, yet he was familiar with most of the classical Western philosophical systems before he graduated from college (despite the fact that no classes were offered in the subject). His primary education was not received in the natural sciences, yet his writings clearly indicate wide readership in the field and respect for the scientific method. Again, his work offers extensive evidence of his rapport with art and literature. A person whose ideas defy precise or terse description, he nonetheless may be viewed as a mystic-activist and theologian of the highest caliber. He was thoroughly versed in the history of mysticism, East and West. He had an intimate knowledge of the development of Christianity and its missionizing and categorizing impulses. He was naturally immersed in the oral and written tradition of African Americans, and familiarized himself with Native American and African history as well.

Among the many intellectual forces that affected Thurman's thought, a few lines of influence stand out to connect him to some of his contemporaries and near contemporaries. His overall approach to mysticism and social change was significantly affected by the growing debate over the inability of Christianity to extricate itself from social conventions — conventions that openly victimized large segments of the population. In their inception these discussions were especially prominent in African American communities, were further extended by Quakerism and the white Christian liberalism of the early twentieth century, and found a convincing ally overseas in the movement against imperialism.

Intimations from Slavery: The Forebears and Nancy Ambrose

Beginning with the wresting of the soil from the Native American, closely followed by the forcible removal of Africans from their indigen shores, the contradictions of America's purportedly

Christian moral and ethical code were made manifest. For the slaves, there was an acute sense of their involuntary presence in the land that became the United States, and an even more fundamental recognition of freedoms denied. Legal and ecclesiastical fiction could never amount to truth; the illicit African progeny of this environment affirmed uncategorically — however sore and severe their trials — that they were persons and never chattel. More than any other people, these uprooted Africans (along with Native Americans) exposed a critical contradiction extant in the American social and religious order: a dilemma of epic proportion — racism — that would rend (and rends) the national fabric.

This protagonistic worldview of the slaves was of course deep-rooted in Africa; in a broader sense, it is reflective of an expression endemic to the human condition. From Central and West Africa, where the preponderance of African Americans originated, came a heritage which denied the absolute division of life and the false dichotomy of sacred and secular constructs.[19] This was based in a strong sense of community, in which individuals understood themselves to be part of a people and where no person could live in isolation, either materially or spiritually. Mundane social concerns and religious experience were considered but aspects of a single reality, a single meaning. Whatever the degree of African retentions presently detectable among African Americans (which issue while vital is not ours to debate), the forebears did bring into their new existence a fundamentally wholistic means of ordering reality.

At the beginning of the twentieth century the African American populace still had direct links to the ante-bellum era. Many were former slaves, thoroughly immersed in the tradition of the "invisible church," which affirmed the worth of self and strove to overcome the degradations of environment. In the aftermath of slavery, these African descendants continued to adhere to their valiant sense of inner freedom and dignity, and the conviction of their personhood.

Thurman's work grows out of this idiom of Blackness, even though a confluence of other traditions came to bear in the future. The preeminent figure to impact his thinking in this regard was his maternal grandmother Nancy Ambrose. She transmitted to Thurman the oral wisdom of the foreparents and gave him the occasion to fashion his own thought by ensuring that he received a formal education.

Nancy Ambrose was not a scholar *per se* but a sapient personality who understood the value of a cultivated mind. As a young girl living on a Florida plantation in the ante-bellum period no prospects for liberty existed, but early on she established the grounds for freedom. Liberty was conferred from without but freedom, she discovered, was founded from within. She never received any formal education yet she was acutely aware of its importance. When the owner's daughter was punished for trying to teach her the rudiments of reading and counting, Nancy Ambrose knew "there must be some magic in knowing how to read and write."[20] Later, she would communicate to her grandson a fundamental reason for obtaining the "magic" of knowledge, sounding this unadulterated message: "Your only chance is to get an education. The white man will destroy you if you don't."[21]

Nancy Ambrose imparted more to Thurman than simply an awareness of the importance of intellectual endeavors. She also impressed upon him crucial theological and psychological insights on "identity." She insisted that religion, whatever else it does, must begin with the affirmation of the individual's dignity and significance. The religious tradition that the masters had profaned, in other words, somehow had to be reclaimed as a religion for all.[22] For Nancy Ambrose this entailed in part at least the informal appropriation of biblical critical methods. She expunged the writings of the Apostle Paul from her lexicon (with the exception of 1 Corinthians 13) but esteemed the Gospels, parts of Isaiah and the Psalms, and especially Psalm 139.[23] Her reasoning was grounded in painful experience. When she was a child, a white preacher in league with the owner would consistently use a text from the Pauline letters, usually "Slaves, be obedient to your masters..." In contrast, the furtive and enabling message which the slave preacher brought to them was, "You are not niggers! You are not slaves! You are God's children!"[24]

This idea of religion speaking to the existential needs of the subject permeates all of Thurman's endeavors. Indeed, in no less significant a setting than the opening paragraph of his first book, *Deep River*, the above-mentioned story is told.[25] It is repeated in *Jesus and the Disinherited*, where Thurman ascribes Paul's often callous disregard for the socially disfranchised to the seduction of social position.[26] Thurman thus owed much of his understanding of self-identity to Grandmother Nancy Ambrose, who taught him that above all else in life one must possess a clarity and certainty about his or her own context. He remained emphatically cognizant of this fact throughout his life.

A Note on Morehouse

Thurman came to Morehouse College at just the period when Black institutions of higher learning had begun (with notable exceptions) to operate under African American administrations.[27] He was exposed to the visions of men who self-consciously felt that they were upon the point of conquering hitherto unknown territories of racial enlightenment and social construction. For the most part, these administrators were vigorous and outstanding scholars, who worked admirably against constraints imposed by too few resources and not enough public support.

In addition, akin to other Black colleges and universities of the era, the Morehouse faculty was undergoing change, wrestling with an admixture of old and new philosophies concerning the education of African Americans. Newcomers such as E. Franklin Frazier and Benjamin Mays were young graduates of eastern and northern colleges, whose penetrating and disciplined approaches to academic investigation often brought them into conflict with the prevailing "exceptionalist" pedagogical tradition so insightfully delineated by Cornel West.[28] The older generation of African American educators were sometimes seen as placing the development of moral character above the development of the intellect. At other times, they reportedly repressed progressive or liberal educational values in order to ensure continued white fiscal support, tenuous and meagre as it was. The young professor of sociology, E. Franklin Frazier, dourly summed up the situation thus: "Negro education in the past, to characterize it briefly, has been too much inspiration and too little information."[29]

Thurman learned much from the religious and humanities emphasis of seasoned teachers, but he divorced it from its metaphysical underpinnings in the exceptionalist tradition. He remained cognizant of the distinctive achievements of African American religion and culture but was insistent that its significance be viewed as more than a conditioned response, however compelling, to white supremacist America. All in all, he attempted to direct the exceptionalist position into a closer relation with the empiricism and causal imputation of the new social sciences, which explains in part his choice of economics as a major.[30] But he still retained his emphasis on the search for the nonsocial or religious matrix of life.

Thurman and American Protestant Liberalism

In regard to Thurman's debt to liberalism, the persons who made a profound impression were his seminary teachers, Henry Robins, Conrad Moehlman, and most importantly, George Cross.[31] In addition, it is clear that he was informed if not influenced by the scholarship of other members of the liberal movement both during and after its zenith.[32]

The empirical language and methodology which Thurman had sampled in college was already well ensconced in white academic circles. The same held true in theological institutions, where scientific principles had made substantial inroads under the aegis of theological liberalism. American liberalism has an involved history, so much so in fact that, as Sydney Ahlstrom has noted, "its influence is very difficult to estimate."[33]

The so-called "older" branch of the American liberal movement, which dated back to early nineteenth century Unitarianism, Universalism and the Society of Friends, and the "younger" Friedrich Schleiermacher inspired branch that infiltrated the larger Protestant denominations, beginning in the 1880's differed in many respects, but what united all major exponents was

the immanence of God in nature and human nature. It tended, in consequence, toward a general human optimism. It made much of a universal religious sentiment — or, increasingly, of the variegated forms of religious experience — that lay behind the institutions, scriptures, and creeds of particular religions and that preceded such formal expressions in order of importance. It valued good works, conceived in either individual or more collective terms, over professions and confessions. Among the traditional doctrines of Christianity, the most important and controlling for liberalism was the Incarnation, which signified and ratified the actual presence of God in humanity.[34]

The impress of liberalism was firmly acknowledged at Rochester Theological Seminary with the addition of Walter Rauschenbush to the faculty in 1897 (where he taught until shortly before his death in 1918). Over the next three decades the school played a significant role in the intellectual development of liberalism, joining ranks with such distinguished institutions and scholars as Colgate and William Newton Clarke, Union (New York) and William Adams Brown, Harvard and Francis Peabody, and Chicago and Shailer Mathews.[35] It was during this era that Cross, Robins, and Moehlman joined Rochester's teaching staff.

Thurman took much of his approach to religious interpretation and action from the liberalist school, even though he strongly disagreed with their assumptions. The impulse dominating liberalism during this period, otherwise known as "modernism," was concerned with an ethically oriented religious understanding that would reduce some of the glaring inequities of modern industrial society and help realign Christian religion in America (the cultural religion *about* Jesus) with the original message of Christianity (the historical religion *of* Jesus). Thurman agreed with this focus on conceptualizing religious behavior within a social and institutional context. For the new emphasis rejected, at least in discourse, the long-standing and misconstrued disjunction between the church and the world, religion and culture, and sometimes even the sacred and the secular.

Thurman's major disagreement with the prevailing liberal current was the fatuous positivism it displayed. Modernism's unmitigated belief in national destiny and world progress served to obscure the malignancy and pervasiveness of domestic evils, particularly as regards racism. For Thurman, a theological stance so readily given to ignoring hostilities directed at vast segments of the population (African Americans, women, various immigrant groups, etc.) was itself seriously impaired. He understood such optimism to be a critical if not fatal departure from social reality, utterly irreconcilable with his own experience as one of the dominated and disinherited. For example, as was noted earlier, despite Thurman's attestation that Cross was the teacher who had a "greater influence on my mind than any other person who ever lived," he remained at variance with the idea of leisurely introspection as the means to human attainment.[36] Thurman observed a similar attitude operative among other professors and classmates. "We were from different worlds, to be sure," Thurman wrote concerning his years at Rochester. However, "the differences not only had to do with the general social climate, but were grounded in the inner prism of spirit and mind through which we gaze out upon the external world."[37] Thurman shared deeply in the concern of Cross and Robins for the centrality of human personality, the universal life of the spirit, and other liberal motifs, but he had to express the "hunger of the spirit" which they encouraged inclusive of his own racial fact.

The Influence of Rufus Jones

The liberal reconstruction of religion and the concern for social disorganization that emerged in the late nineteenth century (albeit selective) was also the inheritance of Rufus Jones.[38] This orientation, combined with his deep roots in the mystical tradition of Quakerism, formed the framework for his thought. Thurman credited Jones along with George Cross as having most prominently "opened a way in my thinking." "He opened up a way for my heart," Thurman conveyed during a lecture on Jones' mysticism, "as the only other great teacher that I had opened up the way for my mind."[39]

Jones' consuming interest in life was to interpret the validity of the mystical experience and the social role of the mystic. He was one of three leading interpreters of mysticism during his time, William James and Evelyn Underhill being the others.[40] He rejected James' (psychological) and Underhill's near obsession with the substantive dimensions of mystical experience, important as this was, for a more deliberately functional analysis.[41] In short, Jones based his commentary on mysticism upon its ultimate effects for good in the human community and in history. He affirmed that mysticism is something special and desirable and may even be elevated to the status of a virtue but with the important caveat, in Tauler's phrase, that "no virtue is to be trusted until it has been put into practice."[42] He contended that the effects of genuine interior mystical experience are exteriorly reflected, that is to say, socially, ethically, and politically manifested in the relationship which obtains between the mystic and the world.

The definitions of mysticism which Jones submits in his numerous (fifty-five) books are essentially variations of his most precise formulation, first stated in *Studies in Mystical Religion*:

Mysticism is the type of religion which puts the emphasis on immediate awareness of relation with God, on direct and intimate consciousness of the Divine presence. It is religion in its most acute, intense and living stage.[43]

Borrowing from his own experience, Jones relates elsewhere that mysticism carries with it a "majestic conviction of objectivity."[44] The mystic encounter, Jones claimed, is not mere sensory experience, but achievable through the most penetrating powers of rationality.[45] Furthermore, the mystic movement which invades the consciousness transforms the character. Ethical and spiritual empowerment occurs; the individual is "possessed with a new and deeper passion to have his life turned into a living radiation-centre of the Kingdom of God...."[46]

Thurman, it will be recalled, had experienced the nuances of mysticism since childhood. The defining of it as such, however, had been unknown to him. He found in Jones' book *Finding the Trail of Life* (published in 1924), the story and experience of an individual whose life's quest nearly paralleled his own. Shortly thereafter, Thurman ventured to Haverford "to find out where I was in my own thinking and what on earth is mysticism."[47]

What particularly appealed to Thurman about Jones, aside from the immense profit gained by exposure to his knowledge and experience of mysticism, was that "He had ... a combination of insight and social feeling."[48] Jones laid the foundation for his awareness that personal mystical experience and social service were not in hopeless and inimical relation to each other. Martin Luther's early reformist insights, John Woolman's anti-slavery crusade, and Elizabeth Fry's prison reform career were among those mystic undertakings which met his criteria for the "affirmation mystic." Moreover, Jones himself offered an extensive social witness through his various protests against the first and second world wars. His disclosure of the beneficial creations and reforms promoted by mysticism, in opposition to the then current clinical descriptions offered by psychology (and, later, sociology), left their mark upon Thurman: "He gave to me confidence in the insight that the religion of the inner life could deal with the empirical experience of man without retreating from the demands of such experience."[49]

Although Thurman gained much from Jones' elucidation of mysticism and from his empirical emphasis, he reacted against his seeming obliviousness to certain social issues:

> The thing that has puzzled me and about which only once did I talk to Rufus, was the way in which the witness of which he spoke so often, growing out of his experience with the inner light, the way that that witness concerned itself to meeting the needs of the desperate, of the destitute, of the whole the things that came about from the ravages of war and pestilence and the guidance about the whole peace testimony. *But I felt that in this emphasis it had no witness for the less dramatic, less obvious sufferings of mankind.*[50] (emphasis added)

This critique sounds so uncharacteristic of Thurman that one might question its authenticity were it not for his own exemplary struggle with the dehumanizing social order. The fact that Jones had a "blind spot" to more mundane social issues is well documented by Thurman. For example, he notes that the struggles of organized labor and injustices linked to racism had little effect on Jones.[51] This was consistent with general Quaker sentiment of the time, which favored involvement in the global issues of war and peace but, rather surprisingly, recoiled against participation in matters specific to labor and race in America.[52] Nonetheless, even this did not diminish Jones' invaluable contribution to Thurman's thinking, namely, that he provided an aperture — mysticism — through which Thurman's own prior understanding of the relationship between religion and social change could pass.

Two Additional Influences: Olive Schreiner and Mohandas K. Gandhi

A fuller account than can be given here would also probe into the identifiable but less direct influences of such thinkers as Jane Steger, Rudolf Otto, Meister Eckhart, Evelyn Underhill, and Bertrand Russell, as well as close friends and associates.[53] Our discussion at this point will concentrate on the impact of two divergent minds, one antedating and the other contemporaneous with Thurman: Olive Schreiner and Mohandas Gandhi.[54]

The influence of Olive Schreiner on Thurman was posthumous. It was not until 1925, five years after her death that Thurman first became acquainted with her writings. "It seemed," Thurman later stated, "that all my life long I was being readied for such an encounter." So great was his appreciation for her insights that he eventually edited a collection of selections from her seven books, entitled *A Track to the Water's Edge: The Olive Schreiner Reader.*[55]

Thurman was strongly influenced by Schreiner's eloquent articulation of the seamless unity of all life and the universality of truth, noting that, "Her writings are invaded by a sense of vastness and timelessness."[56] Reminiscent to his reading of Jones, what was striking to Thurman was the degree to which her writings coalesced with his own life experiences. Two drastically differing social contexts had given birth to markedly kindred spirits.

> As a boy in Florida, I walked along the beach of the Atlantic in the quiet stillness that can only be completely felt when the murmur of the ocean is stilled, and the tides move stealthily along the shore. I held my breath against the night and watched the stars etch their brightness on the face of the darkened canopy of the heavens. I had the sense that all things, the sand, the sea, the stars, the night, and I were one lung through which all of life breathed. Not only was I aware of a vast rhythm enveloping all, but I was part of it and it was a part of me. It was not until I read Olive Schreiner that I was able to establish sufficient psychological distance between me and the totality of such experiences to make the experience itself an object of thought. Thus, it became possible for me to move from primary experience, to conceptualizing that experience, to a vision inclusive of all life.[57]

Schreiner, it will be recalled, was an English-speaking white South African. She held freethinking views with reference to the rights of disparate elements of humanity — women, laborers, the victims and pawns of war and, to some extent, Black Africans — imposing ideas which are even now prescient to some.[58] Her struggles in behalf of humankind, which were numerous, exemplified the dynamism of her ideas. She was never finally able to overcome her ingrained social disposition toward Black South Africans however; the literary evidence of which caused Thurman tremendous "shock and anger."[59] Yet, Thurman accepted the broad expanse of her ideas even as he noted her internal contradiction, "which was never quite resolved." "She was," he decided, "by endowment and philosophy, a universalist in outlook and feeling, being a child of her times as a member of the exploiting and colonizing community."[60] In fine, no reader of Thurman can fail to note his debt to Schreiner's mystic literary philosophy.

Mahatma Gandhi provided yet another reservoir of ideas from which Thurman drank deeply. During the 1935-36 academic year Thurman headed an African American delegation to South Asia, lecturing in some 45 academic institutions. As a result of this trip Thurman met for several hours with Gandhi in Bardoli, India; remarkably, Gandhi broke his fast for the duration of the delegation's visit. It was his first opportunity to engage African Americans in discussion concerning their respective struggles for freedom. Thurman himself returned to the United States with "an enhanced interpretation of the meaning of non-violence."[61]

Thurman may or may not have been equipped with the most rigorous understanding of nonviolent principles prior to his meeting Gandhi, but he had long been committed to their transforming ideals.[62] He learned from Gandhi, "a man who is rooted in the basic mysticism of the [Hindu] Brahma," the life-affirming concepts of *Ahimsa* (compassionate and active non-cooperation in the quest for Truth, or "Love-Force") and *Satyagraha* ("holding on to Truth," and hence "Truth-Force").[63] He found in him a kindred mind who refused to think in terms of a disconnected Truth, God, or Ultimate Reality but focused his attention on that which was pre-eminently practical and spiritual. For Thurman as for Gandhi, unwavering sincerity in the face of strident opposition was grasped as an intensely active and revolutionary endeavor. Thurman has written that

> the acceptance of this alternative is to be simply, directly truthful, whatever may be the cost in life, limb, or security.... There must always be the confidence that the effect of truthfulness can be realized in the mind of the oppressor as well as the oppressed. There is no substitute for such a faith.[64]

The other important contribution that Gandhi made to Thurman's life work was the offering of a global perspective on the human condition. The anti-imperialist movement then surging through South Asia, exemplified by the implementation of ethical non-violence and non-cooperation on the part of the masses, provided the first critical international referent for Thurman's understanding of the relationship which obtains between religion and the social world. Later, other arenas of protest — colonial Africa, Nazi Germany, the Native Indian communities of Canada and the United States — would further sensitize his thinking in this regard.   Thurman's fascinating wartime essay, "The Fascist Masquerade," affords a glimpse into this aspect of his development.[65] This does not deny, however, that his social and religious thought continued to be primarily informed by his experience as an African American.

Isaiah Berlin has classified thinkers in terms of a distinction made by a Greek poet: "The fox knows many things, but the hedgehog knows one big thing." Berlin equated foxes with those thinkers "who pursue many ends, often unrelated." The hedgehogs, in contrast, "relate everything to a central single vision, one system less or more coherent or articulate ... a single universal organizing principle."[66]   Clearly, if analogies are permissible, Thurman was a hedgehog.   Although his thought contained numerous ideas and influences gleaned from as many sources and contexts, they always had to adhere to his single central vision of God.   No one influence was decisive (albeit grandmother Nancy Ambrose came closest).   Rather, what he derived from each were conceptualizations pertinent to the fact of his own experience. How he appropriated each new concept and made them accessible in his own way is part of what defines his expression of mysticism. In the words of Mozella Mitchell, the thought of Thurman makes "us forget the source in that he had his own unique contribution to make. His 'new version' does not keep reminding us how good the original was."[67]

Social Forces

Thurman struggled to find a vantage point from which the integrity of the person in society could be sustained with a maximum of objectivity.   The means he chose was of course largely impacted by his existential situation.   He attempted to be active in the social and religious issues of the day by bringing to bear his experience of double marginality, as a person of African descent and as an outsider in the religious world.   Much like one of his mentors, Rufus Jones, Thurman gained intellectual and spiritual autonomy by engaging in the struggles of society while continually drawing upon his mystic resources.   Periodic spiritual hiatuses gave him the additional vitality to respond to the myriad tensions and confrontations ensuing between the individual and society.

Some of the roots of his method of social engagement may be found in his general background. Thurman came of age in the early twentieth century, a time of profound change on the American scene, particularly with respect to African Americans. He was deeply enmeshed in his family relationships, tied by multiple bonds of emotion and identification not only to his two sisters, mother, and deceased father but especially to his grandmother. There was also the extended family of the African American community, most notably exemplified in the presence of the church. Thurman attempted to clarify his emotions and sort out his commitments by a rich involvement with his family, immersion in an as of then unidentified mysticism, and detachment from hostile white forces.

Thurman pursued a different course in his participation in religious and academic institutions, where repressive and divisive forces were at least as pronounced as those that he had encountered in Daytona. Here he gained attachment in matters social through a fuller immersion, mastering hostile environments by striving for an unambiguous relationship with God. In this respect, he established a profound commitment to addressing the universality of human need.

The New Century

The opening decades of the twentieth century, the years Thurman came of age, were years of profound struggle and despair for African Americans. The tortuous tandem of frustration and expectation that had accompanied the earlier periods of slavery, emancipation, and reconstruction extended into the new century.[68]

By the beginning of the Great War, whatever constitutional rights African Americans thought they had secured were in fact eroded. Racism was rife across the land. In the South and border states anti-Negro hate groups maimed, lynched, rioted and unleashed a furious barrage of bigotry. Social and political deconstruction, North and South, was equally as swift: the denial of the franchise, non-existent or at best deficient educational opportunities, injustice in the courts, discrimination in housing and on public conveyances, and submarginal working conditions. Nature, too, contributed to the grisly spectacle via the ravages of floods and the devastation of the boll weevil. While three fourths of African

America still lived in the rural South prior to 1900, this fraction decreased to one fourth by the last third of the century.[69]

Increasingly, African Americans "voted with their feet" out of the agricultural areas to the industrial and usually Northern cities, establishing a Black urban culturalism. There they encountered the monolith of the industrial complex, sharing in the extant urban crisis of rootlessness and alienation. In the city an impersonal and irreligious, even hostile, social pathology ever threatened. Regardless of background, traditional communal values did not adhere in the urban milieu, creating severe religious, social and psychological displacement.

In stark contrast to the conditions facing African Americans, the early twentieth century marked an era of exuberant reforms of various hues among white Americans. The Populist movement, a radical agrarian alliance of small and poor farmers, opposed exploitation of the farmer by large political and corporate interests. The Progressivist campaign, the urban counterpart to Populism, roused "the people" (which meant the white middle class) to decry the dangerously growing power of political "machines" and economic monopolies. The women's rights movement, whose impetus was largely traceable to abolitionism, abandoned all pretense of interest in racial justice and subsequently received the vote. The labor movement, concerned with upward social mobility, aimed to protect and improve the lot of the common laborer. The social gospel movement changed the emphasis in middle-class churches from the regeneration of individuals to the "Christian regeneration of society." There were numerous other movements contending for the public's attention as well, among which could be counted the socialists and communists, Muckrakers and avant-garde writers, and educational reformists.

The reformers wanted to be concretely responsive to the demands of the day, to infuse their work with a vigorous democratic and anti-elitist spirit. They were intent on celebrating the dynamism, the hopefulness, the optimistic vision of America's future that was sweeping the body politic. But in the process a new and dangerous ideology of subordination was also gaining ascendancy. It went by many names — Anglo-Saxonism, *noblesse oblige,* "the white man's burden," — a myth founded in cultural chauvinism that was exceedingly profitable and amenable to imperialist aspirations. This critical development was a sophisticated variation of course on the "inherently inferior" idea of historic racial chauvenism. In essence, non-white peoples, whether abroad or at home, were still to be relegated to socially and politically passive roles, only now via more respectable condescensions as indicated, for example, by the splendid genteel phrase "culturally deprived." Consciously or not, this new expanded form of racial arrogance substantially informed the national mood, with far greater consequences than short-lived protofascism and a revived Ku Klux Klanism.

Howard Thurman participated in both the African American subculture and larger American culture. Born into one and marginal to the other, he acquired in this tenuous and fragile social position the intellectual and religious resources that enabled him to exercise his several skills, unencumbered by fixed and conventional patterns of social interaction.

The Extended Family Network

"I have often wondered," wrote Thurman, "as I contemplate the experiences of loneliness and shyness, how different my orientation to life would have been had I grown up with brothers rather than sisters — or had my father lived longer. But from the beginning I was surrounded by women."[70]

It will be recalled that the primary responsibility for raising the young Thurman fell to his mother and grandmother. His mother was the breadwinner but the daily care of Howard and sisters Henrietta and Madaline was given into the hands of "Grandma Nancy." His mother and maternal grandmother had an especially close relationship, "so deep that there was never a discernible vibration of tension, or anger, between them."[71] That this was true is attested to by the fact that when Thurman's mother married after the death of his father (she remarried twice), an understanding inhered between mother and daughter that they, and not the men, would assume sole responsibility for his upbringing.[72]

In the person of his mother Thurman was afforded an example of inner quietness, sensitivity and compassion but it was his grandmother's influence that was dominant.[73] He quickly learned to identify with her impassioned Christian witness, which challenged the parochialism of religious authority and substituted a compelling and principled religious experience. She instilled in him a new appreciation for the utter disutility of fighting, which perhaps led to his later rejection of violence (killing for food purposes would always remain a dilemma) and the espousal of pacifism and active non-cooperation.[74] Again, he gained from her inestimable insight into the inherent worth of self and others. Nancy Ambrose had encountered hunger, cold, and the death of some of her children, yet what she imparted to her grandchildren was the realization that they were "not merely a child of Mama Alice and a grandchild of Grandma Nancy, but a child of God."[75] She was all things to young Thurman, an exemplar of dynamic spirituality, a person of account in the community, a supportive friend on whom he could rely:

> She [Grandma Nancy] backed up her word with action and he knew he could count on her. He boasted to his friends of her, saying she could kill a bear with her fist. No one disputed him, though no one felt a need for the test. There was not a person in the Negro community on the shore of the Halifax River who had not at a time of trouble felt anchored by her strength. She was a haven to them all.[76]

Following the death of his father, whom the church had condemned as an unbeliever, Thurman developed an explicit antagonism toward institutional religion. A few years later, he attempted to overcome his tensions by surrendering his life to God, while distancing himself from the church's exclusionary proclivities. Though he was to become deeply committed to the life of the church as exemplified by Jesus, he would never give his assent to its divisive dogmas. The very fact of his commitment to the church he had earlier seen as his enemy "but now knew to be the Way, the only Way for which I was born" was always a paradox: "I believe the seven-year-old has been hard at work all this time to understand that which subconsciously I have never been able fully to accept. He is at home with me and through God's grace, I with him."[77]

The feelings of anger Thurman directed toward the church when his father died were somewhat offset by the intercession of his mother and grandmother, who in continuing to make church participation mandatory also exposed him to its nourishing potential.[78] Thus, despite this severely traumatic event in Thurman's life, the church continued to play an integral role. As the spiritual face of the African American community, social identity and personal dignity were definitely intertwined with its existence. "In the fellowship of the church," Thurman recalled, "particularly in the experience of worship, there was a feeling of sharing in primary community."[79] This "extended family" melded with the life of the larger community in myriad ways. All of the major rites of passage and events of significance transpired within its confines. Thurman's mother loved the church, and among its communicants, grandmother was "Lady Nancy." For Thurman, there were persons who recognized in him special spiritual talents and sensitivities and encouraged their cultivation. The oppressive social environment was enlarged for him by these and other significant people in the community, affirming in him a sense of personal significance.

Thus, freedom stood in the forefront of Thurman's life in the form of his grandmother. She and his mother encouraged a passionate commitment to self-actualization and self-affirmation. In addition, he was nurtured by both church and community. For him the alternative, that is, the thought of a community that could also include whites did not yet exist. They remained external to his realm of ethical and social discourse. Nonetheless, he was instilled with high aspirations from an early age, insights which enabled him to establish a different emphasis within the world he knew, and which ultimately prepared him for a life of profound relatedness in the social and religious world.

The "Forgotten Years"[80]

The post World War I years sobered but did not destroy white American ideological prisms of the past, notably, the myths of "manifest destiny" and innate moral superiority. Meanwhile, the national effort to promulgate the twin virtues of "democracy" and "freedom" went on unabated. The rhetoric of democracy, which guaranteed equality of opportunity to all within the commonwealth, fell on tumultuous times with the crash of the stock market and the national slide into depression. On the world front, the 1917 Bolshevik Revolution portended things to come, with the subsequent linking of the socialist movement to the global struggle against colonialism and neo-colonialism and the limited spread of communist activity to North America. Eventually World War II would resuscitate a somewhat anemic United States, weakened by internal contradictions, to once again rally around the founding cosmogonic documents and ideals. In the meantime, numerous others of the nation's denizens were reaching dissenting conclusions about the validity and integrity of those same ideals, marking a transition in relations between the races.

A noted journalist and economist wrote in 1964 that the years comprising World War II were a "turning point" in United States racial intercourse, in which "the seeds of the protest movements of the 1950s and 1960s were sown."[81]   Indeed, during this period increasing numbers of African Americans refused to be appeased, too long and too deeply offended by the debasements of a nonexistent American equalitarianism.   Having scrutinized the essential transformative capacities of Western forms of democracy and Christianity, they adjudged them to be sorely lacking.[82]   The established structures of American society were deemed a palpable failure, for rarely if at all did they demonstrate the capacity to effect profound and potent change. Stripped of faith in an open, dynamic society, some of Africa's progeny opted for new patterns of community — Holiness and Pentecostalism, Garveyism and Pan-Africanism, Black Moors and Black Muslims, Communism and Socialism, Father Divine and Daddy Grace — but all these were products of modernity still largely submerged in an ocean of tradition. What most African Americans truly sought was that which was already the essential property of the majority of Americans: the rectification of injustices and inequalities through the agency of an inclusionary and responsive social system.

Recognizing the powerful transformative potentials of the time, Howard Thurman sought to champion the *essential genius* of democracy, not out of principled commitment to democratic values as such, but basically because of their compatibility with his own passionate vision for an inclusive community.[83] Like most African Americans he was on the one hand loyal to the national ethos (as explicitly embodied, for example, in the Constitution of the United States and the Emancipation Proclamation), and on the other deeply dissatisfied with the vast discrepancy between preachment and praxis. He questioned the importunity of "making the world safe for democracy," when in fact "the gulf between the dream as uttered and the idea as practiced [in the United States] is wide, abysmal and deep."[84]

Thurman's writings on the social, economic and political situation of African Americans display, as Luther Smith has shown, a belief that continued American oppression of its non-European populations (African Americans, Japanese, Native Americans, partitioned peoples) would undermine the well-being of the nation.[85] He was convinced that as African Americans in particular moved from a position of "anonymnity" to an awakening "individuality" in a recalcitrant society, they would persist as "the perpetual threat and condemnation of democracy."[86] Thurman would give specific content to this sentiment near the close of another United States war effort, Vietnam. He writes that America, still convulsed by division, could cease to be *primus inter pares* as a world power:

> ... it is quite possible that in the major struggle between the Soviet Union and the United States of America the future belongs to that power which is the most convincing witness to the fact that it makes available to all its citizens the freedom of access to a social climate in which the individual not only has an authentic sense of belonging, but in which it is a reasonable hope for him to actualize his potential, thereby experiencing community within himself as part and parcel of the experience of community within the state.[87]

Thurman's strong espousal of democratic virtues, in tandem with his primary commitment to religion, informed all of his endeavors. This was consistent with his belief that "minority groups are in a unique position to be apostles of sensitiveness keeping alive the true genius of the democratic challenge — mark the use of the word challenge."[88] When in his earlier career he was affiliated with segregated institutions in the African American community, he was not so much expressing an acquiescence to the social order but rather acknowledgement of the fact that during this period "a segregated college [could] more nearly create a democratic environment in which Negro students [could] develop the democratic procedure."[89] Paradoxically, Thurman remained to some extent above the battle for racial harmony even while he was engaged in it. He was never a bona fide "group" person although he entered into the social arena. This was because his commitment to the democratic process was mainly rooted in his mystic envisagement of an inclusive and affirming community — one that would not obscure the sanctity and worth of each discrete person.

The Religious and Academic Man

Fairly early Thurman appeared attracted by the worlds of both education and religion. He was at home amidst the intellectual rigors and the lively give-and-take settings made possible by the university. Yet at the same time he was determined to be more than an academician; he aspired to test his ideas and ideals in the church and society. This effort to be consistent within two differing contexts helps to clarify Thurman's distinctive literary and oratorical style. Generally, it has been assumed that the characteristics of his style could be accounted for by his theological orientation. This is assuredly so; however, this fact is further enhanced by consideration of the social role Thurman played within the academic structure and in the general religious community.

Students of Thurman often remark upon special characteristics of his content and style that strikingly distinguished his contributions from those of other leading scholars and practitioners of religion in America. They stress the elegance and brilliance of his literary and oratorical output, but also note the almost studied disregard for conventional systematic exposition.

Mozella Mitchell makes the important observation that "for one reason or another ... perhaps for many reasons, one no doubt being the social limitations he faced as a Black American, Thurman chose a route of development different from the systematic. He chose to remain free of the restrictions of any exact discipline such as literature, theology, psychology, or philosophy."[90] Thurman never altered his ideas to conform either to standard university or ecclesiastical life. Nevertheless, early in his career his contributions were judged to be of high quality, and he quickly attracted the attention of important educational and religious figures.

This general consensus about the high caliber of his intellectual and religious accomplishments was by no means reached just by African American academicians or scholars of religion. In perusing Thurman's books and papers, one is impressed with the wide range of scholars with whom he engaged in intellectual exchanges and realizes the wide cross-section of relationships he established within the academy and the church and across their various disciplinary and creedal boundaries. As a professor, pastor, chapel dean, and university minister-at-large, he related to myriad persons by virtue of his effusive role (a telling contrast to today's more restricted patterns for said positions), touching upon the concerns of disparate intellectual fields. The freedom of his role-set[91] afforded him, in the words of another prominent minister-educator, further opportunity to "conceive of transcending ideas," where he could "create in thought [and action] a construct of another society, another world, another condition for humankind."[92]

Thus, Thurman's involvement with many scholarly and religious circles and audiences, and his many contacts with students and colleagues were in part responsible for his intellectual fecundity. Thurman made it crystal clear, however, that there were other prior resources, internal in essence, that informed his sense of objectivity and creativeness:

> The initial act of standing alone, of establishing a sense of independence of the environment, is one of the prime requisites for participating meaningfully as a person in a collective destiny that involves more and more of the human family. If man were never able to do this, it would be impossible for him to make his home anywhere on the planet, in widely differing circumstances. Control of the environment, and the increasing degree to which this is possible, depend on the making and use of tools, the utilizing of materials given in the surroundings — none of which could be done if in the first instance the graphic distinction between self and not-self had not been achieved. The discipline is not merely in the fact of the achievement, but through it in making the external world an instrument of the private will and the creative mind. The strength to do this comes as a part of the discipline of growth. This is to experience one of the triumphant aspects of growth itself![93]

Not surprisingly, the distinctiveness of Thurman's style was affected by his auxiliary and marginal status in society. As the above statement indicates, achieving mastery over the social environment was a normative and critical activity in his life. The same held true concerning his interactions at both the university and church level. At Boston University, he had to come to terms with the fact that there had been considerable faculty opposition to his appointment on both racial and theological grounds. Even at Fellowship Church he could recount myriad episodes related to the malignancy of prejudice.[94] The experiences of Thurman lend credibility to the maxim of Francis Bacon: "adversity doth produce virtue."

Although Thurman put a great deal of his energies into academic service, it needs to be stressed that he did so with the intent to encourage others in the quest for self-definition and a concommitant social freedom. Students and parishioners alike were privy to the critical distillation of his thought, which emphasized above all else that every person was the primary architect of her or his own experience of truth. He did not attempt to manage or direct others thoughts but rather set in motion the means to broad intellectual and personal exploration. No matter what his audience, he thought it should be axiomatic that the unexamined life is not worth living.

The parallel methods Thurman used to communicate his message were and are non-traditional. His writings are characterized by an amalgam of creative and internally consistent insights that "virtually speak" to the reader.[95] He eschewed all striving for conventional systematization, but applied an unsparing albeit amorphous rational analysis to his own life's struggles. His books and essays, which lack the customary accoutrements of excessive exposition and extensive footnotes, were published by academic and general presses. Again, Mitchell's description of Thurman's literary style is revealing, in which she states that "he took himself as the 'human metaphor' through whom others might be led to share their own primary experience of truth."[96]

What was true of Thurman's writing style was even more true of his oral presentations. All accounts agree that Thurman was considered one of the most brilliant lecturers and orators of his time.[97] He attracted persons from the nost varied of religious and academic orientations; indeed, it is no exaggeration to say that the content and style of his delivery seems to have enthralled his audiences. Former Thurman student and civil rights activist James Farmer writes:

> When this extraordinary man walked into social ethics class, a silence born of awe reigned. It always seemed as if we had dragged him away from private meditation. He would look over the heads of those in class, into space, for what seemed minutes. Then he would open up, in his slow, laborious manner, with a provocative thesis....

> We would leave the class with no answers, but many intriguing questions that had not occurred to us before. It was Thurman's belief that answers must come from within, from the bit of God in each of us.[98]

His biographer relates the kindred effect from the pulpit:

> The feeling of silence prevails as people rise and begin to move away, once more a part of the world. A curious thing has happened: not all may have liked him, but on leaving his presence they find that they are liking themselves better. A scattering of comments can be heard: "I feel as if I'd been with Jesus." A white man holds out his hand to help an elderly Negro woman down the steps. "We were there," a girl says, moving quickly through the crowd as if under some urgency to do what she had seen could be done with an aroused imagination. A man with an unmistakable Southern accent speaks to no one in particular: "He finds his way into everyone's heart." A woman replies, "He stands aside and lets it happen to you." "His words seemed to be coming from God." "A tremendous spirit has expressed itself in words that we can all understand."[99]

Thurman presented his audiences not with an accepted method of exposition, but with a series of often seemingly unrelated insights, testifying to tremendous powers of perception. As we have already indicated, his originality stemmed in part from the marginal position he occupied in several communities. This was in turn informed by an even more fundamental spiritual demand. His ideas generally conformed to the expressed goals of the church, the academy, and larger society, but he had to devise norms for their attainment commensurate with his own needs. Clearly, the contradictions inuring between message and action in the American social structure affected every aspect of Thurman's life. That structure contributed greatly to his innovative thinking and, at the same time, to the cultivation of an activism consistent with his mystical understandings.

Chapter Two

Mystic Passages: Transformed and Transforming

Truth is within ourselves; it takes no rise
From outward things, what'er you may believe.
There is an utmost center in us all,
Where truth abides in fulness; and around,
Wall upon wall, the gross flesh hems it in,
This perfect, clear perception — which is truth.
A baffling and perverting carnal mesh
Binds it, and makes error; and to know
Rather consists in opening out a way
Whence the imprisoned splendour may escape,
Than in effecting entry for a light
Supposed to be without.

—Robert Browning—

The Phenomenon of Mysticism

Like religion as an aspect of human experience, mystical experience and its correlate, mysticism, defy precise and lucid definition. Strong cases can be made — and have been made — that all religious experience is basically the same, inclusive of mysticism. At the same time, to verify that a distinction exists between mystical experience and psychologically similar states is not without its perils. It can even be argued that the concept of mysticism implies a covert metaphysical position that is antagonistic to or at least inappropriate to serious scholarly inquiry. In truth, each of these positions are valid points of contention. Nonetheless, they do not vitiate "mysticism" as a real phenomenon. History of religions scholar Robert Ellwood argues rather persuasively that "the interpretation of [mystical] experience is *part* of the experience as it functions in both individual and social psychology."[1] This crucial insight — that mysticism cannot be delimited on philosophical *a priori* grounds, but only in terms that come out of the experience itself, that is to say, the experiencer's self-interpretation of it — is closely allied with the methodological approach known as the phenomenology of religion.[2]

The task I have set for myself in the present chapter is to phenomenologically highlight the religious/mystical experience of Howard Thurman. In other words, the focus will be on Thurman's own attempt to describe what he variously terms "the creative encounter," "the experience of encounter," and "the religious experience sensed and achieved." Clearly, such an approach will neither prove nor disprove Thurman's delineation of the mystical experience. Nor is this my concern. Rather it is hoped that by eschewing the conventional empirical rush to judgment, comprehension of that which Thurman experienced and expressed as mystic and religious will be appreciably heightened. Given these few brief considerations, let us now attempt to delineate the inner structure and motivations of Thurman's "creative encounters" and how these proved personally (and socially) transforming.

The Creative Encounter

Religion was long a familiar part of Howard Thurman's world. There was to begin with institutional religion, that is, "religious experience ... confined to the holy place, to the religious ceremonial, to the place made sacred by what has happened under its aegis at a given moment in time, identified always with a certain mood, with certain categories that were recognized as religious, a place ..." But there was also the somewhat less conventional experiencing of religion, which aspect Thurman interpreted as mysticism. He reflects thus upon some of his childhood experiences:

> ... many times as a boy I had [experienced] in the woods, growing up in Florida, or all day in my boat fishing in the Halifax River, or wandering half the night along the shores of the Atlantic, ... the dark nights ... the bright stars, and the sneaky way that a storm arises. You know, you are walking along, and you suddenly become conscious that everything is still. Not quiet. There is a great difference between stillness and quiet. Everything became still and you didn't know it until the stillness was upon you and then you were afraid to breathe. ...so that whatever barrier that was in you, that stood between you and the external world could be so relaxed that the mood that

you sensed in the environment and what was emerging inside of you became one. ...the whole environment seemed like a vacuum; the waves were no longer doing their business, coming and crawling back: they just stopped. The sea grass up on the sand dunes froze: you could hear the world breathe. And then, you could hear the wind coming now, ... and in five minutes the waves would be ten feet high.[3]

Years would pass before Thurman began to identify this early and almost unconscious "sense of Presence" with mysticism. As a young seminarian and pastor he encountered the works of Olive Schreiner and Rufus Jones, which resulted ultimately in the understanding of his own religious experience as mystic. One should recoil, however, from too hastily attributing Thurman's conceptualization of mysticism to these or other seminal minds, especially since the veracity of their ideas was generally validated by the content of his own primary experience. In reference to his nascent nameless encounters, Thurman states, "my reflections on mystical experiences were reflections after the fact, dealing with meaningful dimensions of the raw materials of my experience without being able to designate them in any particular category."[4]

Over the years Thurman continued to have, what were for him, mystical encounters. The well-known theophany in the Khyber Pass (1935) was one of the most singular developments in his life. It was an invasion of life-changing proportion:

It [the Khyber Pass experience] remains for me a transcendent moment of sheer glory and beatitude, when time, space, and circumstance evaporated and when my naked spirit looked into the depths of what is forbidden for anyone to see. I would never, never, be the same again.[5]

This revelatory event in the mountains overlooking Kinchinjunga, India and Afghanistan, was, notes Thurman, "the piece de resistance."[6] In *Footprints of a Dream*, Thurman interprets further the significance of his conversion-odyssey:

Near the end of our journey we spent a day in Khyber Pass on the border of the northwest frontier. It was an experience of vision. We stood looking at a distance into Afghanistan, while to our right, and close at hand, passed a long camel train bringing goods and ideas to the bazaars of North India. Here was the gateway through which Roman and Mogul conquerors had come in other days bringing with them goods, new concepts, and the violence of armed might. All that we had seen and felt in India seemed to be brought miraculously into focus. We saw clearly what we must do somehow when we returned to America....[7]

Thurman's experiences of mysticism were not confined solely to the natural environment, but occurred as well in the context of interpersonal relations. Two examples must suffice here. The first accounting took place while Thurman was still in India, during a day of profoundly intense exchange with Dr. Singh, head of the division of Oriental Studies at Shantiniketan University:

> That afternoon I had the most primary, naked fusing of total religious experience with another human being of which I have ever been capable. It was as if we had stepped out of social, political, cultural frames of reference, and allowed two human spirits to unite on a ground of reality that was unmarked by separateness and differences. This was a watershed of experience in my life. We had become a part of each other even as we remained steadfastly individual.[8]

A second example is equally expressive of Thurman's experience with mystical religion.   He relates the following experience in meeting with the Federation of Indian Chiefs of Saskatchewan, Canada (1962).   It was the Saskatchewan Chiefs' first encounter with an African American. In addition, most of them had had little or no previous exposure to English.

> My first lecture came in midmorning of Monday. As I was being introduced I made a sudden decision to dispense with the interpreter. When I told him of my wish, he was completely astounded. "Only two or three of us will understand what you are talking about," he said. "But I'll listen very carefully and then summarize your address for the men when you have finished." At first the atmosphere was tense and disconcerting. It was quite clear that the men didn't understand my words and were puzzled by the unusual procedure. My words went forth, but they seemed to strike an invisible wall, only to fall back to meet other words flowing from my mouth. The tension was almost unbearable. Then, suddenly, as if by some kind of magic, the wall vanished and I had the experience of sensing an organic flow of meaning passing between them and me. It was as if together we had dropped into a continuum of communication that existed *a priori* long before human speech was formed into sounds and symbols. Never before had I found a common path through such primeval woods. When I finished, there was a long breath of silence as if together we were recovering our separate rhythms.

Thurman then gives this final accounting of the gathering:

> On the last night of the conference, I was awakened by a man who brought a message that the men wanted me to say a few words in the morning before they left for home.

When I came down for breakfast, the dining room was empty. The men were standing around in clusters, chatting and smoking. Their cars were packed and they were ready to leave. While I was having my coffee and toast it was announced that I would make a closing speech. When I finished, each man came by my chair. Some took my hand, some gripped my shoulder with unspoken feeling, and at last an old chief, his two long braids falling over his shoulders, looked down at me, his eyes holding mine, as he stroked the top of my head with his right hand. And through it all, no man uttered a word.[9]

This scattering of experiences as recounted by Thurman are but faintly suggestive of the many important meanings deriving from his comprehension of mysticism. For instance, it should be noted in passing, that Thurman did not conceptualize mysticism in terms that stressed the primacy of spontaneous experience or strong sensation, as important as these may be. Nor did he characterize it as a rare and exotic experience limited to the lonely apostate or the specially chosen. As Thurman was wont to point out, "this may be a common experience for everyone."[10] Finally, as has been illustrated, mysticism was not depicted as an experience devoid of empirical and social consequence. In fine, Thurman's autobiographical accounts of mysticism are highly indicative of the kind of latent meanings issuing from the primordial experience of encounter.

The Power of Love

In the opening paragraph of his first published statement on mysticism and social change, Thurman wrote:

In the *Function of Criticism*, Mr. T.S. Eliot suggests, with reference to literary criticism, that the only critic who is qualified to interpret another's writing, is one who in some sense stands in the same stream of fact. It seems to me that this position applies very definitely to an interpretation of mystical insight. I do not claim to have scaled the heights of rarified illumination so vivid to the mystic in his moments of clarity, but I have lived for a long time in the stream of the mystic's experience and am convinced that there is available to me some significant and relevant clues as to his interpretation.[11]

What Thurman said about his experience of mysticism on this occasion remained a constant all his days. Throughout the course of his life, therefore, he attempted in a variety of ways to make articulate the nuances of his mystic insights.[12] Though his reflections scarcely qualify as systematic in the conventional sense, they convey a logic of their own that is at once profoundly creative and strikingly consistent.[13]   A closer look at Thurman's delineation of the mystic's experience is now in order.

Without question, Thurman believed that the whole of his life was informed and validated by his encounter with mystical religion. He defines mysticism as

> the response of the individual to a personal encounter with God within his own spirit. Such a response is total, affecting the inner quality of the life and its outward expression and manifestation.[14]

Interestingly enough, Thurman similarly defines religious experience as "the conscious and direct exposure of the individual to God. Such an exposure seems to the individual to be inclusive of all the meaning of his life — there is nothing that is not involved."[15]   In fact, broadly speaking, Thurman never distinguishes between mystical and religious experience. The implied meaning of his definition of mysticism seems to coincide with Ellwood's as "the cardinal means toward ultimate transformation." Religion in general, on the other hand, is regarded as "a means toward ultimate transformation."[16]

Thurman's definition of mysticism is, sans modification, basically that of his mentor Rufus Jones.[17] Beginning with a rather traditional theistic statement, he goes on to give more full and eloquent expression elsewhere to his own broad ruminations. We must note here, however, that Thurman seems to have deliberately downplayed the labeling of the experience in order to focus on that which was to him of far greater import: the content of the experience itself. In fact, he states in so many words that this was the case:

> I'm still self-conscious in using the term "mysticism" even, because it is a term that came into my life long after the experience. I think there's something so wonderful and free about being able to experience life, or reality, or religion without being bothered about how you label it. I thought, after I was acquainted with the term mysticism and its categories and so forth and so on, that for long stretches of time I neglected my own inner familiar altar, until I found that term was just a term. The important thing about it was the quality of the experience.[18]

Again, the basic point is simple. Thurman was reluctant to make too much of distinctions in such subtle matters as religious and mystical experience because of the potential for reifying categories that, in the final analysis, may be artificial. For related reasons, he tells us that even extraneous attempts to justify mystical experience seem to detract from it. "The mystic's claim does not rest on the degree to which he is able to establish empirical verification of his experience, if by empirical verification we mean a body of separate evidence," is how he puts it. Mystical experience is its own validation, affirming itself by virtue of "the mystic's claim of having in his encounter touched that which is vital, total, and absolute." Not only does the experiencer know that he or she has somehow touched the reality behind the outward manifestations of religion; they have been exposed to direct unconditioned knowledge of all that *is*.[19]

Mysticism and Personal Integration

Yet despite the self-validating quality of the mystic's experience, Thurman indicates that the felt necessity to communicate said experience persists. The experience of mysticism — that of infinity, the ultimate and absolute — may be personal and private, but it must not and cannot be completely "other."[20] This is Thurman's discreet way of acknowledging an attendant yield of mystical experience, perforce, the discursive engagement of the human mind.[21] As a participant in mystical reality, the rationalizing mind must have opportunity to conceptualize and verify that which is experienced as most profound, elemental, metaphysical, and religious:

> And here is the interesting dilemma and the fascinating paradox. The mind insists that all experiences fall into order in a system of meaning. What the mystic experiences within must somehow belong to that which is without. It is reasonable then for the individual to expect to validate his claim of truth by his experience of life in the world. What he experiences in the world must not seem radically different from the quality and the kind that takes place within. ... the necessity for trying to find external validation and vindication can never be relaxed.[22]

A valuable interpretation of this integration of the mystical and rational is supplied by John A. Taylor, former Thurman assistant at Boston University's Marsh Chapel and successor at Fellowship Church. He finds a certain attitudinal prerequisite in such religious experiencing, namely "the willingness to be torn and mended, wounded and healed, exhausted and renewed by the dynamics of the rational and the mystical in one body."[23]   Thurman, for his part, draws attention to an even broader spectrum of events that need be accounted for in the experience of mysticism. Stimuli of various sorts — inspiring natural environment, a religious setting such as a church or temple, participation in spiritual disciplines, the tenor of one's thought, conscious or otherwise, a life crisis — all of these may "place the individual in candidacy for spiritual awareness and insight."[24]

In Thurman's case, the lack of status historically accorded persons of African descent in the national body clearly qualifies as a critical constituent factor. The background settings for his mystic experiences and ruminations often serve as vivid reminders that here was a person continually confronted by his liminal status in American society.[25]   To be certain, the stabilizing influences of his internal counter-structure, the "idiom" of Blackness, were always in evidence. "My roots are deep in the throbbing reality of the Negro idiom," writes Thurman, "and from it I draw a full measure of inspiration and vitality."[26]   Thus, out of the faith of Negro spirituals forged in the fires of oppression he encountered "... a source of rich testimony [concerning] life and death, because in many ways they are the voice, sometimes strident, sometimes muted and weary, of a people for whom the cup of suffering overflowed in haunting overtones of majesty, beauty and power..."[27]   In the final analysis, however, Thurman's intense acquaintance with the root meanings of African American religion also moved him to utter protestation. "I believe, with my forefathers, that this is God's world. This faith has had to fight against disillusionment, despair, and the vicissitudes of American history."[28]

The bitter and seemingly permanent proscription which Thurman experienced by virtue of being African American is an open portal to comprehending the nuances of his mysticism. Similar to the experience of mysticism, the African American estate is itself a counterstructure of consequence, a rupture or break with the conventional and the ordinary, however these are construed. For Thurman, life was deeply oriented by the gifts of African American culture. These were in turn undergirded and encompassed by what he regarded as an even more focal and fontal mysticism.

Thurman's status in society as part of a racial-ethnic counterstructure may thus point toward his accessibility to mystical realities. Nothing definitive can be said on this matter. What can be said, however, is best heard from Thurman himself. "[The individual] carries his struggle for selfhood into his relationships with the world of nature and with the social order.... Things become immoral that defeat this achieving individuality."[29]   Referring elsewhere to these same internal buffetings, Thurman adamantly counsels, "launch out into the open sea or get beaten to death."[30]

In short, it appears that for Thurman the encounter with a sense of Presence had an immediate twofold effect. On the one hand, the debilitating effects of racial discrimination were transcended. On the other, self-centeredness was transformed to God-centeredness.   In Thurman's terms, revelation meets intuition; God possesses the person; a new value judgment is ushered in:

> Now things are not ethical or unethical merely because they aid or take away from his [the mystic's] achieving individuality but because they are now viewed as ways that lead to the mount of vision or away from the mount of vision. The meaning of life is for him summarized in the vision of the good which he has experienced. He must stand ever in immediate candidacy for the reception of God.

And again:

> The judgment of God stands now where the judgment of the self as the rationalizer of experience formerly stood. Things are no longer merely ethical or unethical — they are sinful or righteous — a religious quality has appeared in morality.[31]

As Thurman indicates, it is the mystic's encounter with God, settled down in the very lees of the human spirit, that provides the person with the conviction that however important and thoroughgoing or even devastating the contradictions of life, they are not ultimate and final. An apodictic truth is gleaned, namely, that life has its own restraints against that which stings and casts down. The unity of life, no matter how contradictory on the surface, must yield to the control of God. Thus, grounded in the apperception of divine reality and empowered with "a proper sense of self," the individual can now begin to act.

Mysticism and Moral-Ethical Concerns

There was for Thurman an unrelenting third yield from the mystical experience. Stated simply, the process of transformation entailed the integration of said experience into the rest of life. As we have observed, the initially inchoate but powerful mystical account seeks appropriate and authentic expression. From Thurman's purview, the interpretation is not simply extraneous to the experience, but reflects the complexities of mixing the energies of the experience with the realities of ordinary and often impersonal life. His description of the residue from the mystical encounter utilizes a number of metaphorical expressions.[32] However, the most powerful and moving of all his metaphors have to do with water. He writes:

> It is very striking to me that there is a fundamental paradoxical relationship between the waters of the land and the sea. All the waters of all the lands are fed by the sea and all the waters of all the lands go back to the sea. The goal and the source of the river are the same. The symbolism that is most striking to me of what the Christian mystic achieves in his union is that of the gulf stream moving through the waters of the sea, a part of it in a sense unified with the sea, participating in all of the basic manifestations of the sea but in a sense, it remains the gulf stream.[33]

Thurman's water metaphor illustrates the creative and transformative possibilities awaiting the life established in the reality of spiritual Presence. To begin with, he describes life so experienced as teeming, surging, ever-flowing into new territories. It is dynamic, imaginative, always potential, forever unfinished. Equally important, in the wake of this process a transvaluation of all moral, ethical and religious conventions occurs; goodness, unity, justice and wholeness are experienced as "a growing edge of hope." The now luminous human spirit in quietness and confidence affirms that life is not yet made, and that it will respond, it will yield, it can be shaped. Theologian S. Paul Schilling offers the following commentary on Thurman's liquid ruminations: "Like the waters of the river, which come from the sea and return to the sea, we come from God and return to God, but since God himself is constantly creating anew we too are on a never-ending journey."[34] Thus, in Thurman's representation of mysticism, the very malleability of life is impressed upon us as its vitality.[35]

For Thurman, the dynamics of transformation involved moving beyond the demands of theoretical exposition and personal affirmation (without ever finally leaving either behind) to realization of the moral-ethical component of the experience. To echo Thurman's own metaphor, what he came to discover was that utter immersion in the currents of the river of life was both necessary and inevitable to retaining consciousness of the mystic vision. What is ascertained in the divine "moment," in other words, requires actualization and equilibrium in the ongoing "moments" of persons. In the river one discovers that life denies bifurcation; the dichotomies projected by society — black and white, sacred and secular, church and world, and the like — are conclusively proven false. Thurman declares that our conceived separations and divisions are in truth but aspects of a single reality, a single meaning. Yet not one in the sense of a dull determinism, but in the harmony of a universe with a profound degree of openness and freedom.

> My testimony is that life is against all dualism. Life is One. Therefore, a way of life that is worth living must be a way worthy of life itself. Nothing less than that can abide. Always, against all that fragments and shatters and against all things that separate and divide within and without, life labors to meld together into a single harmony.[36]

There are, of course, many mystic commentators who have emphasized in their definitions that mysticism is an experience of oneness. Thurman sought to satisfy his own hunger for unity in two ways: through such introspective means as the spiritual disciplines and through interpersonal relationships. In the latter regard, he quotes (from memory) a passage from Charles Bennett's essay, *A Philosophical Study of Mysticism*:

> Every lover knows that in love he has somehow touched finality, a foretaste of his destiny. Lovers come to realize that that they can only keep the meaning of the experience by letting it go. It is fatal to try to keep dwelling in it. The meaning of love must be worked out; for love is a metaphysical experience discovering to one not only the beloved but making all things new. The new truth has been grasped but it must be assimilated. So with the relationship between the mystic and God. If he is to retain what God means, he must let God go, that is, *he must surrender the exclusive direction of the mind upon God and establish in the world the God to find whom he left the world.*[37] (emphasis added)

The above analogy adopted by Thurman is important for understanding his relationship to social change. This passage indicates, in no uncertain terms, that the valid God-encounter must move beyond merely inspiring revelation to interpersonal intimacy and social accountability. Similar to the intense experience between lovers, God is experienced as love; even more, God *is* love. Thus, the person who is loved by God and receives the blessings of God's presence as an act of grace is impelled to continue the sensation in interpersonal relationships.   So, too, the discovery is made by persons who are free to love that they are more fully in possession of themselves.   In coming to themselves within, they become the very embodiment of the unifying impetus for love.

I shall return to this theme momentarily. Earlier in this chapter, it will be recalled, we touched on Thurman's interpretation of the eternal paradox confronting the mystic: the reconciliation of mediated (mind) and unmediated (spirit) reality.   For Thurman, this problem extended as well to several interrelated levels — the inner and the outer, the one and the many, the personal and the social. In the final analysis, he resolved these tensions by pro-actively participating in the affairs of the world.

Rufus Jones applies the term, "affirmation mystics," to those individuals concerned with working out in a social frame of reference the problematic realism of their mystic experience.   Thurman has a similar perspective on such mystics, referring to them in at least one writing as "mystic-ascetics."   The preferred designation here, of course, is "mystic-activist."   In any case, all three phrases convey something of the more basic motivations underlying Thurman's own radical mystic undertakings.[38]

> ...the principle of alternation is in the very structure of all experience. The mystic discovers this in a most extraordinary fashion. He is a man — he is a part and parcel of all the world of nature — he has warring impulses within and participates in strife without. He sees that the world of things and men does not conform to the unity which he has experienced in his vision. Was his vision false?   Was his experience genuine or was it merely an illusion?   He finds that the two worlds must in some sense be one because he participates actively in both at the same moment but he is convinced that the meaning of the below is in the above.
>
> With such a conviction, asceticism no longer means withdrawal from men but rather it means a steady insistence that one's human relations conform more and more to the transparency of one's inner graces, one's inner equilibrium in which is his consciousness of the active presence of God. Humanity is viewed as a unit within which are particular individuals all of which must be yielded to the control of God.   This calls for the highest possible ethical demands for one's own conduct, for one's outgoing relation.   Often it leads one to cut right across all social forms, all social behavior patterns, all conventions.[39]

The preceding passage shows Thurman's conceptualization of how the world view and lifestyle of the mystic interact. Undoubtedly, however, a most critical addendum to the explication of this interaction is the theme of love. As we have seen, human love is for Thurman a valid analogy for the passionate quest for the omnipresent Beloved. In fact, he sees love as the major dynamic in sustaining awareness of God; it is the *sine qua non* of the mystic's experience:

> In the kind of religion I have been describing, which is essentially the religion of the inner light, the individual has a sense of experiencing the love of God. He senses that he is being dealt with at a center in himself that goes beyond all of his virtues and his vices. And it is this which he seeks to experience with his fellows.[40]

This statement is immensely important for its disclosure of the theistic theological bent of Thurman's mysticism.[41] For him, God must be personal and so meets the experiencer as Love in the internal and external dimensions of life. In the realm of social interactions, the experience of personal encounter led Thurman to see himself as now more integrated with larger humanity because he had experienced the One who confirms and integrates. His desire was to share the simple but important truth of his discovery, which was that "self-love is the contagion."[42] As much as was possible, the sensation had to be shared, repeated, made accessible in the lives of others.

> To love means to have an intrinsic interest in another person. It is not of necessity contingent upon any kind of group or family closeness. True, such closeness may provide a normal setting for the achieving of intrinsic interest, but the fact that two men are brothers having the same parents provides no mandatory love relationship between them.... Men do not love in general, but they do love in particular. To love means dealing with persons in the concrete rather than in the abstract. In the presence of love, there are no stereotypes, no classes and no masses.[43]

Thurman's exposition of the relation inhering between mysticism and love is emblematic of his extreme sensitivity to the human condition. The period in which we now live is characterized by a complex of factors, prominent among them technology, bureaucratic organization and the rationalizing, pragmatic mind-set that goes along with it. Increasingly, modern persons are confronted with their own anonymity, the result of depersonalization, anomie, alienation, and the like. It may even be said that, in a most haunting sense, we have become detached from ourselves and thus find it ever more difficult to relate meaningfully to others.

Thurman proffers his observations on this fundamental callousness so endemic to the the modern mood. They are sounded as a caution, even a warning.

> There is no substitute for hard understanding of more and more of another's fact. This serves as a corrective against doing violence to those for whom we have a sense of caring because of great gaps in our knowledge of their fact. This is generally the weakness in so much lateral good will in the world. It is uninformed, ignorant, sincere good will. It does not seek to feed its emotion with a healthy diet of facts, data, information from which insights opening the door to the other person's meaning are derived. I think that this is why it is impossible to have intrinsic interest in people with whom we are out of living or vicarious contact.

And a further admonition:

> To speak of the love for humanity is meaningless. There is no such thing as humanity. What we call humanity has a name, was born, lives on a street, gets hungry, needs all the particular things we need. As an abstract, it has no reality whatsoever.[44]

Mysticism and Social Change: A Glimpse Ahead

Mysticism has often been portrayed as at cross-purposes with the dynamics of change. In Thurman's case, for certain, it can confidently be said that not every mystic avoids interfacing with the environing society. As an experiencer of mystic realities, he did not surrender to the various apparatuses and attitudes that dominate modern life. So, too, was no place given to those cognitive expressions of reality which diminished his inner sense of freedom. Being thus concerned with ultimates, he did not hesitate to break with socially constructed reality — or at least that reality in all its ambiguous impurity. Instead, he sought to make manifest in the midst of the world the profoundest meanings of his inner experience of oneness and love, ideologically parting company with those accepting (at least in a tacitly provisional way) of extant social values and arrangements. In fine, Thurman's transformative experience of perfect love was matched by an equally transformative freedom, which not only enabled him to serve as a spiritual resource to the world, but also to participate in social action with "quietness and confidence." I adumbrate the topic of a later chapter with this socio-mystical statement of Thurman's:

> Social action, ... is an expression of resistance against whatever tends to, or separates one from, the experience of God, who is the very ground of his being....
>
> The mystic's concern with the imperative of social action is not merely to improve the condition of society. It is not merely to feed the hungry, not merely to relieve human suffering and human misery. If this were all, in and of itself, it would be important surely. But this is not all. The basic consideration has to do with the removal of all that prevents God from coming to himself in the life of the individual. Whatever there is that blocks this, calls for action.[45]

PART TWO:

MYSTICISM AND SOCIAL CHANGE

Chapter Three

Thurman and Fellowship Church

"Western religion has stressed social progress toward the kingdom, while Eastern religion has emphasized personal growth toward the enlightenment of the individual's soul. The modern believer is going to need both dimensions, somehow harmonized. Howard Thurman ... has stated convictions which suggest the future of American theology."

—Deane William Ferm—

Having examined both the social and phenomenological underpinnings of Thurman's mysticism in considerable detail, it is time to reconsider my original contention, namely, that the contours of Thurman's mystic activity, while many, betray an undeniable capacity for serious engagement of the social world.

We have accounted for Thurman's own venture and response to what he described as the "experience of encounter." To be sure, little question remains that he not only regarded mystical religion as foundational but emphatically personal and private. Yet it is equally clear that he regarded as problematic certain notions of structural insulation and segregation, particularly along the lines of religion and race. The point to be consistently remembered in the latter connection is Thurman's stress on the futility of seeking to retain the vitality and equanimity of mystic experience *in vacuo* from others. "For this is why we were born," he avers, "Men, all men belong to each other, and he who shuts himself away diminishes himself, and he who shuts another away from him destroys himself."[1] So stated, there is little reason to doubt that Thurman's experience of mysticism engendered or at the very least fostered participation in communal and societal concerns.

Victor Turner: Communitas and Worship

To part company with the conventional wisdom of sociology, which eschews a viable relationship between mystic experiencing and group worship dynamics may at first glance appear to be indefensible. Indeed, I would be the first to admit that the complexities deriving from such an arrangement make absolute quantification of such impossible. However, there can be no denying of the fact that mystical experience often has been and remains significantly associated with intentional group worship. Thus Ernst Troeltsch notes, if begrudgingly, in his discussion of seventeenth-century England that "the Quakers overcame the natural, anti-social, or rather individualistic, tendency of mysticism."[2] In fact, he says, they exercised "an unequalled power in the general life of the English people."[3] D. B. Robertson's commentary on the same period is even more forceful, stating that the Quakers "became an instrument for repudiating the tyranny of church power and all power which oppressed the lives of men. Mysticism repudiated tradition, in so far as tradition and precedent were oppressive or limited the individual in his approach to God."[4] Other examples can be cited, but this precedent is confirmation enough that through the mystic's participation in intentionally religious group practice public conditions may be deeply affected. The mystic's experience, to repeat, is not without considerable sociological consequence.

Philosopher Robert C. Williams, in a most insightful essay on the modalities of worship, suggests that any valid recounting of the experience and meaning of worship must focus on three elements central to the situation of the worshipper — "that is, *where* the worshipper worships, *who* the worshipper is, and the *nature of order* generated by means of the experience of worship." Each of these conditions, he posits, has to do with the "inner nature of the worship experience itself."   Williams' views on the interactive nature of worship are in substantial agreement with our own. It is important to indicate that the nucleus of his ideas — as well as those of several other scholars noted herein — derives from the work of cultural anthropologist Victor Turner.[5]

The work of Turner is far too involved to thoroughly explicate here. But his point of departure is highly provocative, in that he posits the existence of two primary modes of human interrelatedness in society, "structure" and "anti-structure" respectively. The first of these interactions is well described by theologian J. Randall Nichols:

[It] is the familiar everyday world of organization, hierarchy, more-and-less, differentiation of functions, values, and positions — in short, what we loosely call the social order. Its dominant characteristic is *structure*: it has shape and predictability and, even with all its vicissitudes, regularity. It is where we spend most of our time. Most sociological and anthropological theory has interpreted "social" to mean "social-structural" in this sense.[6]

The second mode of interrelatedness as defined by Turner is "society as an unstructured and relatively undifferentiated *comitatus*, community, or even communion of equal individuals..."[7] Basically, what Turner is arguing for are categories of societal interpretation that are seen as processual rather than static. In his analysis of ritual, for instance, he indicates that individuals and collectivities alternate between fixed and "floating worlds." This creative dialectic, often ignored by the social sciences, provides Turner with an important perspective on personal and social dynamics.

Communitas is a fact of everyone's experience, yet it has almost never been regarded as a reputable or coherent object of study by social scientists. It is, however, central to religion, literature, drama, and art, and its traces may be found deeply engraven in law, ethics, kinship, and even economics. It becomes visible in tribal rites of passage, in millenarian movements, in monasteries, in the counterculture, and on countless informal occasions.[8]

As can be seen in the above statement, Turner's more formal designation for the social modality of anti-structure is "communitas." "Communitas" is the social counterpart to "liminality" (noted earlier), to be distinguished from "community" in its more political or geographical senses. Akin to the transformation of social-structural status that is experienced by the individual undergoing liminality, communitas generates its own process, "stripping" and "leveling" persons and making heteronomous all prior understandings. So interpreted, communitas indicates human relations when all the structures that separate people are abolished, and where hindrances to intersubjectivity and the inward desire to actualize relatedness (or love) have been largely if not altogether dissipated.[9]

> Major liminal situations are occasions on which, so to speak, a society takes cognizance of itself, or rather where, in an interval between their incumbency of specific fixed positions, members of that society may obtain an approximation, however limited, to a global view of man's place in the cosmos and his relations with other classes of visible entities.[10]

Again, the implications of Turner's ideas while far more searching than can be summarized here are significant for a new and fuller interpretation of the interaction between mysticism, worship, and society. Turner himself, no less, advances our line of reasoning in this regard, applying certain of his own insights to the context of worship. For one, he perceives communitas as having the special ability to encode itself in special symbol systems:

> Liminality, marginality, and structural inferiority are conditions in which are frequently generated myths, symbols, rituals, philosophical systems, and works of art. These cultural forms provide men with a set of templates or models which are, at one level, periodical reclassifications of reality and man's relationship to society, nature, and culture. But they are more than classification, since they incite men to action as well as to thought. Each of these productions has a multivocal character, having many meanings, and each is capable of moving people at many psychobiological levels simultaneously.[11]

From this crucial insight Turner develops a more formal conceptualization of worship. His conclusions are startling, in that the very symbols generated in and through communitas bear about themselves the potential capacity to reinvoke or reenact said experience.

> ...under favorable circumstances some structural form generated long ago, from a moment of communitas, may be almost miraculously liquified into a living form of communitas again.

And again:

> The vain task of trying to find out in what precise way certain symbols found in the ritual, poetry, or iconography of a given society "reflect" or "express" its social or political structure can then be abandoned. Symbols may well reflect not structure but anti-structure, and not only "reflect" it but contribute to *creating* it.[12]

The categories of interpretation utilized by Turner and since adapted by others offer valuable clues for studying worship as a social correlate of religious and mystical experience. To recall just a part of the position advanced by Turner and echoed by Williams, worship has the power to "incite men to action as well as thought."[13] We now turn our attention, therefore, to determining such meanings in the mystic-worship of Thurman.

Howard Thurman: Worship and Community

In contemporary Western culture, the worship event is increasingly regarded as somewhat removed from the pressing concerns of the everyday world. Akin to mysticism itself, worship is construed as privatistic, if not outright escapist and "otherworldly." From Thurman's standpoint, such sentiments could hardly be further from the truth. At its best, group worship is invariably heightening and liberating, a stimulus and guide to socially responsible involvement:

> The center of our undertaking, the heart of our commitment, summarizes itself in terms of the worship of God.... I mean [by] the worship of God, the immediate awareness of the pushing out of the barriers of self, the moment when we flow together into one, when I am not male or female, yellow or green or black or white or brown, educated or illiterate, rich or poor, sick or well, righteous or unrighteous — but a naked human spirit that spills over into other human spirits as they spill over into me. Together, we become one under the transcending glory and power of the spirit of the living God.... And even for those who are not believers, something happens, a sense of being related to a power that is more than I am, that is not the generation of my mind, that is not the generation of my desires, that is not merely the ground of my wishful thinking, but a vitalizing, purifying, exciting moment of presence.[14]

The relation of mysticism to the collective worship experience is, as has already been noted, a most intricate one. Quite clearly, however, a number of important correlations do exist. The commonality is perhaps best evidenced in the need that both have for outward expression of the inward experience. As Robert Bellah has noted, religious encounter, however and wherever experienced, requires some sort of symbolization to "complete the experience."[15] Obviously religious experience, even that belonging to the mystic, has a context, and context can only be communicated via concepts, mental images, group affiliations — the media of language and culture in the broadest sense.

There is thus an indispensable need which almost inevitably links the individual experiencer to the community of worship. For

Thurman and those who gathered around him, it may be said that the symbols of worship adumbrated, in the language of Turner, a state of "communitas" in which all social contradictions to perfect human intercommunion were reversed. In essence, worship was synonymously experienced as a "heightening" and "leveling" event and, therefore, positively democratic and equalitarian.[16] The social character of Thurman's mystic worship is even better understood when observed in its social context as an expression of devotionalism. The experience of one worshipper at Thurman-pastored Fellowship Church provides an illuminating "for instance" of this idea. I recount her story at length:

> A scattered few still stand before the church. Meditation Service is over, and those who have been quietly waiting on the sidewalk or in the short hallway that terminates in the doors to Fellowship Hall, have moved on up the stairs that rise to the left and right of the doors. One little lady feels a special sensitivity today as she moves up the stairs. She pauses on the double landing to which both stairways lead, nods "Good Morning" to some familiar faces, mounts the short wide flight to the level of the sanctuary, where the black-robed choir members press back in the little entry, waiting their signal to march down the center aisle, singing the processional hymn.
>
> Today she is to become a member of Fellowship Church. She is moved by a pervading sense of quiet gratitude, of a warm sense of belonging to this place, to these people, to this fellowship. And she knows with an unusual confidence that this feeling will withstand the analysis and scrutiny to which her well trained modern mind may subject it. At last a sense of real kinship, without a hint of compulsion. Of her own volition — without fear of being subjected to didactic creed, of hidden financial or social pressures, of being caught in an atmosphere of "doing good" — of her own volition, she will sign a little book and become a church member.
>
> She has moved down the aisle to the front row on the left, where seats are reserved for her and the other new members-to-be. She exchanges a smiling glance with the man to her left and with the lady who represents the membership committee.
>
> The prelude is over; the choir moves down the aisle; the congregation rises to join in a hearty "Joyful, Joyful We Adore Thee." Now the invocation ... simple words yet so meaningful in Dr. Thurman's tones ... the responsive reading in which his deliberate voice ranges from depths of seriousness to high singing joy. The second hymn is followed by the period of meditation, that period of quiet which had embarrassed her at first. Dr. Thurman speaking to God so intimately ... too intimately for public gaze, she had thought. And how ... how precious, how moving these few quiet moments ...
>
> Oh, yes, here he is announcing it ... We are to sign the book in which our names are printed. Just five of us ... I come third. Quickly done! Yes, I dedicate myself. For the first time in my life I dedicate myself in fellowship. Now the reading of the commitment by the whole congregation: "I affirm my need for a growing understanding of all men as sons of God, and I seek after

a vital experience of God as revealed in Jesus of Nazareth and other great religious spirits whose fellowship with God was the foundation of their fellowship with men. I desire to share..." I am a member ... desiring to share.[17]

In this narrative we are made privy to an occasion in the life of the worshipper during which the usual structures of church and society have fallen away. Ordinary barriers of creed, caste, gender, and the like — so important in larger society — have been transvalued and become, at least for the moment, of non-effect. For this new member, the scenario of cohesive worship conveyed elements of both symbolic and actual completion via mystical interpretation, that is to say, Thurman's interpretation of life: "Experiences of spiritual unity are more compelling than the things that divide."[18]

Later, there will be occasion to examine other statements supportive of this woman's perceptions. And while the worship experience of persons associated with Thurman may or may not be considered mystical in and of itself, what is apparent about the correlative group worship is a particular *mood* reflective of his mystic understandings. Fundamentally, this mood has to do with claiming worship as an experience of sanctuary, where persons can come together in communitas, apart from social-structural distinctions, obligations, and rights. Thurman's thoughts relative to the meaning of his own sermons bear out this view:

> The preaching deals almost always with the practices of religion and man's encounter with the Spirit of the Living God. Very little of the preaching concerns itself with social issues as they are generally conceived. It is never forgotten that we are a church and not merely some kind of social whip and protest group. We propose to offer experiences of deep moment for the spirit of man during which he can reestablish his sense of direction, lift his sights, renew his commitment and get strength for the struggles of life at the point of his vocation and function.[19]

Up until now, I have made no direct reference to Thurman's concept of community. This is because his expressions of corporate worship and community are so radically and organically intertwined as to make distinction largely superfluous. In essence, Thurman's description of community incorporates the same motifs as Turner's communitas, that shared experience of intersubjectivity, interpretive values, and creative paradigms made potential in the (liminal) state of worship.[20] As we have noted previously, it was incumbent upon Thurman to somehow perpetuate the experience of his mystic envisagements. In fact, his lifelong passion was to make accessible to other persons conditions generally supportive of their respective movements toward authenticity and freedom. He testifies that "community is the native climate of the human spirit. It is for this reason that we seem most our true selves when we are deeply involved in relations with other selves." There is little doubt that the experience of corporate worship is vehicular to such an awareness:

"The key to community must be fashioned of a common understanding of life, a common faith, a common commitment." Every person is at long last concerned with community. There is a persistent strain in the human spirit that rejects the experience of isolation as being alien to its genius.[21]

In sum, it may be argued that mystical experience is finally personal, with its most intimate variables deriving from the individual personality, yet it can lead to a cloud of witnesses. Thurman-generated examples are, to say the least, in abundant number. Our focus here is on one particularly lucid dimension of that witness — the Fellowship Church.

Institutional Mysticism

In 1952 Thurman made the following pronouncement:

"It is possible to develop a religious fellowship that is so creative in character, so convincing in quality, that it inspires the mind to multiply experiences of unity, which experiences become over and over again more compelling than the concepts, than the ways of life, than the sects, than the creeds that separate men."[22]

The context for these remarks was the mortgage burning of The Church for the Fellowship of All Peoples. The Fellowship Church community offers one of the most compelling examples of how mystic experience can become socially reproduced.

In no small measure, Fellowship Church is the sociological transmission of Thurman's mystic worldview. As one of the primary means by which his relation to society became articulate, the church functioned in at least two ways. In the first place, it served to enhance the worth of each of its participants while militating against contrary social winds. Secondly, the Fellowship experience provided each communicant with an alternative angle of perception or transcendence. This establishment of a qualitative difference between ultimate and societal constructions of reality was key, providing incentive for creative and compelling responses to extant social problems.

Peter Berger and Thomas Luckmann, in their oft-quoted work *The Social Construction of Reality*, speak of the never-ending dialectical chain so informative of human life in society.[23] One of their points is that the reality of society and its world views are so imposing that they are believed by many to be the only reality. However, as Ellwood observes in his commentary on the subject, and which Berger and Luckmann corroborate, "not everyone is equally 'taken in.' Nearly every society has its alienated individuals who march to a different drummer, as well as its true believers, who embrace the social vision with an untoward passion."[24] The distinction that Ellwood makes between deviant and true believer is rather amorphous and arbitrary — depending on the circumstance they may very well be one and the same — but there is little question that his comments otherwise reflect the very meanings and intentionalities present in the Fellowship Church.

Fellowship Church was established in 1943 and formally organized in 1944 in San Francisco, at a crucial juncture in the history of the nation. The country was caught up in the throes of a war for democracy overseas, while at home racial segregation continued unabated as *de jure* and *de facto* policy. During this same period the Pacific basin and particularly San Francisco underwent considerable population shifts. There was in the first place the unjustified deportation of thousands of California's Japanese to relocation camps in the center of the country, a direct and irrational consequence of the so-called "yellow peril." Secondly, and equally portentous, there occurred an influx of Black migrants whose movement was attributable chiefly to the abundance of jobs in national defense industries but also the government mandate to promote integration for the general good of the nation. In actuality, of course, such decrees were seldom advanced beyond public rhetoric.

For the Golden Gate city, the rapid demographic changes meant that the city found itself face-to-face for the first time with large numbers of African Americans. To make matters worse, the city already had to contend with a fairly sizeable ethnic population of Chinese, Japanese and Mexicans. As one white citizen put it, "I feel squeamish and uneasy when I move around the city now because everywhere I look I see a Negro." Notwithstanding, San Francisco rapidly developed a reputation for being uniquely tolerant, even liberal, in matters of race and ethnicity. For example, after conducting a survey of race relations in the city, the noted sociologist Charles S. Johnson concluded, "a better solution may be arrived at [here] than has been found in large Eastern and Midwestern or Southern cities." Soon thereafter, the city received even more widespread idyllic recognition when it hosted the first meeting of the United Nations (1945). In brief, this was the social setting which gave broad impetus and encouragement to the Fellowship Church idea.[25]

In terms of organizational structure, Fellowship Church was from its inception an innovative institution, differing as it did in emphasis from other religious communions. It was, after all, a laboratory, "a pilot development of the integrated church movement in America."[26] Beginning from a membership of less than 35 persons, within eight years the number of active members stood near 350, surpassing the seating capacity of the church. In addition, two types of membership arrangements were in place, "resident" for local persons and national "members-at-large." In both cases, persons were encouraged to maintain dual affiliations with Fellowship and with their originating church:

> ...the purpose of the dual membership was two-fold. First it provided an opportunity for people who lived in San Francisco and were active in local "segregated" churches to experience a racially-integrated fellowship, religious in character. They would thus be able to share this experience in the church of their original fellowship....
>
> The second purpose ... was to provide some way by which people who lived in different parts of America and the world might be related to the development of this dream in San Francisco, as participating individuals. Through them the idea behind our venture would spread, and men and women who were despairing of the church in this aspect would be lifted up and strengthened.[27]

With conspicuous exceptions, the function of resident dual membership did not turn out to be wholly practical. For a combination of reasons, many members were either unwilling or unable to effectively divide their loyalties between two churches, generally opting to devote the entirety of their energies to Fellowship. On the other hand, at-large dual membership became an increasingly vital instrument for communicating the social viability of the Fellowship witness. By 1952, over one thousand persons had become at-large members, representing all walks of life from every part of the country, and such places as Canada, Iran, England, Nigeria, South Africa, India, Japan, Norway, Formosa, New Zealand, and Turkey. Among the members-at-large were such persons as South African writer Alan Paton, Federal Judge J. Waites Waring who opened the lily-white South Carolina Democratic primaries to African Americans, Eleanor Roosevelt, actor and baritone Todd Duncan, educators and social reformers Mary MacLeod Bethune, Benjamin Mays, and Channing Tobias.[28] Thus, through members-at-large and other friends of the Fellowship collectivity word about the work of the church circulated nationally and internationally, kindling "confidence in the practical possibility of our kind of fellowship in their own communities."[29]

During Thurman's tenure the composition of the church remained fairly constant. Resident members were primarily couples or single adults, but a gradual and steady increase in families with children occurred. Approximately 60 percent of the membership was of European origin, 35 percent African and 5 percent Chinese, Japanese, and Mexican.[30] In addition to racial and cultural heterogeneity, the church represented a broad cross-section of the religious spectrum: Quaker, Baptist, Roman Catholic, Presbyterian, Jewish, Congregational, Methodist, and Episcopal, but also those who held no particular affinity. Along the lines of class and education, most of the membership were of non-professional status — shipyard workers, government employees, housewives, and so forth — although there could be counted a few teachers, nurses, and social workers, a dentist and a lawyer, and an occasional businessperson. Early on there were several faculty from local colleges, but these remained only a short time.

In the opinion of one founding member, Muriel Bullard, the outstanding common denominator among the Fellowship Church congregants was that they were "people with an independent mind." Similarly, Thurman notes, "any organization whose membership crosses class and caste lines in the pursuit of common goals, is by that very fact, composed mostly of marginal people. People who live, think, move and feel on the fringe of groups into which the great common culture pattern would place them. They do not 'belong.'" Simply put, Fellowship Church did not conform to the characterization (even now widely held) of being "white-collar" in composition.[31]

The leadership of the church was from the beginning and has remained deliberately interethnic and interracial. Alfred G. Fisk, a Presbyterian minister and professor of philosophy at San Francisco State College was, along with Thurman, co-founder and then co-pastor of the church during its first two years.[32] "It was crucial to discover whether or not there could be developed a bond of such authentic community that — contrary prevailing social patterns notwithstanding — the caucasians would not gravitate to Dr. Fisk's leadership and the non-Caucasians to mine," writes Thurman. "The fact that this kind of gravitation did not take place gave the church, at its very inception, a spirit that sustained it through the many crises that were to come." After the departure of Fisk, the interfaith aspect of Fellowship took on heightened meaning, with ministers from various communions invited to serve in the capacity of associate or assistant. Among these was Adena Joy, a Quaker and former faculty member at Lewis and Clark College, James Brewer and Robert Meyners, Unitarian and Congregationalist internees respectively, and Francis Geddes, who eventually followed Thurman as minister-in-residence.[33]

Of course, church leadership was not confined to just religious professionals. From its very inception the corporate body saw itself as fully participatory in all phases of the work, including the administrative.[34] A "Church Board Pro Tem," consisting of five blacks and five whites had assumed important leadership responsibilities prior to the church's formal organization.[35] Later, the even more pivotal "Committee of Nine," consisting of both women and men — three whites, three blacks, two Japanese and one Chinese — was elected to formulate and recommend statements relative to Fellowship's purpose, goals, commitment, and organizational apparatus. What eventually became the permanent governing agent of the church, the board of trustees, continued to cultivate this sense of inclusivity. For example, at one point the church's rapid growth was responsible for noticeable segmentation among the membership and psychological distancing between the board and the rest of the fellowship. In response, the "town meeting" concept was adopted, wherein full and free discussions were held in the homes of members on a sectional basis prior to regularly scheduled meetings of the entire congregation. There were, of course, various other strategies employed to enhance group cohesiveness. But in the final analysis, what is to be said is that under Thurman's leadership the organizational structure of the church was very flexible and wholly consistent with the group's expressed understanding of its purpose.

Hopefully, it is becoming apparent how Thurman's mystic orientation served as a paradigm and catalyst for the development of Fellowship Church. In a matter of speaking the church is both symbolic and vehicular, a statement and structure attesting to the pastor's mystic concerns. This is not to imply by any means that the group — or the individual members thereof — lacked an interpretative stance of its own; far from it. We are simply stressing the fundamental importance of Thurman's ability to confirm and, perhaps even for some, to symbolize the seamless union of the human and the transcendent. It is in this context and this context alone, for example, that Thurman's atypical acknowledgment of his own leadership must be interpreted: "It is true that in a sense I 'called' the membership, whereas usually the membership calls its minister."[36] He offers a more detailed assessment of this self-understanding elsewhere in his writings:

> The communal growth and development of Fellowship Church marked also my own personal pilgrimage. The unfolding of the pattern here was the scenario by which I was working out the meaning of my own life. In the validation of the idea, I would find validation for myself. All programs, projects, and such were as windows through which my spiritual landscape could be seen and sensed. This qualitative experience I sought for all who shared in the Fellowship community — a search for the *moment* when God appeared in the head, heart, and soul of the worshipper. This was the moment above all moments, intimate, personal, private, yet shared, miraculously, with the whole human family in celebration.[37]

To repeat, then, from a sociological point of view Fellowship represents what in many respects may be called the routinization of Thurman's mysticism. Not all participants in the Fellowship experience were directly concerned with mysticism in the strict sense. However, the membership did share in a general understanding of religious experience as a vehicle of quest or concern for the actualization of each person's latent potential. Such actualization was considered to be of preeminent transformative value at the level of the personal and in the interstices of society. Referring again to Ellwood, some groups "do not so much use mysticism as a means of upholding a consistency-based truth [such as scripture or democracy], as make it a symbol of an expansion of consciousness that may run ahead of certain social definitions, at least, of consistency."[38]

The statement of "Commitment" by Fellowship Church is a prime indication of how the membership assessed corporate religious experience. Here, in concise form, we see the church's salient characteristics:

> I affirm my need for a growing understanding of all men as sons of God, and seek after a vital interpretation of God as revealed in Jesus of Nazareth whose fellowship with God was the foundation of his fellowship with men.
>
> I desire to have a part in the unfolding of the ideal of Christian fellowship through the union of men and women of varying national, cultural, racial, or creedal heritage in church communion.
>
> I desire the strength of corporate worship with the imperative of personal dedication to the working out of God's purposes here and in all places which will be found through membership in this Church for the Fellowship of All Peoples.[39]

The theoretical relationship between mysticism, worship and community was earlier outlined in some detail. At Fellowship Church, this interaction dealt with real personal needs and sustained an atmosphere supportive of the social witness. For instance, in terms of racial and ethnic intercourse the church grew to understand that simple physical proximity or "familiarity of presence" was never enough; "fellowship" was equally called for. Observes Thurman, "contact without fellowship tends to be unsympathetic, cold, and impersonal, expressing itself often in sick or limited forms of ill will; ill will easily becomes the ground for suspicion and hatred." But what the church discovered more and more was that "the reverse is also true. Contact with fellowship is apt to be sympathetic; sympathetic understanding often leads to the exercise of goodwill."[40]

Toward this end the church sponsored myriad activities that were specifically social, cultural and/or educational in nature, such as study groups, intercultural workshops, dinners (in restaurants and in one another's homes), and presentations of the dramatic arts, among others.[41] Below follows a sampling of replies given by the membership in response to the survey question, "What do I expect Fellowship Church to do for me?"

> ...It is difficult for me to separate what I would want Fellowship Church to be for me from what I would want it to be for others.... I think that first of all it should be a place where men may come together to share in the search for a better understanding of God, and through Him of each other, and together in wisdom and maturity, seeking for the enrichment of their own lives and for valid principles of action for the solution of human problems on a broader scale.

> ...My church should provide me with sanctuary; a place where I may come and find this sanctuary either in quiet meditation, dynamic spiritual inspiration, or in noisy social activity. My church should provide for me an island on which I may find spiritual inspiration — spiritual challenge; a group recognition of individual human dignity and decency; and the chance to work for a dream.[42]

The question, "Why did I join Fellowship Church?" evoked similar response:

> ...because I wanted to worship God in a church that is open to all people without regard to race, creed, or culture.... When I found a church where people gathered with a dedication to seek God and know each other with spiritual concern first, I felt a sense of "home-coming" unknown to me.

> ...because I felt the need for spiritual growth; but I had no religious dogma. As St. Augustine said, "my soul was restless" and I hungered for an experience of God, but churches such as I had attended did not feed this hunger.

> ...I joined Fellowship Church because the Commitment reaffirms my belief in the "oneness" of people and the "oneness" of religious faiths.[43]

Thurman makes a most important observation in connection with this 1953 church survey, noting that one of the most persistent insistences of the congregation over the years was that their

witness not take on the appearance of ecclesiastical pretentious-
ness or social exhibitionism. The outward manifestations of religious experience were esteemed by the membership as a natural
and logical outgrowth of a perduring commitment, the duplicity of
human motives notwithstanding. Testified one member, "the
difference the church has made in my attitude toward people is to
increase my confidence in 'oneness' because of the perfectly natural fellowship expressed by those of widely different backgrounds
working together toward a goal of universal love and an integration
of differing religious faiths."[44]

To an extent, then, it is easy to see why a mystic-oriented collectivity like the Fellowship Church has so seldom been cited for its
social contributions. There is little inclination on the part of the
mystic-led church to call direct attention to its experience, except
in the qualified sense of promoting goodwill. And while such an
attitude is perhaps to be lauded, it can and does pose tremendous
investigative difficulties. From the standpoint of the outside
observer, attitudes of discretion are exceedingly elusive and fluid,
defiant of translation, and tend thus to yield hard data of minor and
ephemeral value. Again, the observations of Turner prove helpful:

> We have been accustomed to thinking of mystical utterance as characterizing
> solitary individuals meditating or contemplating in mountain, desert, or
> monastic cell, and to see in it almost anything but a social fact. But the
> continuous operational conjunction of such language with movements of a
> communitas type, — leads one to think that at least something of what is
> being uttered refers metaphorically to the extant social relationships.
> "Withdrawal" there is, "detachment," "disinterest," there is, — but this with-
> drawal is not from humanity, but from structure when it has become too long
> petrified in a specific shape. What is being sought is emancipation of men
> from all structural limitations, to make a mystical desert outside structure
> itself in which all can be one, *ein bloss nicht*, "a pure nothingness," — though
> this "nothingness" has to be seen as standing in metaphorical opposition to
> the "somethingness" of a historically derived structure.... History will of
> course unpack its latent structure, especially as experience encounters tradi-
> tional structures of culture and thought.[45]

Two points by Turner are of special note here. First, the mystic-
communitas conjunction has ramifications for "extant social relationships." In other words, it is altogether possible for the mystic
to move beyond mere metaphorical opposition to the more clearly
manifest. Of even greater consequence for us is his point that

"history will unpack its latent structure." In the case of Thurman-led Fellowship Church, the assembled sought in a number of ways to make specific impact upon the larger community. And always and in every respect the Fellowship community accomplished this on their own terms — terms we might add, that only now are becoming clear.

Sacramental Activism

I have argued that the oppositional potential of the mystic-institutional conjunct becomes operative in and through the formal experience of worship. At Fellowship Church, this occurred as persons from diverse backgrounds shared with others in the grasped truth of "equality of infinite worth."[46] Thurman writes:

> Our worship became increasingly a celebration before God of life lived during the week; the daily life and the period of worship were one systolic and diastolic rhythm. Increasing numbers of people who were engaged in the common life of the city of San Francisco found in the church restoration, inspiration, and courage for their work on behalf of social change in the community. The worship experience became a watering hole for this widely diverse and often disparate group of members and visitors from many walks of life.[47]

The "systolic and diastolic rhythm" of the worship event closely approximates the dialectical process described by Turner. For Fellowship Church, communal worship became the forum for a vitally different assessment of self and society; the elements of unity and inclusiveness experienced re-integrated the worshipper into society as part of an organic whole. It is most important to recognize that the focus of worship was never the polarity or inequality between community (relatively unstructured communitas) and society (excessive and repressive structure), *but rather the elevating and revitalizing elements of community.* More than mere conditioned response to or reaction against society, worship served as that which transformed structure through the agency of worshipping persons. The renewed individual was given the impetus to better the world rather than ignore it, and enabled for consistent and continuous involvement in societal issues. One worshipper phrased it thus:

> When I, as an individual make possible the privilege of abundant life for all
> people, whether on Monday at noon, or Tuesday at twilight, I become myself
> a revelation of the hidden meaning of the corporate worship hour of Sunday
> morning, a part of the true genius of The Church For the Fellowship of All
> Peoples...[48]

It is this sacramental quality — the unremitting consciousness of divine presence in one's life — which is part and parcel of the Fellowship witness. There was a felt incumbency among the communicants to demonstrate the truth of the religious experience in ever more meaningful ways, to act as a conduit or contagion of sorts spreading beyond the perimeters of the local church. Thurman attests that

> even the most radical of our congregation were eager to safeguard the
> centrality of the religious commitment that held the concerns of the spirit and
> the worship of God at center. However, radiating from this center were our
> deepest personal and corporate concerns for the total community; and we
> worked faithfully to implement this imperative of our commitment. We were
> citizens in the classical Greek sense, concerned with all aspects of the welfare
> of the state, responsible but penetrating critics aiding in every effort to make
> the good life possible for all people.[49]

I have chosen to define the Fellowship style of social activism as "social regeneration," because it strives to replicate each individual's experience of infinite and qualitative worth in the social milieu.[50] For fairly ostensible reasons, neither Thurman nor the congregants of Fellowship Church had any need to resort to strategies of definition. Nevertheless, certain key factors do commend our usage of social regeneration. "Regeneration" parallels a number of terms indicating causality — "change," "action," "transformation," and the like. However, internal conditions and primordial processes provide the specific impetus for "regeneration," in contrast to the external motivations more often associated with the latter. Taken together, then, the words "social regeneration" strongly suggest a type of social activism arising out of the fluid experience of religion itself, a vital response to outward situations as an inevitable result of an inward movement.[51] In the case of Thurman and the Fellowship body, this conceptualization more readily identifies the real point of activism: It is not merely to improve society, relieve suffering, or end oppression, as important as these are, but rather to remove anything "that prevents God from coming to himself in the life of the individual. Whatever there is that blocks this, calls for action."[52] A deep and abiding reverence for the integrity of the person *qua* person — and never as a means to an end — is what largely distinguishes the activist orientation of the Fellowship Church.[53]

The best way to illustrate the social regenerative process is to offer a sample of responses by the members of Fellowship to everyday issues. The first incident, involving two members of the church, has to do with the confrontation of racial stereotypes — hardly a commonplace activity at mid-century. As the story is told, these women engaged one of the city's most prestigious booksellers about certain of his merchandise:

> Children's books were to be bought for a community center's library. Those on the staff to use them thought of making the trip to the store ... Three women, a Nesei, a Caucasian and a Negro made up the trio. Two were members of Fellowship Church, the other an irregular visitor. The children's section [of the store] was also featuring dolls of all nations and races. All of them were beautifully formed and daintily dressed except the one representing the Negro. Little black Sambo in small and blown up sizes, a caricature and stereotype, was the only brown doll in the group. Sensitive to the subtle propaganda for continued "separateness" that the stereotype effects, the three sought the manager ... They discussed the social responsibility of the man in business, and it was only as a man in business — that the owner identified himself, not as a business man with a social responsibility. The wife felt a compromise could be reached by requesting the maker of the dolls to send them a brown doll to sell that was not a caricature — not a stereotype. They could not curtail the sale of the book, but they would talk to the salesgirls in the department to try to make them aware of the implications. A word from them now and then to the customers would help, she thought. The trio had not kept silence when a word was timely. "If we don't act on our perceptions (social perceptions) they become atrophied: if we do ... if our actions invariably meet with high success, they become enduring possibilities for choice."[54]

Two other examples have to do with housing. Like most other American cities at mid-century the neighborhoods of San Francisco were firmly segregated along lines of race. Legally, every person was entitled to live wherever they chose. However, white homeowners devised an effective counter strategy for enforcing the separation of the races — to wit, the restrictive covenant:

> A caucasian home owner, who belongs to an intercultural, interracial, intercreedal fellowship on the west coast, was eager to rent her second floor apartment to tenants belonging to one of the minority groups — either

Filipino, Japanese-American, Negro, or Chinese. She wants her action to be intelligible to the long line of neighbors who lived on her "select" street. She had a rather unusual type of "at home," inviting all the neighbors, including many whom she had known before. She explained what she was about to do, insisting that as she respected their intelligence, she hoped they would respect her philosophy of how human beings should live together. The minority group family moved in. The street goes on apace with its quiet living. The neighbor's have constant exposure to a ... religious individual's way of life in action.[55]

Another member relates:

...When I was preparing to lease my home for a year, I made an effort to find tenants from one of the minority groups. I was disappointed to be unsuccessful, but felt the expressed desire may have had some constructive effect through calling a number of real estate firms and having them realize that there are people who want to share their homes with all people. I have stopped dealing with a dress shop that has very good merchandise because they refuse to sell to Negroes.[56]

Examples of social regeneration are not restricted solely to the individual witness of Fellowship's members. The church as a whole was engaged in its own novel expression of regeneration, a kind of corporate activism grounded in the common experience of spiritual discovery. Thurman offers a most poignant illustration of this fact:

One evening I walked past one of the most elegant department stores in the city. There was a window display of a black woman and several children, the stereotypical "Black Mammy and Pickanninies." I was shocked and angered. The following Sunday morning, I invited my entire congregation to go by this store to see the "interesting" window display and react to it in their own way. I was careful not to say what it was, nor why I wanted them to see it. By noon on Monday, the whole display had been removed.[57]

The social conscience of the church was further reflected in the work of its "community relations committee," which informed and counseled the church body on concerns consistent with the church commitment, and cooperated with other organizations more exclusively concerned with such issues. Following are some of the activities undertaken:

The sponsoring of an F.E.P.C. [Fair Employment Practices Committee] Sunday in cooperation with the local Council of Churches ... A special Bulletin on the Alien Land Laws, about which the State was seeking the will of the people, was released and a Nisei lawyer was heard of great advantage....

The committee was the spearhead of a campaign within the church to get representation in and participation in a citizens' group led by the Council for Civic Unity which succeeded in changing a neighborhood attitude in the question of restrictive covenants within that area.[58]

Examples of the social conscience of the Fellowship community can be multiplied many times over. The church's refusal to sign the loyalty oath as a condition to tax-exempt status,[59] the individual undertaking of acts of conscience despite threat of violence,[60] and many other demonstrations of social concern served as a constant challenge to social and religious parochialism.[61]

To be sure, it should not be inferred from our discussion up to this point that the activism of Thurman and the Fellowship community took on the implications of a major social movement. In conventional terms, the church was and is a small-scale effort, compiling an effective yet limited protest record. What is being argued rather, to re-emphasize the point, is that the church and its constituent members offers convincing evidence of a discreet and exceptional mode of activism defining its own sociological import, the unorthodoxy of which has defied conventional social analysis. Again, this mode of activism is best described as "social regeneration," for it operates out of an intersubjective principle of *relatedness between persons* that can bear manifold consequences and is part of the infinite network of interactions that comprise society. So interpreted, what Muriel Bullard said of Thurman's means to social change may be equally true for the entire Fellowship community: "He could talk so convincingly and yet with respect for the other [offending] party. He didn't come in and pound on tables and say 'You get that thing out of there' that caused them to comply."[62] A statement from Thurman concludes this portion of our discussion:

From what has been said, I do not mean to suggest that there has been any great social shift in the city because of the existence of Fellowship Church. These specific illustrations [of social regeneration] simply point out some of the ways by which the people of our land can at last find freedom in democracy. The existence of the church has become a beacon of truth in the minds of many, many people who in their entire lives will never enter its doors nor be involved in its active program, but who, nevertheless, came to know from our experience that the unity of fellowship is more compelling than the superstitions and credos that separate.[63]

Postscript: Fellowship Church Today

In 1953 Howard Thurman left Fellowship Church to accept a pivotal post as Boston University's Dean of the Chapel and Professor of Spiritual Disciplines. In the intervening forty or so years, the congregation has attempted to maintain its viability as a social regenerative force in the community. It has endured difficult times of late in struggling to envision the future, yet continues to "maintain views that ... have been regarded as religious and social heresy" and which remain largely unappropriated by the wider church community.[64]

Fellowship Church has secured the services of about a dozen clergy during those years, male and female, black and white, moving from "co-pastors and no pastors" and back again.[65] Also, the church experienced a substantial drop in residential membership (while at-large membership remained relatively high) and the average age of the church's participants rose significantly. Recently, however, the church has begun to gain again somewhat. Under the current leadership, membership has seen an increase and a youth program has been instituted. Relationships which once flourished with the Jewish and Buddhist communities are being rekindled. The arts and intercultural activities continue to be important. So, too, there is clear evidence of involvement with social movements reflective of the prevailing maelstrom of problems and dilemmas — nuclear proliferation, the environment, sanctuary, apartheid, and the homeless — as well as the more long-standing concerns of racial, gender, religious, and ethnic parochialism. In sum, Fellowship continues its creative pursuit of the vision of wholeness, inclusivity, and transformation, an institutional metaphor affirming in myriad ways that the things that bind persons (and all living things) are more compelling than those that separate.[66]

Chapter Four

Thurman and the Social Order

"...if there be any government or social institution of whatever kind that operates among people in a manner that makes for human misery, whether of the mind through fear and despair, or of the body through the freezing of the freedom of movement, or of the spirit through the destruction of any sense of the future, such a government or such a social institution, without regard to its sanctions, is evil. To the extent that it is so, it cannot survive, because it is against life and carries within the seeds of its own destruction. The moral law is binding. There is no escape..."

— Howard Thurman —

The relationship between Thurman and the Fellowship Church offers undeniable confirmation of the social significance of mystic orientation. In one respect, the almost nondirective authoritarianism of Thurman was instrumental in establishing a cohesive and stable yet not highly formalized church organization. As mystic-pastor, he was able to reduce areas of decision-making tension in the church, while stimulating through example the virtue of mysticism or vital religious experience. The congregants themselves no doubt reinforced and validated one another's religious experience, but Thurman's objectification of extraordinary verities was of especial import. As one who believed that his experience of encounter put him in a relation to society (and to himself) sufficiently different than that which society legitimated, his social interactions — in all their unambiguous acceptance and affirmation of others — lent authenticity to the nature and meaning of vital religious experience. Thus, as a self-affirmed person, Thurman's sociological status became itself a symbol for the legitimacy of subjective values evoked by the mystical experience. As we have already documented, this stimulation had direct and discernible social ramifications for the Fellowship Church community and surrounding environ.

The relation of Thurman's mystical experience to society was hardly exhausted, of course, by just one institutional expression. In one way or another, his involvements at Howard University, Boston University, the Howard Thurman Educational Trust and elsewhere were all indicative of his desire to make exteriorly manifest that which he found to be internally and personally legitimating. As well, he engaged the social order by a variety of other means, through the arts and letters and in association with such community-wide organizations as the Conference of Christians and Jews, the Urban League, and the Martin Luther King Memorial Center for Social Change.[1]

Significantly enough, with each new objectification and reification of his experience, Thurman "learned an old lesson, with new implications: how difficult it is to trust the genius of an idea or a movement to grow and to perpetuate itself without finally feeling the necessity to formalize it in some way.":

> There is an intrinsic contradiction between the freedom of the spirit and the organization through which that freedom manifests itself. This contradiction, this paradox, is inherent in the nature of man's personal experience of freedom itself. The sense of freedom exists within the framework of our structured and articulated obligations. If it is to compete with these obligations, then its free-flowing nature must be harnessed so as to compete on an equal footing. It too must be structured and contained within a mold. The only function of the mold is to give substance to the spirit, that we might relate to it as we do to other competing obligations when the pressures build within us to make a choice. But when, inevitably, the mold begins to choke the spirit, the mold is broken and the spirit breaks out anew, only to encrust itself in another mold, and so the process continues. This has been the historical pattern of religion and all of society's creative expressions.[2]

Insofar as Thurman was concerned, then, no single form could exhaust the veracity of the mystic experience. Each organizational affiliation was taken as an opportunity to further his mystic vision of community. However, the very nature of the vision also called for a posture and commitment not finally dependent on any one group or movement which, to here get ahead of ourselves somewhat, was what Thurman most sought: emancipation from all forms of social discontinuity — even those sanctioned by activism — for the sake of a more ultimate continuity. In short, Thurman's mystic activism involved a profoundly subtle combination of communalism and individualism. Our attention at this point is given to critical individual facets of his witness.

The Concept of Charisma

It would be difficult to further discuss Thurman's engagement of the social milieu without giving some brief attention to the concept of "charisma" — the "gift of grace." Max Weber first gave the term sociological prominence when he ascribed it "to a certain quality of an individual personality by virtue of which he is set apart from ordinary men and treated as endowed with supernatural, superhuman, or at least specifically exceptional powers or qualities."[3] Talcott Parsons followed Weber's lead in part, defining charisma as a quality of things and persons that sets them apart from the ordinary and the everyday (correlative to Durkheim's "sacred").[4] Peter Worsley argues that the appeal of an individual labeled as charismatic is multifaceted, being composed of her/his acts and messages in addition to personal attributes.[5] More recently, Bryan Wilson has emphasized the fact that even if the message need be congenial, it is not everything; there may also be a demand for a person whose exemplary lifestyle (or, as the case may be, supernatural powers) is the only guarantee that the followers' desires will be fulfilled.[6]

Charisma is certainly one of the most critical and most debated concepts in social science literature. One does not need to assent to any one of the above perspectives, however, in order to see the valuable insights that each contributes. From my point of view, the lack of unanimity between these and other definitions is to a considerable degree overcome by recognizing what is the often implied or stated relational and transactional character of charisma. Benjamin Zablocki writes, for instance, that "charisma is both real and primordially social ... and it is based upon the human capacity to invest the self into other persons or larger collectivities."[7] Similarly, Aldon Morris points out that the charismatic propensity is for "strong face-to-face personal relationships that foster allegiance, trust, and loyalty, and give rise to a shared symbolic world that provides an interpretation of earthly affairs."[8] Equally important for social activism is the fact that the charismatic element owes no allegiance to particular persons, groups, structures or norms; it therefore has real potential as a device in society halting, even reversing historically immutable situations.

This is not to imply that the above limited conceptualization of charisma is definitive for every context. The sheer number and variety of interpretations indicate that the concept is still far from well understood, and not likely to be exhausted by any one discussion. However, in the framework of our analysis there is little doubt that charismatic authority more rightly denotes an emphasis on relationship (between the endowed and the participants) than on personality *per se*. I would contend, further, that the charismatic person and/or group evokes a larger identification of persons, whether this be their principal aim or not, primarily because they are anchored in the center of the ebb and flow of the social and cultural forces critical to their community.

A final theoretical point concerning charisma has to do with the amount of social influence of the charismatic-bearing individual. As already intimated, mystics are hardly a topic of widespread interest in sociological circles. To speak about any of them, therefore, as in a league comparable, say, to that of the founders of the world's major religious systems or historic military and political strategists might seem highly irresponsible, or in any case, irrational. However, the difference in the charismatic attributes of certain select persons, mystic or not, is more often imagined than real, which is to say, uncritically linked to issues of magnitude and visibility as opposed to efficaciousness and scope. As Zablocki so astutely notes in his discussion of the same, "a difference in degree, no matter how vast, does not automatically qualify as a difference in kind."[9] It is in this sense, if none other, that Thurman as a mystic-activist and "social regenerator" demonstrates many of the relational and collective properties associated with charisma.

A Track to the Water's Edge

The words that Thurman often shared with others are of more than passing relevance: "the individual must not relinquish his sense of responsibility for the total life of his country or nation."[10] This statement strongly underscores Thurman's own attitude, a consistent and purposive involvement in the everyday mundane concerns of persons and society. So, too, it supports our truncated definition of charisma, insofar as Thurman's life endeavors are being increasingly celebrated, appropriated, and actualized by others. This is not to ignore the fact that for others Thurman may still be no more than a religious anomaly — a mystic who proactively impacts the world.

We have now observed for some time how Thurman regarded himself in relation to his experience of God. It was in the experience of encounter where he made the deepest and fullest discoveries about himself. In particular, he believed that so long as the self is experienced only as the separate, isolated self, it remains shallow and less than complete. Only by involving the self in a larger context of reality, most notably the social as informed by the transcendent, can authentic being be realized. It is particularly important to note that as far as Thurman was concerned, this sense of interdependence is not given from without, but is inherent to human being itself. Hence, in the realest sense the experience of God is also the coming of the person to oneself. This perception permitted Thurman to develop some distinctive insights and paradigms for ordering interpersonal life and social concerns:

> It's interesting that we think of love in terms that are external, in terms that are sociological, in terms that are in a sense even ethical. We do not think of it in terms of moving to a center in another human being that is beyond all their faults and all their virtues. And it means, then, going down in you and coming up in them. Not going this way, that's the network. Now when you do this, then you look out on the context that the other person is living and functioning and believing and practicing, you look out on what they are doing through their own eyes, not through yours, and you discover that the only way that any man can be at home anywhere, is to be sure that he is at home somewhere.[11]

Thurman's approach to interpersonal relations is sensitive and complex: a mix of high vision, quietistic discourse, and practical intimacy. Carlyle Stewart refers to the Thurman mode as "intuitive," a kind of spiritual-ethical liberation,[12] while Luther Smith notes that his "convictions are not adopted systems of belief, but convictions which have been shaped, tested, and proved within life experiences."[13] However stated, it is manifestly clear that Thurman embraced a compelling, consistent, intersubjective mode of human interaction in the world.

> So I start in my feeling and thinking with the inner meaning of my own reli-
> gious experience for all the God that I can ever experience, sense, be aware
> of, come to understand, know or love is there first ... So therefore it is not an
> accident that the Book says that on that great day of Pentecost all of the
> people in Jerusalem of every kind, they heard the word. How? "In their own
> tongue." Not in the tongue of Peter, James, John, they heard it in their own
> tongue. And if I can hear in you the tongue, the sound that is in me, then
> whatever separates us is negotiable. If I don't, I can have all of the schemes,
> all the philosophies, all of the theologies, all the other ologies and I am still ...
> lost.[14]

The gist of Thurman's argument is that the basis for moving
toward others is fundamentally interior and inseparable from the
cultivated inner life of the individual. The awareness of self and, by
implication, other selves can be deepened, made ever more thorough through an inexorable journeying inward to the center of
one's own religious experience. Says Thurman, "a regular experience of religion obtained over an indefinite time interval, having
within that time interval numberless repetitions of the encounter
— all of this will in time make certain structural changes in the
behavior pattern of the nervous system itself."[15] It is from this new
vantage point that a profound concern for the internal climate of
other human beings issues.

One must ask, then, what is the actual significance of Thurman's
interpretation for social interaction? Ellwood surmises, "we are
social beings and what we often want most to find is people who
have found self and God."[16] Often, people are either drawn or led
to the charisma-bearing person or group in hope of having a corre-
sponding experience, whether achieved directly or vicariously. In
the case of Thurman, his ability both to personify and expound an
alternative view of reality was of preeminent attraction. Indeed for
many his mysticism-laden utterances concerning God, equality,
community, inwardness, freedom, and authenticity did strike a
challenging and liberating chord. For instance, Francis Hall, a
leading Quaker thinker of this century, recalls the personal emancipation inspired by Thurman's message:

> The call: "follow me." These words of Jesus were spoken by Howard
> Thurman who was still young in his ministry at that time ... He had held me
> entranced each day by his deeply meditative style of speaking. You felt the
> creative spirit at work; indeed it was the Spirit of Christ that was speaking
> through him. I hung on every word as it was given birth and waited eagerly
> for the full sentence and the total message.

Thurman did not speak from an obvious outline, in a systematic way, and in this next to the last message of the conference he began to weave the call of Jesus in and out of his elaborations. I do not recall those elaborations but know that the call of Jesus was beginning to echo in my heart. ...suddenly the words were no longer being transmitted by Howard Thurman. They were the living words of Christ and they sank deep into my being where they exploded and infused me and gripped me. In that depth of my being was a glad response, "I come!" Tears rose in my eyes; a tingling ran up and down my back; I seemed to be lifted out of myself...[17]

Rabbi Joseph B. Glaser attests that Thurman also had a significant impact upon his life. Both in his presence and in the ambiance of his life he found a very special confidence and self-knowledge. He writes that

... Thurman was interested in roots — not his roots, *my* roots. And he with Rabbi Fine and Rabbi White opened my *Jewish* eyes for me in a way no one ever had, and few have ever since. He had a contagious reverence for Judaism and such a profound understanding of it that I have yet to see the equal of his 1965 address on The Covenant before the Union of American Hebrew Congregations. In any event, he produced a rabbi and whatever this rabbi has produced bears the mark of Howard Thurman as it travels down the current of Judaism in the mainstream of life.[18]

A final example comes from the pen of E. Pauline Myers, a freelance writer. She tells of a most fascinating experience from her youth, when she was chosen to represent her school (then Hampton Institute) at a Young Mens Christian Association conference being led by Thurman. The time was the early 1920's. Only recently has she felt able to share her experience outside of her family. I quote her retrospection in part:

Dr. Thurman drew from his pocket a small book and began to read from it in modulated tones: "I'm going to begin our meditation," he said, "by reading from Olive Schreiner's, *A Track to the Water's Edge*." I heard the first two lines, — when suddenly and without warning, something quite unexpected happened to me:

I felt, it seemed, that my physical body was levitating in air and I was standing alone facing the sky. Never had the firmament seemed so luminous, so radiant. It was all too awesome to describe. Then, as if in a flash, I was encompassed by a cloud, appearing as a dense fog. The cloud wrapped itself about my body holding me in firm embrace. All my oxygen appeared to be cut off and all sensations ceased. But, I was not afraid...

... More than a half-century has passed since that ecstatic experience. All else concerning the YMCA conference and the persons who attended it have faded into oblivion. But, if I should live to be a hundred, I guess I shall never fully comprehend the depth of meaning and revelation contained in that mystical experience on Mt. Cheaha with Howard Thurman. I only know that ever since that day I've been on a ceaseless search for truth.[19]

A comparison of these three experiences — examples of which can be multiplied many times over — strongly point to the importance of considering the experience of the mystic personality as illuminative for other individuals.[20] Each of the three considered what happened to them as somehow associated with spiritual ultimates, and each found in Thurman's presence and persona an environment congenial to their apprehension. We must, however, take care to note that none of these person's experiences were fully *de novo* and spontaneous, but occurred subsequent to a period of spiritual questing, followed up by continued growth. In short, none of the three sought to equate Thurman with salvific or messianic themes. While highly esteemed as an interpreter *par excellence* of supernal insights, he was not revered as the source of all-encompassing truth.[21]

Religion scholar Joachim Wach, citing the work of noted mysticism student William Ralph Inge, avers that "true religion is not taught but caught from somebody who has it."[22] This was Thurman's insistence, not only with respect to the specifically religious but also in terms of the range and scope of human interaction. For him, religion, the individual, and community were not mutually exclusive entities. Rather, the three were close and complementary to each other, indeed blending into each other, and not radically different aspects of being. What follows from essential religious or mystical experience is a disposition, a propensity to communicate with others through a deep-seeded receptivity. In punctiliar moments of contagiousness, the radical disclosure of life's universal connectedness — inclusive of human coexistence — is somehow transmitted and effected:

> God has not left himself without a witness, and my job is to wait and try every door, wait in season and out of season, wait, wait until at last the very urgency of my own spirit will pull up out of your center that which responds to me. I can't manipulate it — I can have all the systems, all the schemes, all the propaganda, it's wonderful but it isn't going anywhere. I must smell it in you, I must catch it from you, and if I can't catch it I have to wait. I can't organize a system that will bring it out. I can try that to keep busy, but ... that's the one great radical distinction between God and those of us who have been

created in His own image, is that God alone knows and understands how to wait.[23]

Interpersonal Activism in an Impersonal Order

At this point it must be reiterated that Thurman was not particularly interested in a full or systematic exposition of either religious experience or human activity and behavior. His mystic assessment of human nature simply did not call for it. Thus it comes as no surprise here to find that his ruminations on relatedness offer little evidence of an external uniformity or grand social formula. Consistent with the mystic experience itself, his energies were more concentrated on the interpersonal and, by extension, the small-scale.

> ... for me, it is a spiritual quality to feed a hungry person so that the hungry person knows that *he* is being addressed, not merely his hunger. Perhaps with my kind of background and my history, I have my kind of biases. I admit that. It is not that I don't think the large scale impersonal operations will take over and salvage the common life in terms of all of the environment, and all of this ... But the way my life is conditioned and projected I have to feel that the person who is helping me knows that I am there. Not just my hunger is there; or my nakedness is there. But *I* am there.[24]

As this statement indicates, Thurman strongly believed that abstract impersonal arrangements between human beings, the normative mode of larger societal functioning, are devoid of fundamentally substantive meaning. Genuine human relations, on the other hand, are defined by a love born of spiritual sensitivity, situated in critical proximity to the inner and outer facts of another. These interpersonal relations are the foundation for a growing, diffuse collectivist "movement" that traverses and, consequently, challenges "official" social boundaries on the basis of a common dynamic centering experience.[25] What Thurman did, in effect, was to identify the individual — a creative unity conjoined to kindred persons — as the catalyst for propelling society beyond its own limitations, in juxtaposition to the large scale "impersonal operation." He is properly cautious when he states that the potential inter-individual, inter-group dynamic "requires a special kind of honesty, a special kind of integrity."[26] Nevertheless, he remains unswerving in his advocacy of collective unity, community, as the impetus and starting point for profound social change. To recall the concluding sections of the previous chapter, the Thurman mode of social change is "regenerative" because it is encouraging of persons to actively work toward a world in which always, under any and all circumstances, "personhood" is meaningful.

Luther Smith discusses an important dissenting viewpoint in this regard. He points out that Reinhold Niebuhr, the mid-twentieth century exponent of neo-orthodoxy, had sharp words for optimists like Thurman who seemed to insist that relations between individuals were determined by the same ethical considerations as those governing inter-group relations. To summarize his argument, which was particularly intended for the protestant liberalists, it is in order to quote a well-known passage:

> Our contemporary culture fails to realise the power, extent and persistence of group egoism in human relations. It may be possible, though it is never easy, to establish just relations between individuals within a group purely by moral and rational suasion and accommodation. In inter-group relations this is practically an impossibility. The relations between groups must therefore always be predominantly political rather than ethical, that is, they will be determined by the proportion of power which each group possesses at least as much as by any rational and moral appraisal of the comparative needs and claims of each group.[27]

Smith provides further elaboration on Niebuhr's stance, observing that "a group is not just the sum total of its individual members; a group can have a consciousness (ego) and value system which differ from those of its individual members."[28] Thurman readily acknowledges both the saliency of Niebuhr's position and the shortcomings of his own individual-centered approach to social change. Notwithstanding, it should not be supposed therefrom that he was a naive advocate of personalism. Like Niebuhr, he too distinguished the individual ego from the collective consciousness. It was on the question of how the individual is connected to society "in real terms" — the issue of sociocultural context — that there was a marked difference; a point which will be explored shortly.

To return to the issue at hand, it should be noted that early on Thurman concluded "the problems of human relations can never be solved merely by the radical transformation of individuals in society."[29] And even in his final years, he continued to struggle with this enduring "gray area of compromise."[30] A most revealing "for instance" occurred in 1947 at the State College of Pine Bluff, Arkansas, where Thurman had been invited to deliver the commencement address. The details of this little known conundrum bear repeating:

> When we arrived at the campus, I noticed that even though it was 2 o'clock in the morning all the lights were out all over the campus, even the lights on the sidewalk, everything. The campus was dark. As we turned in to the campus, we had been driving about three minutes, when in front of the headlights stood a man with a rifle, and he came over and identified us and we were passed on. A little further along, someone else did this, and finally we came to a place I didn't know. ...The young man said, "this is where you get out. You're spending the night here with this family."
>
> ...It was the home of a young lady who had lived with us when we were living in Washington at Howard University, and when she saw me she fell on my neck and began to weep. ...We walked through the darkened hallway into a center room where there was light, and here was her husband seated by a window, with a rifle. Then they told me a very tragic story. They said that a few days before a blind man had been killed in the police station, and there was a great deal of unrest in the city. The policeman who was responsible had been discharged, and feeling was very high. He had gone out with the threat that he would organize a group and come out and destroy the college. The mayor had suggested that the president of the college perhaps should postpone commencement until this thing passed over, but he didn't, he stayed. And that night, Saturday night, the night they allegedly were coming, all the men who lived on campus armed themselves to wait for the coming mob.
>
> My host said, "This is the second long night of our vigil. You have been riding all day and part of the night, so suppose you take a shower and take a nap for a couple of hours, and then you relieve me." Now, I have not had my hands on a rifle since I was a boy with a 22. So I showered, took a nap, and then at the proper time I was awakened and I sat at the window with this shotgun, waiting. In that interval I had one of the most amazing experiences of a long lifetime. All of my commitment, all the ups and downs of my own journey trying to find a way to affirm the positive and creative meaning of life and the highest dimension of clean human relations — I went back to 1922 when I was a boy in college and I joined the FOR [Fellowship of Reconciliation] and walked all the way through the years — and I said, "Here I am now. What am I going to do?" I didn't know. After I admitted that, I was able to think about it. I had two choices as I saw it: one, if they turned the corner coming toward this house, I could wait and take my time and as they drew near and opened fire I would return the fire until I fell. That was one option. The other option was that if they came, I could turn the porch light on, leave the rifle at the window, and walk out on the porch in the light. When I settled these two alternatives, I was at rest. I didn't know which one I would do. But they didn't come.[31]

Thurman finally weighed the implications of the dilemma thus:

> ... when all possible methods of social action have been exhausted without
> any appreciable relief or change in a given condition, then what does one do?
> I must select what seems to me to be the critical moment, when my maxi-
> mum sacrifice will make my ultimate contribution to the relief of human
> needs and suffering. And you know, I don't think that any of us ever know
> what we will do under such circumstances.[32]

On this "long night of vigil," Thurman's sensitivity to the ultimate logic of his approach — martyrdom — is startlingly apparent.
In other of his writings there exists evidence enough to posit that
he viewed the individual-society problematic from at least two
perspectives. Not surprisingly, his first focus was on the imponder-
able and insistent deficit which plagues the human will. "The crux
of the problem," he writes, "is not merely that we desire the right
and find it difficult to achieve it, but it is also true that, again and
again, we do not desire to *desire* the right."[33] Likewise, "what is
needed is not more information, more facts, but an *aroused will*."[34]
In the second place, there was concern about the relative omnipo-
tence of socio-political entities and the resultant vitiating of human
life:

> When the powers of this world begin to make demands of surrender,
> what do you do? Of course, if you have no thing, no transcendent Person
> that has already inspired in you a willingness to surrender, then you give
> yourself to the highest bidder...[35]

He elaborates elsewhere:

> One of the great despairs of our times is the way in which the large-scale
> nature of the operations of the modern state takes from the ordinary man
> any responsibility for the state beyond the payment of taxes and service in the
> armed forces. This withdrawal of responsibility from the individual deper-
> sonalizes him. With the loss of a sense of responsibility there has been a
> corresponding stifling of free social initiative and a destruction of any sense of
> the future.[36]

Unfortunately, Thurman's assessments concerning complex,
large-scale structures are in need of considerable refinement; and
invariably, his treatment is too brief.[37] Again, Thurman was well
aware that his analysis of macro conditions suffered from a lack of
real precision. There was little doubt in his mind that oppressive
social structures, rooted in the vagaries of history and largely self-

sustaining, had to be dismantled but he was less than direct on the question of how.

Was, then, Thurman one to simply avoid or ignore the validity of structural causes? If anything, the above statements are suggestive of a position more deeply conceived and astute than is generally recognized. As one with a principled committment to root values (such as personhood and the democratic ethos) Thurman, it appears, felt less compelled to attend to socio-structural explanations and schemas in order to keep track of that which was in his estimation even more subtle and complex. His mystic orientation affirmed structural analysis, but he was not a social theorist. Life, he enthusiastically contended is the more fundamental category — not society — and it is individuals who are the constituents and vehicles of life.[38] One need but refer in this instance to one of his key declarations, that "life itself is alive."[39]

Thurman quite clearly recognized the mutual contingency of the individual and society. The tension for Thurman occurs when, to use sociologist Roland Robertson's words, the "experience of being partly an individual and partly more (or, perhaps, less) than an individual" is not mutually and symmetrically reflected in both milieus: turmoil, anomie, and meaninglessness are inevitable.[40] To re-emphasize an earlier point, what Thurman sought most was a mode of individual-society relatedness that would safeguard the freedom of the individual to pursue her or his own spiritual reconstruction and completeness; ergo the prophet's dream:

> Now it is true that again and again we are overwhelmed by our sense of insignificance because we are taken in by the lateral classification of society, on the basis of which it seems so many of our utopias are projected. But not the prophet. He said there shall come a time when the lion and the lamb shall lie down together and the little child will put his hand on the whole of an asp and the asp will relax his self-regarding impulse and not sting the child. Why? Because there has been a rehabilitation of the economic order, as important as it is? Because suddenly there is health everywhere, as terribly important as this is? No, the prophet says, because the knowledge of God will cover the earth as the waters cover the sea.... And time is running out.[41]

The Civil Rights-Black Consciousness Movement: An Appraisal

As we have indicated from the onset, the failure of scholars to take seriously mystic experiencing among "marginated" communities in the late twentieth century United States — especially from an *in situ* perspective — is lamentable but not surprising. One of the few scholars to address this issue has been Ellwood, who writes in reproving fashion that "there is a purist view of mysticism and a type of mysticism studies that seems to want to limit the subject matter to a rather small circle of elect souls..."[42] Without casting aspersions on the absolute value of such works, and many are of extreme benefit, we need but point out the conspicuous absence of mystical experience by African Americans and others of the disinherited, among whom Thurman must be prominently numbered.[43]

Thurman's fierce insistence on the freedom, cognitive and moral-ethical, of the individual was not without good cause. Unlike other twentieth-century religious figures who inherited the mantle of liberalism, his appraisal of social progress could ill afford to be illusory. On this point, it seems, he has long been misunderstood. From a personal point of view, Thurman was intensely aware of how the collaborative forces of bigotry and the social and ecclesiastical order were set against he and his idiomatic community, African America. Thus his realism, optimistic as it was, made him wary of any group or entity claiming jurisdiction over matters pertaining to the whole of human life.

> ...I have long since abandoned any hope that from the institutional arrangement — whether it is church or corporation or any of these things — the *initiative* for the changing of the social order will take place. I don't have much confidence in that myself.... It has meant for me a very difficult and strenuous kind of discipline and exercise, because there is nothing in my history that gives me a great deal of confidence in the fact that those who control the vast impersonal operations of the social order can take into account my needs as a person who was born and lived primarily as an outsider in American society.[44] (emphasis added)

In Thurman's thinking the situation as regards the "outsider," and particularly the person of African descent in American society, was so involuted that there was *prima facie* little leverage upon the issue of societal self-consciousness. However, mystical experience, as an ontological and epistemological reordering, was permitting of a reinterpretation of one's self in relation to society whereby the individual could not only contribute to the wider collectivity, but on the most distinctive and indigenous of terms. There is no need here to repeat earlier elaborations, except to stress Thurman's primordial conviction: vital religious experience provides an aperture for operating with integrity relative to both the individual and societal level.

Thurman's convictions were severely tested during the years of the modern Civil Rights-Black Consciousness movement (early 1950's - early 1970's). During this period, the very processes guaranteeing of African American anonymity in the early part of the twentieth century were themselves powerfully and widely implicated. The spirit of African American protest and conflict is historic of course, but the scope and magnitude of the new protests — initially non-violent in strategy — were of a scale previously unknown. There were thus set in motion powerful and prolonged processes whereby African Americans sought in the main to dismantle the institutional apparatus of racism.

The history of the Civil Rights-Black Consciousness movement will not be dwelled on here, as it is richly documented in other sources.[45] In the immediate context all that we seek is to ascertain Thurman's relationship to "The Movement," and vice-versa. As Lerone Bennett and others have noted, there were those in the African American community who believed (and believe) that Thurman was not substantially concerned with the pressing social issues of the time.[46] From Thurman's vantage point such charges had no founding and, in any event, seldom required response. On those occasions when he did address the criticisms directed at himself, Thurman was likely to share the following somewhat humorous story:

> When I was at Howard University, among our list of preachers was Reinhold Niebuhr. Because the University had no guest business, they always stayed at our house, the guest preachers. One night, when Reinhold came, we were having the typical no-holds-barred discussion about religion and our society and social action and all the rest of it. On Tuesday in his lecture at Union, he referred to this discussion, and there was one Negro fellow in his class. After Reiny finished making this reference, this fellow had a rather important comment to make, which Reiny passed on to me that night by way of the telephone. He said, "I was talking about drawing some illustrations from our experience, ... and this young fellow said, 'when this Thurman fellow came up out of Florida and began to talk around, many of us who were much younger were sure that at last someone had come who would be our Moses. And what did he do? He turned mystic on us!'"[47]

Negatively intended comments were taken in stride by Thurman, who felt it wholly possible to participate in activism by means other than through a highly visible leadership. His basic testimony was that "I work at giving witness in the external aspect of my life to my experience of truth. That's my way — the way the grain in my wood moves."[48]   Nonetheless, his unconventional stance was interpreted by some activists as ambivalent and, in any case, short on resolve with respect to racial injustice and discrimination. Ironically, Thurman was being widely lauded by larger society for his successful establishment of "color-blind" (read: "non-African American") religious fellowships. It did not take much for angry young African Americans to infer from such plaudits that the elder leader intended, in all probability, to transcend the racial issue altogether. Many thus chose to ignore him; while others remained less sure of where they — or he — stood. It was another of the elders, W.E.B. DuBois, who probably best expressed the sentiments of his younger contemporaries when he remarked with exasperation, "what Howard Thurman *really* believes I have never been able to find out."[49] (emphasis added)

What Thurman actually believed concerning social change hardly conformed to what many of the younger activists wanted and expected to hear. He began from

> the fundamental proposition inherent in any concept of social change ... that the individual is a part of a larger social construct, larger whole; that he is rooted in that larger whole: what he thinks, feels, does can affect that larger whole but what he thinks, feels and does may not, *may not* influence the larger whole in ways that conform to his notion of what the change or the shift, or the influence of his life may be.[50]

Thurman saw a disturbing and potentially destructive trend emerge in the African American community during the Civil Rights-Black Consciousness movement. The paradoxical consequence of the movement was its relatively simultaneous demands for the elimination of segregation, on the one hand, and cries for a "self-determined separateness," on the other — acts which were in complex respects interwoven, but which effectively polarized the African American community and wider society as well. The dilemma, at least as Thurman interpreted it, was to find a means to change which did not have as its sole or even primary purpose the societalization of African Americans, which is to say, a less than critical desire and demand for: (1) inclusion in the national body (civil rights orientation) or (2) the establishment of separate socio-political structures (black consciousness theme). As far as the ongoing struggle for equality and freedom was concerned, the most critical underlying factor, in Thurman's estimation, was to remain "inwardly motivated, not ambitiously oriented."[51]

Thurman was especially disquieted by the lack of "a binding sense of identity" among the new generation of African American disenchanted. In his opinion these young activists, while certainly aggressive and motivated, all too often failed to make the essential connection between their struggles and phenomena or experiences not transparently in evidence. Even more damaging, he took it as a matter of inviolable primal reality that the inadequacies and failures of the older generation are visited, in no small part, upon the children. During the movement years the mounting disinterest on the part of African Americans to infuse moral-ethical concerns onto socio-political conditions was, therefore, scarcely incidental. Under no uncertain terms does Thurman exempt white society from this judgment, but his primary interest in the present context has more to do with self-understanding in the African American community, both inside and outside the institutional church. Speaking in what were for him unusually sharp tones, Thurman charges:

> It is a great irony that the Negro Church has figured so largely as a rallying center for the civil rights movement in the South primarily because of its strategic position as an institution in Negro life; *it has not become a civil rights rallying center because of its religious ethical teaching as such.*[52] (emphasis added)

In time, the rewards of civil rights proved less than the goals appeared to promise. Modest social and economic gains accorded some African Americans gradually led to an unquestioning acceptance of general societal values, complete with their often adverse effects. One of the underlying and rightful assumptions of civil rights orthodoxy was that African Americans were entitled to full participation in the American socio-economic context. But rarely was there a sustained discussion or recognition, Malcolm X being a notable exception, about what kind of people, morally and spiritually, such "progress" might produce — namely, middle class, white collar, communally disdainful and culturally amnesic African Americans.

Far more immediate in impact were those social attitudes and arrangements which continued to relegate the vast majority of African Americans to underclass status. It is at this point that the frustration and rage of African Americans, long present in latent form became catalytic and, momentarily, cathartic in the movement toward a new black consciousness. Thurman reflects on the implications of the new mood:

> In the contemporary push on the the part of American Negroes to elevate blackness to a place of supreme significance in self-identity, we see at work an effort to reclaim the body as the home of the self. The battle cry, Black is Beautiful, is an effort to deal with this central issue. In its preliminary stages, the slogan is an attack on the white world which has made of "white" an absolute. It is this absolute that for so long a time has been the key for the identity of the Anglo-Saxon. With such an absolute as a rallying point for the personality, the grounds for establishing a sense of community, exclusive in character, are guaranteed. Under the aegis of this absolute, the categories for all non-white peoples are defined. The sense of belonging which any non-white peoples are permitted to have can very easily be measured by ground rules established by so-called white supremacy.[53]

Thurman's critique of American attitudes during the sixties and seventies, especially those of African America, augurs ill of what happens to a people (or movement) increasingly estranged from their deepest indigenous ("spiritual") resources. Inevitably, the forces of change brought to bear on the "other," in this case white racist society, become couched in attitudes, behaviors, and instrumentalities reflective of inward realities. In the decade of the sixties "Black" America made a clear and conscious break with the norms of its "Negro" past. Into the void of forsaken values and meanings "a new offensive was born," a metaphysics of immediacy which by and large supplanted the more gradual (and, in hindsight, often too gradual) bridge building efforts of the past. "Freedom, now" and "by any means necessary" denied the utility of non-violence, reconciliation, and the reflective disciplines. "Black power," "power to the people," and "fight the power" cavalierly dismissed extant repositories of wisdom — inclusive of the primal/spiritual/cultural — as evidenced in the enthusiastic (and long overdue) embracing of African history to the exclusion of a prior historicism. So, too, was favored a fragmented collective confrontation with corporate and institutional structures. Reported Thurman in this vein: "Up to and including the present time, no creative way has been found to accomplish the specific ends of identity and healthy self-estimate that is devoid of the negativisms that seem to be inherent in the present struggle."[54]

Thurman felt that one potential vehicle for effecting constructive change was non-violence, not as employed by movement leaders — Martin Luther King, Jr. being a conspicuous exception — but a more involved commitment to non-violence as discipline *and* technique. He casts non-violence as a creative, ethical approach to change, capable of producing specific ramifications in society. In the first place, it is immanently practical: "the purpose of shock treatment is ... to hold before the offender a mirror that registers an image of himself, that reflects the image of those who suffer at his hands." While at the same time, it serves an explicitly transcendent function, which "is to tear men from any alignments that prevent them from putting themselves in the other person's place [and] to remove anything that prevents the individual from free and easy access to his own altar-stair that is in his own heart." The importance of both factors must not, however, be misconstrued, for as Thurman makes manifestly clear, not even non-violence as a collective device can guarantee social change. Rather, the major contribution of non-violence is that it creates and maintains a "climate" wherein protagonists may be brought into a single commitment. To paraphrase Thurman, nonviolence affirms the existence of the "other," however defined, whereas violence embodies a will to non-existence which, translated at the level of society means non-community, even war.[55]

Thurman's discussion of non-violence again connects empirical conditions with cosmic concerns. To accept his premise means that the incentive for non-violent strategy must issue from a spiritual base and, accordingly, out of a profound sense of one's personal and cultural deep-rootedness. Crucial insights are always to be gained from the political and intellectual spheres — culture, church, history, the social order, and so on — but the compelling vantage point, finally, must be inclusive of and beyond the particular, even long-lived social concern. Without this holistic uniting of the objective and subjective, the inner and the outer, Thurman believed it impossible for any movement to maintain the necessary increment for incentive — social or otherwise. Any line of reasoning that is void of Presence and dogmatically self-protecting prohibits persons and groups, African American, Native American, Hispanic or whomever, from fully investing in their potential. If the exigencies of head *and* heart are not activated, the results are certain to lead to self-deception and self-defeat:

> Always I must have available my place of retreat where I can refuel, where I can renourish, where the need itself will not be so overwhelming that I become uprooted. Now this is important. Because, you see, if I become uprooted in my response to human need, then there is no core out of which I'm relating to anything. I become anonymous.[56]

Aldon Morris, in his groundbreaking work *Origins of the Civil Rights Movement* presents a most convincing argument that "a new 'nonviolent black'" was created specifically for the civil rights aspect of the movement, whereas previously "nonviolence was practically unheard-of in Southern black communities." What's more, he is careful to document that "it took time to create the nonviolent protester." What is of particular interest in the present context is that not every demonstrator was able — or willing — to suddenly turn the precepts and training of nonviolence into a way of life. We can do no better than to quote from his interview with long-time activist and minister Hosea Williams:

> I'm not ashamed to say that I've never believed in nonviolence as a philoso-phy of life. And I don't know nobody else who did but Martin Luther King, Jr. Andy [Young] jumped on me one day, physically — knew he couldn't whip me — and if you think Ralph [Abernathy] is nonviolent, back him up ...

Morris then brings the discussion to fruition, by asking:

> How did Southern black Americans suddenly become nonviolent when the civil rights movement unfolded? The answer, of course, is that they did not. Rather, through continuous nonviolent workshops and constant appeals to the nonviolent tradition rooted in the black church and in the life of Jesus, blacks were persuaded to accept nonviolence as a tactic to reach a specified goal.[57]

To be sure, it should be indicated that Morris' overall thesis is that the civil rights movement had a significant and positive impact on the life of the nation and the world. But the fact of the matter is that there was always a clear ambivalence among civil rights activists and an even stronger disdain among black consciousness proponents with respect to the merits of nonviolence. In fact, Thurman himself corroborates the contention that non-violence was a relatively alien concept in the African American community. He offers these pre-civil rights observations:

> For many years Negroes for various reasons have tended to be far too docile. Their docility has been confused with an alleged meekness and cowardliness. Of course, this overall picture is not true, but so deep is the resentment of many Negroes to this overall picture that the technique of nonviolence is regarded by them as being an expression of cowardice. The problem, therefore, is to maintain a non-violent action and increment of courage that would be disassociated from the so-called hat in the hand attitude. I am quite enthusiastic about any attempt on the part of interracial units to combine directly nonviolent action and a program of constructive adjustment in group relations. Grave indeed, is my concern as I watch the mounting tension all over the country. I have traveled some 13 or 14,000 miles since early June, and the picture is the same everywhere — sporadic outbursts of violence, meanness, murder, bloodshed, and a great paralysis in the presence of it all. It seems to me that one of the important solutions is to be found in the work of small groups in communities all over the United States demonstrating courageous, peaceful action, carefully planned and carefully executed.[58]

Increasingly, and especially in the latter stages of black consciousness, movement activists focused and defined African American identity in ways which intentionally opposed the debasements of American society. However, intentionally or not, the call to black consciousness at times mirrored the negating and marginating propensities of larger society, sanctioning the desecration of the identity of others. "Burn, baby burn," "white reparations" and similar expressions were fiery, necessary responses that had been long simmering in the steaming cauldron of America's social proscriptions and racial posturings. But while these slogans were most certainly grounded in an arresting sense of oneness, the functional forms they took were fiercely retributive, sometimes vengeful, and finally proved incapable of dismantling the nation's virulent system of racial preferment. Thurman offers a most prophetic summarizing analysis:

> Whether you assume that by violence the barrier can be removed, or that by non-violence the barrier can be removed — the great critical question, particularly for the man of religious insight is, who will have the right to stand at the moment of panic of the collective psyche when the barrier is gone and the awareness of its non-existence breaks into the mind? If there is any

judgment that rests on the church, I think it is the judgment of God that it has so lost the moral initiative that it may not have the word at the moment of panic. It may be that those of us who are struggling for social change must have a little reservoir of energy left ... that when the tank is empty you throw a little gadget and you can get another gallon of energy. For those who are engaged in the struggle which is so exhausting and exhaustive, which makes such a primary and absolute demand upon all the resources of one's life, there must be provisions made for some little pocket of energy untapped, ready to move in at the moment of exhaustion when the wall comes down. *This* may be the way, the faith, the givenness of God which will assert itself in our time. And may we find a way to be ready.[59]

A Most Significant Witness

> Between the idea
> And the reality
> Between the motion
> And the Act
> Falls the Shadow

> — T.S. Eliot —

It has been stressed to this point that Thurman, often queried concerning his apparent lack of participation in civil rights and other social causes, never advocated an introverted mysticism or privatistic approach to life. To dismiss his contributions to the social arena as only at best minimal is to greatly misread his life's work. "Individuals themselves must trouble the waters," he clearly states, "but nothing must be taken for granted."[60] Unexpectedly, however, it is Gandhi's words to Thurman which provide the best conceptualization of his role as mystic-activist:

> I devoted my life; I withdrew from politics entirely, withdrew from anything having to do with the mechanism of social change and my mandate for carrying out the truth in terms of its ethical and moral significance, and devoted my time to this other — *an energy building thing for the masses of the people so they would have enough vitality to be non-violent.*[61] (emphasis added)

What I want to draw attention to here is that the most distinctive contribution Thurman made to social change was his very "fact" and "for instance" as an exemplary mystic figure. He was not one to shake history through the founding of a large movement based upon a mass following, although he actively engaged the social milieu. Rather, as one in deep association with the transcendent (and, as well, in partial dissociation from society), there were seen as resident in him qualities that were authenticating and motivating of others. On the one hand, he helped others to generate in their own lives the capacity to withstand much of the coerciveness and perniciousness which dominates larger society. On the other hand, he imparted to others — by precept, example, and presence — strength for the long haul in the active engagement of society. Thurman writes:

> It was my discovery that more than campaigns or propaganda, however effi-
> cacious for creating the climate for social change, my gifts moved in the direc-
> tion of the motivation of the individual and what could be done by the indi-
> vidual in his home, in his life, on his street.[62]

And this well-known statement:

> I have never considered myself as any kind of leader. I'm not a movement
> man. It's not my way.... I don't prescribe for anybody else; and I'm willing to
> make available any resources I have to help people who have other ideas.[63]

Thurman relied heavily on his familiarity with the internal *topos* in contributing to broad-based social movements. As the above statements indicate, the main direction in which his activism tilted was to affirm collective direct-action and other approaches through his individual witness to the truth. It follows quite naturally that the import of his role should be easily observed. This is precisely the case, especially if the attestations of many involved in the civil rights aspect of the movement are taken seriously. Benjamin Mays asserted, for instance, that Thurman didn't have to march to prove his freedom — freedom leaped out at you from every direction. Samuel Gandy declares that it was not for everyone to be on the picket line; someone — a Thurman — had to be the dynamic inspi-rational source for others. Otis Moss, for his part, states that while Thurman seldom marched, he more strategically "participated at the level that shapes the philosophy that creates the march — and without that people don't know what to do before they march, while they march or after they march." Jesse Jackson puts it yet differently, saying, "he [Thurman] did not have to work to be black, he was black without effort; and so he focused beyond ethnicity on that which is ethical, that which is efficient, that which is excellent, that which is essence; for these areas — the ethical, the efficient, the inner essence, required effort."[64] Undoubtedly, however, the most radical and revealing of characterizations comes from Lerone Bennett, who says "Howard Thurman ... was *more than* an activist, he was an activator of activists, a mover of movers."[65] (emphasis added)

Numerous persons of every description have found and continue to find in Thurman an exceptional challenging social witness. Landrum Bolling, Alice Walker, Roy Wilkins, Rabbi Alvin Fine, Whitney Young, J. Anthony Lukas, Vernon Jordan, and William Jovanovich are only a few of the prominent professing to having been profoundly affected by his testament. It is now known, of course, that Martin Luther King, Jr. received counsel, renewal and inspiration from Thurman.[66] Even more recently, Jesse Jackson made the message of Thurman's book, *The Search for Common Ground*, the central theme of his presidential campaign.[67] So, too, scholar-activists such as Vincent Harding, James Cone, Nathan Huggins, and Sam Keen count themselves among the transformed and the transforming. Without question, however, it is the broad constellation of persons, seldom receiving of widespread recognition, whom Thurman has impacted most. To all of these individuals, Thurman personified a commitment and consciousness that ran (and still runs) consistently ahead of social definitions. Reciprocally, through them — and kindred seekers everywhere and in every station and walk of life — rested Thurman's hopes for the full integration of vital religious experience with societal and cultural change.

A brief word needs to be said concerning Thurman's personal wrestlings with "the powers of this world." It is true that Thurman was for many the organic embodiment of that which he articulated as religious truth, a concrete reservoir from which one could drink deeply the life-nourishing sustenance of infinity. Nevertheless, such accolades must not overshadow the fact that Thurman had his own outward journey. He engaged in individual challenges to social wrongs wherever and whenever these impeded the demands of the ontological bedrock, the essential and irreducible center. This meant, at once, that all interests were allowed and all impediments eliminated — even when not immediately or transparently evidenced at the level of the socio-political. Says Thurman:

For I believe that there is always something that can be done about any thing. What can be done may not alter the situation, but the individual may relate to unalterable situations within the context of his own choosing. In other words, I am saying that a man need not ever be completely and utterly a victim of his circumstances despite the fact, to be repetitive, that he may not be able to change the circumstance. The clue is in the fact that a man can give his assent to his circumstances or he can withhold it, and there are a desert and a sea between the two.[68]

Thurman's own sense of freedom thus served as the basis for effective confrontation, quiet but confident challenges to segregated religious and academic institutions, hotels, mortuaries, and hospitals.[69] He furthered his concern for world peace through involvement in such human rights organizations as the Fellowship of Reconciliation.[70] On occasion, he physically joined the struggle for civil rights, traveling to survey conditions across the South and, later, participating in the 1963 March on Washington.[71] Funds given him by friends and alumni of Howard and Boston Universities were used to establish the Howard Thurman Educational Trust, which by 1979 had established scholarships for African American youth, primarily in colleges located throughout the South.[72] Thus, Thurman, remaining true to the essential resources of his own life, consistently and actively engaged society through the transforming experience of mystic encounter.

Chapter Five

Activism and Beyond

"Mysticism can finally be the only guarantor of any future to religion..."
— Robert Ellwood —

The focus of this final chapter begins, appropriately enough, with a reflection from Thurman. It concerns "the miracle of the working paper" and the life significantly lived:

> Wherever there appears in human history a personality whose story is available and whose reach extends far, in all directions, the question of his working paper is as crucial as is the significance of his life. We want to know what were the lines along which he decided to live his life? How did he relate himself to the central issues of his time? What were the questions which he had to answer? Was he under some necessity to give a universal character to his most private experience?
>   Our attention is called to such a figure because of the impact which his life makes upon human history. For what is human history but man's working paper as he rides high to life caught often in the swirling eddies of tremendous impersonal forces set in motion by vast impulses out of the womb of the Eternal. When a solitary individual is able to mingle his strength with the forces of history and emerge with a name, a character, a personality, it is no ordinary achievement. It is more than the fact that there is a record of his life — as singular as that fact may be. It means that against the background of anonymity he has emerged articulate, and particular.[1]

It is, of course, the "working paper" of Howard Thurman — his perspective on and praxis of mystical verities — which has played such a critical role in this study. Our work began by identifying a basic problem: the general dismissal of mysticism/mystical religion as vehicular, at least potentially, to radical social change. For the sake of clearer exposition it was determined that the reason for this is closely linked to several factors, and two most especially. The first has to do with the view that mysticism is inherently asocial or anti-social, a position widely accepted in the social sciences. While a second and far more insidious factor has to do with the continued diminution and skewing of the *sui generis* significance of the cultures and contributions of marginalized peoples, including African Americans. The latter observation, it must be said, also but by no means exclusively applies to the social-scientific community. Both of these notions, more than implicit in the literature, we find expressly challenged and disconfirmed by the life and work of Thurman.

A Sociology of Mysticism?

In the appendix following these pages considerable attention will be given to conceptual considerations in the sociology of religion, but of vital interest for the moment is the relationship between mystic orientations and social engagement. The constellation of questions which arise with respect to mysticism and society can be succinctly stated: Are mystics the agents of change, passive reflectors of change, or reactionaries? It is of interest to observe in this connection that the ideas of two seminal thinkers, Ernst Troeltsch and Max Weber, have acquired generalized analytic status in sociology. Unfortunately, this has occurred without adequate dissection of the pragmatic and theoretical issues implied in their respective views on mysticism. As a result their constructs have proven formidable (but not insurmountable) in further reconsidering the sociological apparatus of mysticism.

Church historian Martin Marty makes a point which throws into sharp relief the above problem. In addressing the importance of Thurman as a twentieth century mystic-activist Marty says:

> We can fault Troeltsch for failing to anticipate many developments in the modern sociology of religion. He did not foresee clearly or, as a European, understand the meaning of denominationalism. He did not see how "individualists" of various sorts could be bound into profound, not accidental fellowships. When he assigned this category to people of privileged social classes he did not know, for example, of black slave religion in America. It was not churchly, since no integral community was permitted. It was not sectarian. Indeed it was voluntaryistic, but it was not purely a "parallelism of spontaneous religious personalities."[2]

The formulations of Weber are equally if unintentionally indicted under the terms of Marty's reasoning. Hence, the fact that both of their positions on mysticism should continue to have a heavy impact on contemporary theorizing seems at first encounter puzzling. Again, however, the strong emphasis of Anglo-American sociology of religion on purely institutional studies or, conversely, altered states of consciousness — to wit, classifications of church, sect, and cult — coupled with the prominent neglect of social and cultural paradigms from the "underside" of American society goes a long way toward explaining this prevailing impairment in judgment about mysticism. Thus, as far as most sociologists are concerned the phenomenon of mysticism constitutes a limiting case, capable of contributing little to social understandings. However, in order to avoid charges of exaggerated interpretation from social scientists, I invoke the counsel of Werner Stark:

> Modern man, pan-scientist that he is, has often been helpless and hopeless in his half-hearted efforts outside the confines of science. He has tried to investigate by scientific means what is not, in common sense, amenable to scientific investigation. You cannot put the human psyche under the microscope, nor yet can you scan God through the apparatus of radio-astronomy. The last centuries have sadly neglected, for instance, the methods of sympathy and empathy as well as the methods of mystical experience and metaphysical speculation. In these respects modern man can still learn a good deal from other kinds of man, if only he will be great and generous enough to go to school with him, which he should not, of course, be reluctant to do.[3]

The significance of mysticism as a phenomenon of social consequence thus remains largely uninvestigated in the North American context. Ironically, perhaps the most persuasive argument to pursue such studies comes from Latin America and the work of anthropologist Roger Bastide, who in his classic *African Religions of Brazil*, contends that investigations of cross-cultural interpenetration and mysticism are (analogously) possible in other settings. It should come as no surprise, therefore, to read his brief but studied opinion on the whole matter: "There is a sociology of mysticism."[4] With this assessment and its searching implications we cannot agree more.

Mysticism and Ecclesiastical Change

Careful examination has established that Thurman challenges our conventional understandings of mysticism and social change in at least two ways. First of all, by pragmatically conjoining his worldview to communitas type organizations and movements and, secondly, through an exemplary individual witness. Insofar as the former is concerned, the Thurman-led Fellowship Church provides exceptional evidence of the mystic made manifest. Since the Thurman years, however, Fellowship has struggled in its efforts to continue envisioning the future. This leads us to ask the question what, if any, is the enduring meaning of Fellowship Church? And what of Fellowship's currency as a model for the larger religious community in the United States? Our query is intimately bound up with the recognition that half a century and many founderings later, inter-racial and inter-faith communions are now common-place ideals, but they remain no less rare realities.

A charge frequently brought against Fellowship Church is well expressed by one journalist who wrote, "although [Fellowship] is courageous and pioneering, it can be questioned as a 'pilot development of the integrated church movement in America.' Not every city is San Francisco, and not every minister is a Howard Thurman."[5]   Smith further elaborates upon this sentiment, observing that "Fellowship Church did not have to struggle continually with denominational politics; and since it was founded upon inter-racial and inter-cultural principles, it did not have to confront a tradition, history, and people whose experience with that church had been completely contrary to its inclusive tenets."[6]

This is not to suggest that there were no obstacles at Fellowship Church. Thurman notes, for instance, that there were persons who left Fellowship out of "profound disappointment in the church because it was a *church* and not merely a social-protest group." As well, the congregants had to continually wrestle with their own "deep-seated and ... unconscious racism," Thurman not excepted.[7] Thurman nowhere directly refutes doubters and detractors, but his response speaks for itself: "Be assured of one thing, that it is possible to develop under God such a community in the midst of an environment that is not conducive to such a development."[8] To put the matter succinctly, to isolate Fellowship Church as "peculiar" or anomalous is to miss what is fundamentally at issue:

> The contribution of Fellowship Church to a stream of American religious experience is *the articulation of confidence in the possibility* of uniting men and women of varied backgrounds in a common religious experience before God and as a corollary to that the accumulation of a small but precious body of data as to techniques, methods, by which the implications of the religious

experience may be worked out in the fabric of the common life.[9] (emphasis added)

Similar to the mystic-activist orientation of Thurman himself, the historic importance of Fellowship Church resides in what Roland Robertson would refer to as its "synergic" characteristics — that is, "in erecting a model that facilitated individuals conceiving of their making a simultaneous, positive contribution to self and society."[10] Thurman's own convictions relative to the systemic transformation of the church in America are quite clearly expounded in the following statement:

> For the church this means a radical internal organization of policy, of structural change. I am realistic enough to know that this cannot be done overnight. My contention is that if the will to segregate is relaxed in the church then the resources of mind and spirit and power that are already in the church can begin working formally and informally on the radical changes that are necessary if the church is to become Christian. This of course may not mean that there will be no congregations that are all Negro, or that are all white, but freedom of choice which is merely a sense of alternatives will be available to any persons without regard to the faithful perpetuation of the pattern of segregation upon which the church in America is constructed.[11]

As has been noted, the Fellowship community was little inclined toward replicating itself, whether by way of aggressive missionizing or denominational type cloning. Moreover, as Thurman readily concedes, "this experience has not provided a final or complete answer to the question of the exclusiveness of the church both as to conditions of belonging and of race. But it gives me confidence about the direction in which to continue the search."[12]

Thurman's basic expectation for the church was that it would serve as a kind of institutional contagion, a relatively organic or natural system which in certain crucial respects works as a leavening agent "out there" on its own. What he and the Fellowship community believed, in other words, was that the social regenerative influence — as opposed to singularly lateral or socio-political means of change — was not only authentic but operative enough to enable others to envision, confer and implement their own distinctive intent to community.

The oblique leavening process of social regeneration raises a number of issues worth reflecting on. As Smith suggests Fellowship Church, by virtue of its unpretentious stance, "may have missed the opportunity to stimulate change by its failure to become more aggressive in promoting its insights."[13] On the other hand is it possible that this church, whose authentication diverges from society, offers a transcendence of sectarianism yet prophetic, the results of which are not even now appreciable? To put the matter another way, despite the fact that Fellowship Church has waned in influence, whether its actions will be viewed as merely reformist or radically transformative *in the long run* remains to be seen. No matter, here at least is a "realized alternative" to the social divisiveness ever threatening to engulf our nation. One of the most crucial developments in twentieth century American religious life, the lessons of the Fellowship Church "experiment" can scarcely afford to be neglected any longer.

Mystic Contours and Global Change

Whatever else may be said, Thurman's primary interest in social change was not to provide *the* model for a different order of society. In fact, his preoccupation with the inner life makes it difficult to escape the fact that he emphasized personal rather than social reform. Yet belying the seeming individualism, even conservatism of some of his activities was his emphatic identification with persons and situations portending of change. Just how strongly this is the case may be seen in his linkage of the struggle of African Americans to "the worldwide stirring of subject peoples. It is a phenomenon that seems to me to be the winds of God blowing across the people."[14] After returning from an extended trip to West Africa in 1964, Thurman made the following remarks:

> ...in America we seem to have lost sight of what the real condition of mankind is in the rest of the world.... My mind moved around the world as I had seen it in the last four years, Hong Kong, Manila, Bombay, Cairo, Japan — poverty, hunger, deprivation. That our land had never been ripped open like a ripe melon by bombs ... that we were unable even to imagine six million human beings like us being put in gas ovens, of children being buried alive and every form of creative cruelty beyond imagining; that American Indians had been almost completely emasculated and all their ancient values destroyed; that American Negroes had been exploited, raped, lynched and systematically often suppressed. And again and again with the basic sanction of the state and sometimes even the sanction of religion. All these things moved through the forest of my mind like a huge crawling python.[15]

For Thurman these and many other situations of gross inhumanity, while devastating and far-reaching, were not without their own regenerating force. He cogently connected each of them, finding much that reverberates with respect to the relationship between nonwhite peoples and the Western tradition of conquest and domination. Ever since his 1935 trip to India, in fact, he had been bearing witness to the reality of something other than sheer submission taking place around the globe; everywhere the colonized were rejecting the debasements of the West while constructing new modes of "being" in and for the world.

> This new and widely spread awareness undermines the fear of violence. When a man knows that what he may suffer can be and will be shared vicariously by many others, this gives to him a strange new courage. He enters into a fellowship of sufferers and he does not seem to be alone. The degree to which this suffering is shared by others marks the potential that such suffering may itself become redemptive.[16]

Again, I am drawing attention to the fact that Thurmans' insights concerning social change have not been sufficiently examined. Akin to revolutionary movements in Oceania, Native America, Africa and elsewhere, Thurman's mystic constructs prophetically point out the seeming inability of the West, inclusive of its religious myths and structures, to know and name itself without simultaneously devaluing others.[17] There can be little doubt, of course, that not every situation of contact has issued in a critique of the modern world of specific religious quality. Yet the fact remains, at least for Thurman, that the creation of new or renovated forms of human "being" in the world finally and ultimately rest not on the interpenetration of cultures, but on the irradiating "centering experience."

> ...this is the essence of freedom and it is this that unlocks the door and therefore, you see, it is not anything that is bestowed upon you. It isn't anything to be given to you, it is something that is intrinsic in the essence of your being and this is, from my point of view, ... one of the blind spots in all the psychology that is at work in the revolution that is going on in our part of the world, the notion that political and economic and social rights are something that are conferred upon underprivileged people by privileged people....
>
> A sense of alternative is freedom. The opting of the alternative is the actualizing of the freedom.... It is a riding sense of alternatives and options and it is not of necessity related to the fluid character of the option itself. And this is the story all over the world, everywhere I have been ... it is the same story.[18]

A more ambitious exploration of the parallels between Thurman's mysticism and religiously promoted forms of global change must await another occasion. However, before leaving this theme let me emphasize that a variety of "non-classical" forms of mysticism exist in the United States — among women, Native Americans, African Americans and others — which, in addition to mysticism-laden movements elsewhere, present modalities of change deserving of further study. The following hypothesis by J. Needham especially merits attention:

> When a certain body of rationalist thought has become irrevocably tied to a rigid and outdated system of society, and has become associated with the social controls and sanctions which it imposes, then mysticism may become revolutionary.[19]

The Challenge to African American Religion

We have looked at the case of mysticism in some detail because, for reasons indicated before, of its real and radical potential for social critique and transformation. Of particular and personal concern are those mystic translations which bear directly on America's communities of African origin. I am convinced that African America, for reasons intrinsic to its situation, has much to gain in drawing on insights from its own mystic culture — a culture owing to Africa, the slave forebears and, more recently, Howard Thurman.

For African Americans, much of the legacy of the Civil Rights-Black Consciousness Movement is now in doubt. It is crucial to recognize that this ambivalence issues from a complex of cultural and political factors, none more prominent than the contradicting impact of larger societal values. For the first time, beginning with Lyndon Johnson's "Great Society," sufficient numbers of young African Americans have been deemed socially and intellectually qualified as to make *crossover* (in opposition to the less savory historical activity of *passing*) a meaningful phrase. Meanwhile, a recent resurgence in racial pride and ethnic awareness has also occurred, primarily among African America's youth, suggesting a new permutation on the theme of black consciousness.

As America's communities of African descent prepare for the new century, numerous questions await response. Will the hope of

African Americans continue to rest largely in strategies and under-standings associated with the Civil Rights-Black Consciousness Movement? Are African Americans of necessity limited to the cognitions and motivations of the sixties? Put differently, have we become unquestioningly mimetic in our current praxis, incapable of expanding on the liberation modalities of an earlier period? Or are there prospects for new modes of activism, forms capable of moving beyond divisive penultimate social realities? Is an African American consciousness emerging that is prepared to emancipate, elevate, and liberate — collectively?

It could be argued that much of the evidence to date — the emergence of the urban griots of rap music; the social message of Afrocentricity and a proliferation of African American cultural groups; political identification with Black South Africa, Mauritania and others of the Two-Thirds World — reflect changes of major moment. Yet, one need but point to the fracturing of African America into two extremes — the prosperous and the desparate, the haves and have nots, the already-haves and never-will-haves — to realize that the above-named indicators alone surely will not suffice in the African American quest for dignity and well being.

It is difficult, therefore, to determine whether or not a new African American consciousness is now coming into existence, in large part because we are not all that far removed from the move-ment years of civil rights and black consciousness. With an eye toward better assessing these contours of change, we again turn to Howard Thurman. What significance, if any, does he hold with respect to the future of African American religion, culture, and politics? The essential perspective proposed here bears repeating, that there is much to be gained in taking seriously the mystic envis-agement, the holistic reason, of Thurman.

Throughout this book, I have endeavored to show how Thur-man's diagnosis of the African American condition and, generally speaking, of all humankind now seems more timely than ever. Hard questions arise, some of which have already been examined; others of which I am regrettably not in a position to pursue here. One cannot help but wonder, for example, when African American leadership will come to see the critical connection between mate-rial and immaterial realities. How and by what means, in the strug-gle for dignity, identity, justice, and empowerment are the

uprooted — children, women, and men — yea, all of us to become
better rooted and established? What I am implying, of course, is
that profound and enduring social change need be anchored in the
wellsprings of community. Indeed, as concerns the African American estate, where the demands of the social and the spiritual have
been radically separated from each other or seen to work at cross
purposes, a people suffer. Nevertheless, for many the alliance
between the two orientations remains uneasy, not profound.

Common Ground

We have come to the end of our inquiry relating Thurman's
mystic praxis to social change. Sorting out the variables has been
anything but simple, for as I have tried to show, Thurman's
approach to activism — namely, social regeneration — is a complex
mixture of primordial experience plus interpretation, an interpretation fueled by feelings and associations evoked by the experience
but nonetheless situated in a particular place and time.

Undoubtedly, caution is the key word to employ in understanding the social role of the mystic-activist. Care must be taken to
insure that the mystic's degree of involvement is not overstated,
nor his or her conservative impact as such overlooked. With
respect to Thurman, we recognize that his articulation of the
mystic quest — in all its intersubjective aspects — can easily be
misappropriated in behalf of "pop" causes, voguish self-realization,
and as an opiate for the oppressed; yet, none of this is inevitably
true.

What of the future meaning and significance of Thurman?
Undoubtedly, in a major sense the world of modernity is characterized by fragmentation and increasingly attenuated forms of individualism. But at the same time the groundwork has been laid, at
least in part, for a trajectory of individual-social regeneration. The
potential importance of Thurman — and mysticism — for the
coming days is well-stated by scholar-activist Vincent Harding:

> I have a feeling that Howard Thurman's greatest contribution is going to be
> to the future of black religious thinking because, as I see it, what Howard was
> trying to say to us, especially through works such as *The Search for Common
> Ground*, was that it is possible to take all of the struggles and the sufferings of
> the black experience and recreate them in such a way that they can be used to

open up a whole new arena of human encounter and human relationships. I think that is the direction he felt we fundamentally had to go in order to find our own wholeness as a people. He thought that the whole movement towards black religion, black identity, black theology was a necessary but temporary stopping ground. For whatever we do out of our blackness, and whatever others do out of their Native Americanness or Chicanoness or Europeanness in creating, in a sense, rooms in the American house, there has somehow got to be a common foundation for all of us — Because his conviction was that we came out of a common center and it is towards that common center that we must continually be moving. And I feel that has tremendous political implications.[20]

I have employed several different determinants in my attempt to reinterpret Thurman's role as mystic in society, most notably, history, sociology, and phenomenology. This symbiotic approach has been advantageous in maintaining a clarity of distinction between the confluence of factors informing Thurman's mystic involvements. In the final analysis, whatever can be said about Thurman as mystic defies easy description. Yet it is clear that his is a most distinctive contribution to social change, dictated by a vision inclusive of and beyond conventional activism, a movement effected in concert with other vitally transformed, transforming persons. We end with these benedictory words from Thurman's final work:

And this is the strangest of all the paradoxes of the human adventure: we live inside all experience, but we are permitted to bear witness only to the *outside*. Such is the riddle of life and the story of the passing of our days.[21]

APPENDIX

Mysticism and Society:
Sociological Perspectives

"The practice of detachment for the sake of meditation need not be more than a stage in the training of the mystic; it does not imply that mysticism is quietism. One need not suppose that such detachment, or meditational practices in general, have an adverse effect on the other activities a person engages in. But the opposite need not be true either — that meditation improves one's performances in other respects ... Of course, sitting quiet is always healthy in a society based upon strife.... But at a deeper level, all such questions can only be dealt with at a later stage of the exploration of mysticism.... [T]he view that mysticism is connected with passivity and/or irresponsibility is pure prejudice."

— Frits Staal —

In this final essay I focus on the role which sociology has played in defining the relation of the mystic to society, identifying past and present points of departure. As has been stated throughout this work, it is my contention that mysticism can actively and significantly impinge upon the social milieu. Such a position, to put it mildly, has hardly been the conventional consensus (from my reading) of sociology. For the sociologist of religion, mysticism is typically regarded to be asocial, even antisocial in outlook.[1] As I shall discuss, this limited and less than favorable social assessment is largely traceable to the classic European characterizations of mysticism as forwarded by principals Ernst Troeltsch and Max Weber. The following analysis briefly reviews the constructs offered by both scholars, takes issue with elements of each, and draws on recent insights vital to our objective of establishing a nexus between mysticism and social change.

The Ideal Type

Requisite to any substantive discussion of mysticism as delineated by Troeltsch and Weber is some understanding of the latter's

notion of the "ideal type" (*Idealtypus*). For both researchers the
ideal type was the central conceptual tool for what were in important respects diverging perspectives on mysticism.

Weber recognized an inherent dilemma in the traditional
German idealistic or Kantian approach to the social sciences and
historicism. On the one hand, explanations concluded from overly
generalized social scientific concepts tended to overlook the
distinctive elements of a phenomenon. On the other hand,
however, the particularizing propensities of historical method
seldom allowed room for comparison with related phenomena.
Weber thus sought to establish greater rapport between the social
sciences and the historical disciplines through his notion of the
"ideal type." Virtually all the implications of his concept are
suggested by the following formulation:

> It [the ideal-type] is a conceptual construct which is neither historical
> reality nor even the "true" reality. It is even less fitted to serve as a schema
> under which a real situation or action is to be subsumed as one *instance*. It
> has the significance of a purely ideal *limiting* concept with which the real situ-
> ation or action is *compared* and surveyed for the explication of certain of its
> significant components. Such concepts are constructs in terms of which we
> formulate relationships by the application of the category of objective possi-
> bility. By means of this category, the adequacy of our imagination, oriented
> and disciplined by reality, is *judged*.[2]

This passage illumines several pivotal points in Weber's ideal-
typical analysis, which may be summarized in the following manner:

(1) An ideal type never corresponds precisely with the spatial-
temporal, that is, historical reality. Rather, it is a limiting concept
constructed out of relevant elements of reality to form an empirically manageable, logically precise and coherent whole. It is
framed in terms of two criteria: the knowledge that is available to
the investigator in the initial stages of study and that which is
derived from the actual empirical situations under consideration.

(2) Conversely, whereas an ideal type can never be found fully
embodied in empirical reality, neither is it ever foreign to it. "An
ideal type is formed by the one-sided accentuation of one or more
points of view and by the synthesis of a great many diffuse, discrete,
more or less present and occasionally absent *concrete individual*

phenomena, which are arranged according to those one-sidedly emphasized viewpoints into a unified *analytical* construct."[3]

(3) The third factor is a corollary to the second, namely, that the ideal type involves an accentuation of selected mundane courses of activity or "the conceptual heightening of certain elements of reality."[4] Ideal types are deliberately abstract and synthetic, but always founded upon the probability that component actors will engage in expected social actions. They fulfill the function of delineating at the level of pragmatic illustration the particular features of a given relationship.

(4) An ideal type is not intended to conform to moral or ethical imperatives, but rather the "objectively possible" or what may be deemed the "sociologically adequate."[5] The comparisons made then between the ideal type and real situations or actions is analytic and not evaluative.

(5) Finally, and as a crucial addendum to the first four points, it should be noted that ideal typology is not meant to be either static or transhistorical. Once the phenomenon under consideration has received "an understanding 'inside look'" (*verstehen*), the ideal type loses much of its utility; newer and ever more exhaustive and complete understandings are required.[6] "At the very heart ... lies not only the transciency of all ideal types *but* also at the same time the inevitability of *new* ones."[7]

Thus, in Weber's schema, ideal types are analytical devices that enable the investigator to organize the data of research for the ascertainment of similarities and deviations in concrete circumstances. In other words, from ideal typological constructs hypotheses both necessary and appropriate for comparative study are developed. Moreover, through this means meaningful and precise reflection upon the unique components of phenomenon is made possible above and beyond the determination of correlations and causal imputations.[8] Julian Freund aptly summarizes the profundity of Weber's conceptual tool: "Being unreal, the ideal type has the merit of offering us a conceptual device with which we can measure real development and clarify the most important elements of empirical reality."[9] Bearing these distinctions in mind, we now turn our attention to analyzing relevant components of the Troeltsch and Weber typologies.

Ernst Troeltsch

Central to any discussion of Ernst Troeltsch is his altering of Weber's church-sect typology through the introduction of mysticism as a third type. It is pertinent to indicate that Troeltsch, who was first and foremost a church historian and theologian, gained the preponderance of his insights into the emerging discipline of sociology from Weber.[10] To the point, it is Troeltsch's appreciation for Weber's ideal type moreso than his appropriation of the church-sect distinction which undergirds his own thinking about mysticism. Let us look briefly once again at Weber's construct:

> The ideal-type is an attempt to analyze historically unique configurations or their individual components by means of genetic concepts. Let us take for instance the concepts "church" and "sect." They may be broken down purely classificatorily into complexes of characteristics whereby not only the distinction between them but also the content of the concept must constantly remain fluid. If however I wish to formulate the concept of "sect" genetically, e.g., with reference to certain important cultural significances which the "sectarian spirit" has had for modern culture, certain characteristics of both become *essential* because they stand in an adequate causal relationship to those influences. However, the concepts thereupon become ideal-typical in the sense that they appear in full conceptual integrity either not at all or only in individual instances. Here as elsewhere every concept which is not purely classificatory diverges from reality.[11]

It is important to note from the above passage Weber's methodological injunction (echoed in our earlier quote from Julian Freund) that the basic sociological purpose of ideal type analysis is not "classification" but "clarification." Hence, precisely at the point where the question of "genetics" is raised do concepts lose their purely classificatory significance. In Weber's thinking, the genetic notion does not automatically deprive concepts of their taxonomic precision, but makes them accessible for additional and broader ends. Specifically, he translated this into a concern for the "practical significance" of ideal types as they operated within the limiting framework of "objective possibility." A prime example of Weber's analysis in this regard would be his brilliant proposition — established through mental experiment and comparative study in other cultures — that modern culture could probably not have developed without the sectarian spirit.[12] This by no means implies that Weber identified the sectarian spirit as *the* cause of modern culture, only that it must be considered as *a* cause.

This theoretical digression calls attention to the fact that the analytical precision for which Weber pressed could and did clarify the process by which the past has yielded and shaped the problematic of the present. Troeltsch, seeing the utility of Weber's ideal typical analysis, made sagacious use of his entire conception. The actual effect of his appropriation of the notion, however, was a treatment of church and sect which differed significantly from that of his friend and colleague.

Mysticism has a long heritage in religious traditions, of course, but credit for its first prominent association with sociology belongs to Troeltsch. In 1910, he initiated the inaugural meeting of the German Sociological Society, offering the paper *"Das stoich-christliche Naturrecht und das moderne profane Naturrecht."*[13] The twenty-five page essay was Troeltsch's first formulation of his famous trichotomy of religious forms — church, sect, and mysticism — partially inspired by Weber's germinal church-sect dichotomy.[14] Two years later he elaborated the typology in full in his seminal work, *The Social Teaching of the Christian Churches.*

Thus, Troeltsch's interpretation of the history of Christian social thought is based on a trio of types which may be outlined as follows: the *church type*, distinguished by a relationship generally supportive of and in fact normative to the environing society, which sociological form is related to Christianity's universal symbols; the *sect type*, by a somewhat divergent relationship with society, which sociological form is related to Christianity's demand for ethical perfection; the *mysticism type*, by the lack of both concern and potency with respect to society, which sociological form is amorphous and tends to work at cross-purposes with more definite institutionalizations. In the conclusion to *The Social Teachings* Troeltsch summarily juxtaposes the three types:

> The Church is the holy institution and the institution of grace, endowed with the result of the work of redemption, which can absorb the masses and adapt itself to the world, since, up to a certain point, it can neglect subjective holiness in exchange for the objective treasures of grace and redemption. The Sect is the free union of stronger and more conscious Christians, who join together as the truly reborn, separate themselves from the world, remain limited to a small circle, emphasize the law instead of grace and in their circle set up love as the Christian order of life with greater or lesser radicalism, all

of which is the preparation for and the expectation of the coming Kingdom of God. Mysticism is the intensification and the making immediate of the world of ideas solidified in cult and doctrine into a purely personal and inner possession of the heart, whereby only fluid and completely personally limited group formations can assemble, and in which the remaining cult, dogma and connection with history tend to become so fluid that they disappear.[15]

From the above passage it is evident that Troeltsch views both the sect type and the mysticism type as contradistinctive to the more decisive church type. However, he affirms that each type is rooted within the current of Christian tradition, the latter two arising as complementary correctives to the first. Troeltsch also states that each type has had a dominant impact in differing periods. Overall then, Troeltsch wishes to use the church-sect-mysticism trichotomy as an instrument for ordering the data of the *history* of Christianity. So, too, we shall see that he saw the mysticism type as at once the most elusive and the most portentous of the three.

The Characteristics of the Third Type

Troeltsch somewhat haphazardly delineates the characteristics of mysticism in his discussion of "the pure individualism of the Protestant Dissenters," during which period the third type achieved its "universal historical significance"[16]:

> In the widest sense of the word, mysticism is simply the insistence upon a direct inward and present religious experience. It takes for granted the objective forms of religious life in worship, ritual, myth, and dogma; it is either a reaction against these objective practices, which it tries to draw back into the living process, or it is the supplementing of traditional forms of worship by means of a personal and living stimulus. Mysticism is thus always something secondary, something which has been deliberately thought out ... [I]t always contains a paradoxical element, a certain hostility to popular religion and its average forms of expression, an artificiality which, however, is again extinguished by its own thirst for direct communion with God ... It expresses itself in ecstasy and frenzy, in visions and hallucinations, in subjective religious experience and "inwardness," in concentration upon the purely interior and emotional side of religious experiences.[17]

The broad imagery of mysticism which Troeltsch offers here is fairly consistent with general understandings of mysticism. Among other things, he emphasizes the individuality and inwardness of mystic religious experience and notes its inferior social capacity.

Nonetheless, this portrayal is merely prefatory to his argument for a more precise characterization of the concept, in which he indicates that "we must seek to distinguish mysticism in the narrower, technical concentrated sense in which it is used in the philosophy of religion from this wider mysticism with its immense variety."[18]

Troeltsch thus sets out to differentiate between two analytical forms of mysticism. The "wider form of mysticism" to which he refers is common to all historical expressions of religion. In Troeltsch's view, this wider form is the result of the basic human quest for unity with the divine; it is the realization of "the natural universal religious consciousness." This mysticism form can be "combined with every kind of objective religion, and with the customary forms of worship, myth and doctrine. They contain no kind of doctrine and theory about themselves; at the very most, all they possess is a primitive technique of religious self-cultivation and the production of a certain tempor." Troeltsch's standpoint here is not at all difficult to deduce: wider mysticism is generally supportive of the prevailing religious structures since its practice does not oppose them.[19]

However, it is mysticism in the "narrower, technical concentrated sense," which Troeltsch seeks most to critique. He contends that this narrower form derives from the Protestant Reformation, and especially German Lutheranism. This narrower mysticism has its own sociological import, an independent principle that undercuts existent religious structures and sometimes leads to the formation of new but less absolute or stable groups.[20] Correlative with this form is the development of an entire religious philosophy, that is to say, the construction of a fairly complete *Weltanschauung* cognizant of both "absolute and finite being."[21]

This portrayal of Troeltsch's mysticism, while far from exhaustive, does afford a substantial glimpse into the ambivalences accruing from his formulation. Mysticism is characterized by and, as we shall discuss shortly, periodicized as a duality of "wider mysticism" and "narrower, technical mysticism." Mystical proclivities within both the church and sect types (potential wherever intense and direct religious feelings are located) are subsumed under the first form, while the "pure" mystic (isolated or at best ephemerally related to other mystics) is best represented by the second. Sociologically, then, to the extent that mysticism supplements or intermingles with church and sect types through its provision of religious individualism, it is positive and constructive. However, to the extent that mysticism undercuts the other forms as mere reaction to ecclesiastical contingencies, it is negative and destructive. In Troeltsch's rather convoluted schema, "wider" and "narrower" mysticism are cast as analytical forms with antithetical tendencies, one serving to support and the other to weaken religious structures. I should emphasize again, however, that it is mysticism in its "narrower" form which preeminently occupies Troeltsch.

The Modern Form of Mysticism

As has been noted, Troeltsch's discussion of the third type occurs within his broader treatment of the rise of Protestantism, during which epoch the third type achieved its "universal historical significance."[22]   Troeltsch concluded his monumental survey of Christian thought with the eighteenth century, remarking that after this time "Church history entered upon a new phase of existence."[23] This "new phase of existence" was extremely troubling to Troeltsch, especially with regard to the role of mysticism in the ongoing development of Christian social thought and practice. William Garrett takes notice of the fact that "Troeltsch approached the future with a considerable measure of pessimism and apprehension, founded in the main on his stalwart conviction that mysticism would very likely surface as the prevailing modern religious form."[24]

Indeed, although Troeltsch ended his survey of Christian social thought just prior to 1800, he could not refrain from discussing the predicaments facing modern Christianity. The radical religious individualism of mysticism, which he contended emerged as an independent sociological type from the Protestant Reformation, became both critical and focal to his observations on "the infinitely difficult situation of Christian social doctrine in the modern world."[25] Christendom was in a state of veritable disintegration; a new "compromise between church and culture" was not yet apparent. With somber apprehension, therefore, Troeltsch braced himself for what he believed to be the ineluctable rise of the third type:

It is neither Church nor sect, and has neither the concrete sanctity of the institution nor the radical connection with the Bible. Combining Christian ideas with a wealth of modern views, deducing social institutions, not from the Fall but from a process of natural development, it has not the fixed limit for concessions and the social power which the Church possesses, but also it does not possess the radicalism and the exclusiveness with which the sect can set aside the State and economics, art and science.

... Gradually, in the modern world of educated people, the third type has come to predominate. This means, then, that all that is left is voluntary association with like-minded people, which is equally remote both from Church and sect.[26]

Only if one is clear regarding Troeltsch's use of the third type can the full import of this and similar statements be grasped. Troeltsch believed that modern mysticism's movement beyond historic religious individualism was as potentially devastating as it appeared inexorable. At least two factors would be responsible for the unleashing of the third type's socially ambivalent propensities: 1) a growing restiveness with the institutions of church and sect, and 2) an increasingly sophisticated and individualising culture.

In general, ... the modern educated classes understand nothing but mysticism. This is due to the reflex action of the atomistic individualism of modern civilization in general, of an individualism which in non-religious spheres of life is already losing its hold, and is beginning to develop into its exact opposite. In its depreciation of fellowship, public worship, history, and social ethics this type of "spiritual religion", in spite of all its depth and spirituality, is still a weakened form of religious life ...[27]

For Troeltsch, the rise of contemporary mysticism was a signal to the probable demise of so-called Christian civilization. Its major deficiency, an absence of socially formative power, is compounded by an equivalent lack of social concern. Moreover, the modern mysticism form is parasitical and incapable of holistic existence apart from the other types (of course, the same could be said of the other types). Thus, in the case of Christianity about the best that Troeltsch could hope for was the emergence of some new socio-religious structure or development which, in the spirit of ideal typological usage would also render obsolete his tripartite conceptual framework:

In the mutual interpenetration of the three chief sociological categories, which must be united with a structure which will reconcile them all, lies [the] future tasks, tasks of a sociological and organizing kind, which are more pressing than all doctrinal questions.[28]

There is little question that Troeltsch's evaluation of mysticism, particularly when considered in light of such twentieth century examples as Thurman, Mahatma Gandhi, Rufus Jones and others, is wholly inadequate for current sociological investigations.[29] What is more, it is plain that Troeltsch himself had no plans for his typology to be extended beyond its specific historical (if not cultural) utility. This does not negate the fact, however, that the legacy of his third type contains kernels of insight significant for tempering current understandings of the mystic's relation to society. Troeltsch's fear that mysticism's atomizing tendencies would be increasingly evidenced in the foreseeable future remains little more than a matter for speculation. Yet his concern about the destructiveness of a post-Reformation mysticism separated from socio-structural constraints — perhaps best evidenced in some cultic milieus — continues to merit close attention.   That Troeltsch's pioneering efforts in the sociology of mysticism have borne fruit will become more apparent after our review of Weber.

Max Weber

Significantly, the earliest recorded occasion of Weber addressing the subject of mysticism was his response to the paper offered by Troelsch at the initial meeting of the German Sociological Association in 1910.[30] In the ensuing discussion, Weber interjected a most critical albeit subtle change into the grounds for investigating mysticism as a sociological concept. Arthur Mitzman's observation with respect to Weber's participation in the colloquium is persuasive, stating that "the opportunity of discussing the significance of mysticism precipitated an intellectual *tour de force* that carried him well beyond the perspective of his studies on Calvinism and set the framework for some of his most important work in the next decade."[31] Thus, for all practical purposes, Weber's appropriation of mysticism as an analytical component may be understood as part and parcel of a considerable intellectual reciprocity which occurred between himself and Troeltsch.[32]

Weber's initial commentary on Troeltsch's paper seemed to strongly endorse his introduction of the third type. He proceeded, for example, to identify the substratum upon which Greek Orthodoxy and Russian Literature is established as "a very specific classical mysticism."[33] In actuality, however, his very interest in what he elsewhere calls "the oriental Christian church" had to do with its marked emphasis on brotherly love, a phenomenon of communal consequence far removed from Troeltsch's depiction of an individuated mysticism.[34]

Hence, while identifying somewhat with Troeltsch's three-tiered format, Weber simultaneously shifted the emphasis of the typology. More than that, later in the colloquy he introduced, whether intentionally or otherwise, a new and even more provocative conceptual framework based on salvational forms:

> The most extreme contrasting poles which exist are, on the one hand, the forms of world-rejecting religiosities ... which are preserved in those spiritual movements of which I spoke earlier and were also characteristic of certain parts of primitive Christianity: a kind of "acosmic" love of man, that is the one possibility. On the other hand, there is its most extreme counter pole: the Calvinistic religiosity which finds the certitude of being God's child in the to-be-attained "proving of oneself" *ad majorem dei gloriam* within the given and ordered world. In other words, we have on the one side the completely amorphous formlessness of acosmic love; on the other side that unique attitude extremely important for the history of social and political practice, that the individual feels himself placed within the social community for the purpose of realizing "God's glory" and therewith the salvation of his soul.[35]

Roland Robertson, whose work will be considered momentarily, notes that Weber's fullest development of this new typological system occurred in later of his expositions, when "mysticism as a counter to asceticism [was conceived] within the context of the inner-worldly/other-worldly distinction."[36] These essays, written between the years 1912-1915, are clear evidence of the heightened prominence that the mysticism concept held in some of Weber's final reflections. For example, in his essay on "Religious Rejections of the World and their Directions," he focuses his attention on the "constructed types of conflicting 'life orders'" as represented by asceticism and mysticism in the spheres of economics, politics, aesthetics, and the erotic. He offers additional explication of these "polar concepts" in "The Social Psychology of the World Religions" and in several sections of *The Sociology of Religion*.[37]

What Weber seeks to distinguish in these essays are two main directions for those seeking salvation — mysticism and asceticism. The first may be said to constitute a rejection of or at least an indifference toward the social cosmos ("acosmicism"), while the latter seeks to master said world. Garrett's assessment of Weber's typology rightly underscores the fact that these basic paths of action orientation "functioned to define the antipodal options available to men and societies in their quest for a meaningful stance toward the ultimate structures of reality, however differently those structures might be interpreted by separate religious or philosophical traditions."[38]

The overall picture of Weber's treatment of mysticism is filled in with the addition of the other-worldly — inner-worldly tandem. First, Weber states that asceticism may be a "rejection of the world" (typified by the Hindu Yogi), involving a formal withdrawal from the world, inclusive of all "creaturely interests." However, it is most notably "inner-worldly" (typified by Calvinism), which orientation leads the individual to participate "within the institutions of the world but in opposition to them." Weber contends that in this situation, "the world is presented to the religious virtuoso as his responsibility." On its part, mysticism may be characterized as a "flight from the world" (typified by Buddhist mendicants). This type of activity mandates a "subjective condition of a distinctive kind, ... confined to a minority who have particular religious qualifications, and [is] the end product of the systematic execution of a distinctive type of activity, namely, contemplation." Finally, there is the possibility of inner-worldly mysticism, of which Weber all but ignores.[39]

Quite clearly, the configuration of Weber's four basic types of religious orientation — in descending order of social significance from 1) inner-worldly asceticism to 2) other-worldly asceticism to 3) inner-worldly mysticism to 4) other-worldly mysticism — suggests that his estimation of mysticism is considerably less than positive. In fact, it is safe to say that Weber viewed mysticism with suspect, deeming its world-negating tendencies to be essentially out-of-step with modernity and a hindrance to contemporary socio-cultural formation.[40] Ironically, despite Weber's strong anti-mysticism bent, it is his typologizing which offers clues necessary for affirming the mystic's participatory role in the modern world.

Anglo-American Sociology and Mysticism

With few exceptions, the mysticism-related constructs of Troeltsch and Weber have established the parameters for all subsequent sociological characterizations of mysticism. In the foregoing analysis it was noted that the Troeltschian model of mysticism was socio-historically typed, that is to say, its original and empirical frame of reference was Christianity's organizational forms prior to 1800. Influenced by but at variance with Troeltsch was the asceticism-mysticism model of Weber, which stressed salvation as a social-psychological motif. Weber's elaborations, even moreso than his colleague's, belied the potential social significance of mysticism.

It has also to be said that the respective portrayals by Troeltsch and Weber exhibited sufficient congruities. Both recognized that mysticism is part of society (however woefully), that the mystic actor does not exist in an absolute empyrean abstracted from society. In true Durkheimian fashion, the mystic's experience itself may derive in part from the feelings of nonrational oneness engendered from living in society. Finally, and perhaps most importantly, the dual underscoring of the mysticism notion is a clear acknowledgement of the indispensability of individual experience and personal motivation in issues facing the sociologist of religion.[41] Neither Troeltsch nor Weber offer conceptualizations adequate to clarify mysticism's contemporary impact. Nonetheless, this does not render their insights any less valuable as we seek to move the sociology of mysticism beyond rather limited hypotheses to more sufficient inquiry.

In the English-speaking world, and especially in American sociological circles, the approaches of these two standard-bearers have redounded to a rather curious and confusing turn of events. For example, in church-sect theorizing it has been the socio-theological conceptualization of Troeltsch that has prevailed rather than Weber.[42] On the other side, and of more direct bearing here, it was Weber's realignment and decidedly other-worldly characterization of Troeltsch's third type which ensured the relegation of mysticism to sociological oblivion.[43] Whatever the historical reasons behind these developments — and they are quite involved

— it is fairly safe to say that orthodox Anglo-American sociologists have accepted the constructs of the forebearers as normative if not definitive.[44]

As regards contemporary Western mysticism, clearly too little has so far been said in the social scientific literature. Most researchers are apparently convinced that Weber's egoist and escapist — and, to this we must add, dated — depictions of the type are beyond dispute. Thus it comes as no surprise that recent empirical studies in mysticism have, by and large, done little to dispel the deeply entrenched Weberian parochialism.[45] This ongoing denial of a socially engaged mysticism is strongly rejected by religion scholar Frits Staal, who states that "the evaluation of mysticism as escapism may be justified when intended as a psychological evaluation of the attitude of individual mystics. As a general characteristic of mysticism it fails not only because it is not applicable in many individual cases, but also because it approaches mysticism from a perspective which is alien to it."[46]

The wholesale neglect of mysticism by English-speaking sociologists (and, conversely, the current enthusiastic focus on esoterica and the like) is even more ironic given the original use of the Troeltsch-Weber typologies. It is clear from any serious reading of Troeltsch and Weber that they did not construct their models with analytical immortality in mind. Nor, for that matter, did either one claim for their conclusions that they would be definitive in every social context. In fact, among the important regions absent from both investigations are the United States and the then colonies of Europe. As Swatos so perceptively puts it, the reification of the Troeltsch-Weber constructs into "generalized abstractions" and "evaluative stereotypes" opposes the very intentionality of ideal typology.[47] And Weber's own remarks are equally instructive: "It [the type] has the significance of a *purely ideal limiting concept with which the real situation or action is compared and surveyed for the explication of its significant components.*"[48] (emphasis added) Unfortunately, few Anglo-American sociologists have taken seriously the methodological respect which Weber and (even) Troeltsch had for historical and socio-cultural specificity; at least, not when it comes to studying mysticism.

Roland Robertson: Modifications of a Type

The modern period has been characterized by a complex of factors deeply affecting society and religion, including mysticism. Troeltsch and Weber alike recognized that such modern motifs as technology, enhanced individualism, and alienation portended change on the socio-religious landscape. As indicated, however, their expositions contained little more than inferences to the fate of mysticism in the modern context. Outside of an occasional historical note, neither referred to mysticism in the United States. Again, no mention is made of mysticism in connection with the volatile developments attendant to situations of struggle in Africa, Latin America, and elsewhere. The most that can be said about the notions of Troeltsch and especially Weber is that they are correct insofar as they go. The difficulty, of course, is that neither went far enough. Benjamin Nelson notes the resulting lacunae:

> ...Troeltsch is aware of the crossings of mysticism and sect in the late-Medieval and early modern era. Thus it proves that Troeltsch does perceive the important role that mysticism played in the passages toward the illuminous sectarian groups and the extensions of the notion of reason and civil liberties. In a sense it is surprising that Troeltsch's [1910] remarks on mysticism here did not appear to prompt Weber to a larger response.... Weber was so intent upon establishing the unique predominance in the West of the penetration and remaking of the world to innerworldly asceticism that he failed to give enough weight to another fact which he no less than Troeltsch implicitly recognized. Weber does not here or elsewhere in his work sufficiently stress the significance of *innerworldly mysticism as contrasted with otherworldly mysticisms*.[49]

Weber contended, and rightly so, that mysticism as a tradition had been more dominant in Asia, whereas the breakthrough of asceticism received primary elaboration and legitimation in the Occident. Apparently, however, the very grasping of this difference became an *idée fixé* which prevented him from any thorough examination of mysticism's varieties.[50] This calls attention to the fact that Weber, like many another researcher, was not above straying from his own methodological guidelines. Contrary to his well-known stance on value-neutrality and, to a lesser degree, probability, in this instance he chose rather to isolate what he saw as the most consistently patterned and absolute of distinctions, thereby neglecting crucial intermediate conceptualizations.[51]

On balance, then, Weber's passionate but excessive concentration on the "polar concepts" of inner-worldly asceticism and other-worldly mysticism considerably weakened what was in other respects a masterful exposition. Nevertheless, sociology remains largely content with the main thrust of Weber's formula, satisfied that mysticism is void of social implications, at least positive ones. On a more positive note, a handful of sociologists have begun to challenge Weber's venerable but incomplete portrayal of mysticism. Important theoretical reformulations and elaborations have been offered by several prominent scholars, including Benjamin Nelson, Gert Mueller, William Swatos, William Garrett, and David McCloskey.[52] However, in our view, the most fruitful contributions to date come from the work of Roland Robertson.[53]

As a social theorist, Robertson is perhaps best known for his expositions on "cultural sociology," and the relation of the individual to society. He brings to his task a formidable and self-described "post-Weberian" concern, whereby he seeks in part both to critique and advance beyond those normative interpretations of Weber which ignore "the modes and categories of the thought of the 'ordinary' individual in modern societies."[54] To a large extent, Robertson's goal is the reconstruction (but not dismantling) of the more conventional sociological enterprise of viewing action from the standpoint of a conceptual scheme applicable to all situations. As we shall observe, such a theoretical perspective bears greatly on his analysis of mysticism.

Robertson, in a series of articles has persuasively asserted the emergence of a new ethos of inner-worldly mysticism in the West. Obviously, such a reading of mysticism's current position in the West stands in stark contrast to iconic Troeltsch-Weber prognoses. Commenting on Weber's notion of a socially passive and disinterested mysticism, Robertson writes:

> The notion of inner-worldly ascetic mysticism being proposed here indicates a much more activist, *engage'* modality. In other words, in the modern kind of *ascetic mysticism* the emphasis is much more positive, both with respect to the significance of worldly activity and the active quest for personal realization.[55]

Robertson attests that Weber's analytical modes of inner and other-worldly/asceticism and mysticism were, as Talcott Parsons wrote, "radical solutions on a personal basis."[56] At the same time, however, discrepancies in Weber's judgment (see our earlier discussion) eventually rendered his typology less than useful as an exploratory/explanatory device. Robertson thus sets out to modify the imprecision of his definitions:

> In line with much that Weber wrote, and indeed our present knowledge of different forms of mysticism, the basic requirement is to conceptualize inner-worldly and other-worldly directions of salvation such that the first is contingently more conducive to asceticism and the second more conducive to mysticism. From a Weberian standpoint this is very necessary, in that Weber clearly saw inner-worldly asceticism as the polar opposite of other-worldly mysticism.[57]

Robertson is interested in making less ramified the distinctions that obtain between inner-worldly and other-worldly varieties of asceticism and mysticism. He endeavors to accomplish this feat by giving analytic precedence to the understated dimension in Weber's analysis, the inner-worldly/other-worldly variable. As Robertson himself notes, an "empirically more accurate" rendition of the Weberian formulation will effectively illuminate traditionally neglected affinities and influences. This leads him to reprioritize inner-worldly mysticism as a "variation upon a more fundamental form of inner-worldly asceticism and other-worldly asceticism as a variation upon a more fundamental form of other-worldly mysticism."[58] For Robertson, mysticism and asceticism come to acquire a complement of the other in modern societies — an altogether healthy synthesis:

> Speaking specifically of Western, inner-worldly contexts the development of a mystical complement to asceticism involves making good some of the 'deficiencies' of asceticism. Mysticism counterbalances three particular characteristics of asceticism. First, it offsets the ascetic's tendency to execute in society something which he has no time to understand — that is, the ascetic does not from the point of view of the mystic really care about the nature of God. Second, mysticism counterbalances the ascetic tendency to manifest a 'happy stupidity' with respect to the meaning of the world; for the ascetic being a man of inner-worldly action fails to cope, from the mystic's point of view, with the problem of ultimate reality. Third, the mystical orientation provides a counter-point to the asceticist tendency in working for the glory of God to confuse this with self-glory — mysticism facilitating the differentiation of working *for* God from relating *to* God. The latter is a specialty of the mystic.[59]

Robertson insists that this differential development of a contemporary Western mysticism, or *inner-worldly ascetic mysticism*, is foreshadowed in some aspects of Lutheranism.[60] It is a product of the crucial linkage between historic mysticism's promise of self-fulfillment and modern asceticism's orientation towards goals in the future and in the larger society. Unlike other-worldly mysticism, which seeks to transcend (escape) the world, inner-worldly or ascetic mysticism "provides for both immanent active participation in the world and transcendent reflection upon the world."[61] Accordingly, ascetic mysticism seeks to cultivate the self for the purpose of living happily and effectively within the world. At the same time, it endeavors to sustain responsible participation in societal affairs.

It should be apparent by now that in Robertson's estimation twentieth century Western mysticism does not undercut the old ethos of inner-worldly asceticism but instead vitalizes it through the role-motivational strategy of "ultimate completion." The emergence of various instrumentalities for the realization and enhancement of the "self" in the modern context coincide with asceticism, itself a condition necessary for the evolution of the social. In Robertson's words, "society demands individual specialization, while individuals demand wholeness." Hence, the contemporary combination of mystic and ascetic orientations, that is, ascetic mysticism, bridges "the hiatus between societal and self demands in conditions of extensive societalization and individuation."[62] It is in this connection that the shrewd observation of Robertson's former colleague Benjamin Nelson ought to be taken into account: "matters never seem to be going well with us in the West when the two orientations are radically separated from one another or appear to work at cross purposes."[63] Thus, we see underlying Robertson's neo-Weberian stance the old Weber tradition of concern for sustaining the individual actor's sense of credibility — freedom — in relation to a seemingly intractable and increasingly more autonomous social structure.

We have not dealt prior to this point with Robertson's perspective on mystical fellowship. The evidence is clear that while Troeltsch and Weber alike acknowledged such collectivities, neither highly valued their existence.[64] Robertson, on the other hand, shows measurable appreciation for mysticism in more than individual form. He quotes Joachim Wach in this regard:

> Wach argued that because mystical experience is ultimately ineffable (ineffability being one of the most commonly noted of the attributes of mysticism) there are left "mainly two forms of sociality in which the mystic will participate: human companionship in what concerns all daily life and mutual support in the protest against traditional religious forms and institutions."[65]

Robertson is quick to point out that he is speaking of mysticism as a particular orientation to life, somewhat distinguishable, at least for analytical purposes, from mystical experiences *per se*. Nevertheless, it should at least be stated that the connotation of mysticism's "ineffability" does not mean that there is nothing that can be said about it, but only that not nearly enough can be said. In any case, Robertson concurs with Wach's contention that there is a protest nature embedded in one major form of modern mysticism. What is more, in the absence of specific empirical examples from Wach, Robertson proceeds to offer one of his own, the Free Spirits of the Reformation period — an accurate yet rather curious selection, given his stress on twentieth century mysticism.

Robertson thus finds under post-Reformation circumstances ground fertile for the cultivation of relations between mysticism and protest movements. Unaccountably, however, Robertson is reluctant to elaborate on (is unfamiliar with?) any of its forms. Indeed, lack of empirical illustration is the major failing in his otherwise perceptive and penetrating argument. Nonetheless, in rather inadvertent fashion, Robertson does restate his crucial insight elsewhere. He writes:

> Weber's discussions of mysticism, particularly when we consider them against the backdrop of German intellectual history and within the context of early twentieth-century German thought, point the way to our need to bring the sociology of religion more directly to bear on the discontents of modern societies.... One would ... not realize from reading the growing number of studies of modern mysticism that the latter could have much bearing upon such matters as the nature of the modern state, the character of political authority in modern societies, and so on.[66]

Robertson's hints of a dynamic interaction between mysticism and "the discontents of modern society" are most suggestive. To reiterate, however, as intriguing as his argument is, in my opinion it is unnecessarily timid, truncated and not altogether convincing. The position which has guided this book is more adamant and straightforward: *In situations of social unrest, mysticism may be a conduit for the articulation of dissatisfaction with extant social structures and for the introduction of innovations.* It is my conviction that the social transformative aspects of mysticism can at least be elucidated to this extent, mysticism's more conspicuous individualistic tendencies notwithstanding.

Robertson's argument for delineating contemporary mysticism's meaning in the Occident has been a primary stimulus and guide to our own investigations. His perspective not only takes seriously the Troeltsch-Weber tradition, but expands and enhances these conceptualizations in compelling fashion. Again, from my purview, the only real drawback to Robertson's recasting of classic motifs from the sociology of mysticism is his lack of empirical documentation.[67] As Robertson himself acknowledges, his treatment of the subject is "empirically-sensitive" and not explicitly empirical.[68] This shortcoming in no way diminishes the importance of his argument.   But it does highlight the fact that the practical renderings of contemporary mysticism still have to be vigorously identified.

In sum, recent contributions by scholars such as Robertson, Nelson and others have begun to point the way beyond Troeltsch and Weber to a more sociologically responsible and significant approach to the study of twentieth-century mysticism. In light of the post-Weberian criteria set forth by Robertson — and our own focus on Thurman — the task of sociology now is to become more consciously attentive to socially engaged, "activist" forms of mysticism.

Notes

Introduction

1 Examples of accolades for Thurman abound. He was listed as one of the "twelve greatest preachers in America" in *Life*, April 6, 1953, p. 128. This distinctive honor was echoed in July of the following year by the readers of *Ebony*, who named him one of the nation's "ten greatest Black preachers."

2 The range of interpretations of mysticism are broad, so much so that no one definition can hope to do justice to them all. In any case, what I have in mind is somewhat less ambitious, namely, to focus on the specifically sociological meaning of mysticism.

3 The phrase "social change" has any number of connotations, depending on the analytical perspective, i.e., evolutionary or revolutionary, macro or micro, the causes of change, the agents of change, and so on. Correlative phrases include "social transformation," "social reform," and "social activism." All of the above are referred to throughout this study in a more or less general sense. A specific focus of this inquiry, however, will be "social regeneration," which activist orientation takes into account among other things the agent and nature of change. For a much fuller and elaborate definition, see the section later in the introduction on "Methods of Inquiry," and also chapter three.

4 Major sociological studies include Bennetta Jules-Rosette, ed., *The New Religions of Africa* (Norwood, NJ: Ablex Publishing, 1979); Bryan R. Wilson, *Magic and the Millenium: A Sociological Study of Religious Movements of Protest Among Tribal and Third-World Peoples* (London: Heinemann, 1973); and Peter Worsley, *The Trumpet Shall Sound*, 2nd, augmented ed. (New York: Schocken Books, 1968). Offerings in the field of anthropology are Kenelm Burridge, *New Heaven, New Earth* (Oxford: Basil Blackwell, 1980); and I. C. Jarvie, *The Revolution in Anthropology* (Chicago: Henry Regnery Co., 1964, 1967). History of Religions is represented by Vittorio Lanternari, *The Religions of the Oppressed* (New York: Alfred A. Knopf, 1963); and Charles H. Long, *Significations: Signs, Symbols, and Images in the Interpretation of Religion* (Philadelphia: Fortress Press, 1986).

5 Luther E. Smith, Jr., *Howard Thurman: The Mystic as Prophet* (Lanham, MD: University Press of America, 1981), p. 9.

6 Lewis A. Coser, *Masters of Sociological Thought*, 2nd ed. (New York: Harcourt Brace Jovanovich, Inc., 1977), pp. xiii-xvii. There are other studies, of course, which adopt a similar framework. See, for example, the Erik Erik-

son profiles, *Young Man Luther* (New York: Norton, 1958), and *Gandhi's Truth* (New York: Norton, 1969); Frank Manuel, *A Portrait of Isaac Newton* (Cambridge: Harvard University Press, 1968), and more recently, Frederick L. Downing, *To See The Promised Land: The Faith Pilgrimage of Martin Luther King, Jr.* (Macon, Ga: Mercer University Press, 1986).

7   Seminal offerings to this effect are Vincent Harding, *There is a River* (New York: Harcourt Brace Jovanovich, 1981); C. Eric Lincoln, *Race, Religion, and the Continuing American Dilemma* (New York: Hill and Wang, 1984); and Gayraud Wilmore, *Black Religion and Black Radicalism*, revised ed. (Maryknoll, NY: Orbis Books, 1983).

8   The term "Two-Thirds World" while scarcely more definitive than the "Third World," is here viewed as a more positive appropriation for the present, giving due recognition and affirmation to the majority of the world's human and natural resources. Ultimately, "Two-Thirds" attempts to acknowledge that those who occupy the underside of the purchasing and ruling powers in the human community seek a quality of life which, when met by the "One-Third," will indeed equal "One."

9   For an extensive discussion see the appendix.

10 Andrew Greeley, *Ecstasy: A Way of Knowing* (Englewood Cliffs, NJ: Prentice-Hall, 1974), p. 101.

11 *The Pursuit of the Millenium*, revised and expanded ed. (London: Temple Smith, 1970).

12 *Mysticism and Dissent* (New Haven: Yale University Press, 1973).

13 Howard Thurman, *The Creative Encounter: An Interpretation of Religion and the Social Witness* (New York: Harper & Bros., 1954).

14 Howard Thurman, *Mysticism and the Experience of Love* (Wallingford, PA: Pendle Hill Pamphlet 115, 1961), p. 7.

15 Unless, of course, they choose to adopt an evolutionary approach concerning the function and role of religion reminiscent of Emile Durkheim's *The Elementary Forms of the Religious Life* (New York: Free Press, 1965). Essentially, Durkheim contends that the reality experienced by the religious actor as universal and objective causality (the "sacred") is not really religion at all, but society. Society has deified itself; religion is the thoroughly human means of symbolic expression of the total collective life.

16 *Preface to Existentialism 2*, ed. William V. Spanos, p. xiv, quoted in Mozella Mitchell, *Spiritual Dynamics of Howard Thurman's Theology* (Bristol, In: Wyndham Hall Press, 1985), p. 156.

17 Ninian Smart instructively describes the meaning of this stance: "...it is wrong to analyze religious objects in terms simply of religious beliefs. A description of a society with its gods will include the gods. But by the principle of the

bracket we neither affirm nor deny the existence of the gods. In order to get over the cumbrous inelegancies that we are likely to run into in trying to maintain this methodological posture, I shall distinguish between objects which are *real* and objects which *exist*. In this usage, God is real for Christians whether or not he exists. The methodological agnosticism here being used is, then, agnosticism about the existence or otherwise of the main foci of the belief system in question." *The Science of Religion and the Sociology of Knowledge* (Princeton: Princeton University Press, 1973), p. 54.

18 Mircea Eliade, *The Sacred and the Profane* (New York: Harcourt Brace Jovanovich, 1959).

19 Rudolf Otto, *The Idea of the Holy* (Oxford: Oxford University Press, 1958).

20 Smart, *Science of Religion*.

21 Thurman was a product of his time as concerns inclusive language; it was simply not a priority in his ministry. It is well known, however, that women were prominent in every aspect of Thurman's life and work. In addition, his deep regard for and sensitivity to the total personhood of women is well documented. See, for example, the array of essays in "Simmering on the Calm Presence and Profound Wisdom of Howard Thurman," a special edition *Debate and Understanding* (Spring 1982).

22 Thomas Luckmann, *The Invisible Religion* (New York: Macmillan, 1967), pp. 73-76.

23 Some of the sources consulted include Elizabeth Yates, *Howard Thurman: Portrait of a Practical Dreamer* (New York: John Day Co., 1964); Mozella G. Mitchell, *Spiritual Dynamics*; and Luther Smith, *Mystic as Prophet*. The reader is also referred to two major recent studies by Carlyle Fielding Stewart, III, *God, Being and Liberation: A Comparative Analysis of the Theologies and Ethics of James H. Cone and Howard Thurman* (Landham, MD: University Press of America, 1989); and Walter E. Fluker, *They Looked for a City: A Comparative Analysis of the Ideal of Community in the Thought of Howard Thurman and Martin Luther King, Jr.* (Landham, MD: University Press of America, 1989).

Chapter One

1 Lerone Bennett, Jr., "Howard Thurman: Twentieth Century Prophet," message given at commemoration service, Boston University Marsh Chapel, Boston, Ma., 10 April 1983.

2 Robert T. Young, "Howard Thurman: A Vision of Oneness," *Debate and Understanding*, (Spring 1982): 55.

3 The main information for this section comes from three sources: Howard Thurman's autobiography, *With Head and Heart* (New York: Harcourt Brace Jovanovich, 1979); Elizabeth Yates, *Portrait of a Practical Dreamer*; and

Lerone Bennett, Jr., "Howard Thurman: 20th Century Holy Man," *Ebony*, February 1978, pp. 68-85.

4   At the time there were only three public high schools for African Americans in the state; the closest church-supported school was some one hundred miles away in Jacksonville.

5   This episode in Thurman's life is of especial interest in light of the well-known statement by sociologist of religion C. Eric Lincoln, that "no one can die 'outside the Black Church' if he is Black. No matter how notorious one's life on earth, the Church claims its own at death — and with appropriate cere-mony." *The Black Church Since Frazier* (New York: Schocken, 1974), p. 116. For changing trends see Lincoln and Lawrence Mamiya, *The Black Church in the African American Experience* (Durham, NC: Duke University Press, 1990).

6   See Howard Thurman, *Footprints of a Dream: The Story of the Church for the Fellowship of all Peoples* (New York: Harper & Row, 1959), pp.15-16.

7   Howard Thurman, "Footprints of the Disinherited," Black Pentecost sermon given at Elliot Congregational Church, Roxbury, Ma., 31 May 1972.

8   Thurman, *Head and Heart*, p. 60.

9   Ibid., p. 73.

10   Ibid., p. 90.

11   The Student Christian Movement was part of a large national movement occurring on college and university campuses, black and white, with a view toward spreading the Christian message among students. See also Mary Jenness, *Twelve Negro Americans* (New York: Friendship Press, 1936), pp. 145-60.

12   Fisk remained with the congregation for a period of about two years, after which time Thurman shared pastoral responsibilities with interns and co-ministers.

13   (Mills College, Ca.: Eucalyptus Press, 1945), and (New York: Harper & Bros., 1947).

14   (Nashville: Abingdon-Cokesbury Press, 1949; reprinted in the Apex edition paperbacks, 1969).

15   *The Luminous Darkness: A Personal Interpretation of the Anatomy of Segre-gation and the Ground of Hope* (New York: Harper & Row, 1965), and *The Search for Common Ground: An Inquiry into the Basis of Man's Experience of Community* (New York: Harper & Row, 1971).

16   Thurman, *Head and Heart*, p.201.

17 The impetus behind the establishment of the Trust occurred in Thurman's early life. Ibid., pp. 24-25. Note also the dedicatory page.

18 Yates, *Portrait of a Practical Dreamer*, pp. 222-23.

19 A few of the many works addressing the African/ African-American religious and cultural tradition are Joseph E. Holloway, ed. *Africanisms in American Culture* (Bloomington: Indiana University Press, 1990); Albert J. Raboteau, *Slave Religion* (New York: Oxford University Press, 1978); John S. Mbiti, *African Religions and Philosophy* (Garden City, NY: Anchor Books, 1969); and Daryll Forde, ed., *African Worlds: Studies in the Cosmological Ideas and Social Values of African Peoples* (London: Oxford University Press, 1954).

20 Mary Goodwin, "Racial Roots and Religion: An Interview with Howard Thurman," *The Christian Century*, 9 May 1973, p. 533.

21 Yates, *Portrait of a Practical Dreamer*, p. 23.

22 See Bennett, "Howard Thurman: Twentieth Century Prophet," p. 2, as well as the remarks by John R. Silber, President of Boston University, on the same occasion, p. 3.

23 Thurman, *Jesus and the Disinherited*, p. 30. In addition, I have benefitted greatly from Smith's remarks on the subject in *Mystic as Prophet*, pp. 41-42, nn. 50-51.

24 Thurman, *Head and Heart*, pp. 20-21.

25 Thurman, *Deep River*, pp. 11-12, 17.

26 Thurman, *Jesus and the Disinherited*, pp. 30-35, 50.

27 It is somewhat curious to note that none of the critical studies of Thurman have given even the slightest attention to the meaning of the Morehouse years, especially in light of the fact that Thurman himself discusses their importance in *With Head and Heart*, pp. 33-45. Other major sources for this period are Benjamin E. Mays, *Born to Rebel* (New York: Charles Scribners Sons, 1971), pp. 89-93; G. Franklin Edwards, "E. Franklin Frazier," in *Black Sociologists: Historical and Contemporary Perspectives*, eds. James E. Blackwell and Morris Janowitz (Chicago: University of Chicago Press, 1974), pp. 91-93; and S.P. Fullinwider, *The Mind and Mood of Black America: 20th Century Thought* (Homewood, Il: Dorsey Press, 1969), pp. 92-107.

28 Cornel West identifies "exceptionalism" as one of four traditions of African American response to racism in America. He states that "the exceptionalist response to the challenges of self-image and self-determination is this: a romanticization of Afro-American culture that conceals the social mobility of an emerging opportunistic Afro-American petite bourgeoisie.... It generates cathartic and amorphous feelings of Afro-American pride, self-congratulation, and heroism that contain little substance." *Prophecy Deliverance!: An*

Afro-American Revolutionary Christianity (Philadelphia: Westminster Press, 1982), pp. 70, 72-78.

29 E. Franklin Frazier, "A Note on Negro Education," *Opportunity*, March 1924, p. 76. Further observations may be found in his *The Negro in the United States* (New York: Macmillan Co., 1957), pp. 478-97.

30 This rationale also serves to clarify why Thurman was unrelenting in his desire to study formal philosophy at Columbia University. *With Head and Heart*, pp. 43-44. Then, too, he wanted to start his life's work with the broadest possible foundation. He states, "I wanted to come into the ministry with my eyes wide open to the way people have to live." Jenness, *Twelve Negro Americans*, p. 151.

31 Smith provides a thorough analysis of the thought of Cross and Robins. The thought of Moehlman, for whatever reason, receives no attention. We assume that his ideas largely mirrored those of his colleagues. *Mystic as Prophet*, pp. 19-29, 73-77.

32 The evidences are scattered but collectively validate our contention. It is illuminating to note, for example, that Thurman made extensive use of Edgar Brightman's philosophy of Personalism in the classroom. See Howard Thurman, "Religion in Human Culture," n.p., 30 April 1948, course examination key, Howard Thurman Archives, Mugar Memorial Library, Boston University, Boston, Ma. Study groups at Fellowship Church discussed the writings of liberal theologian William Adams Brown during Thurman's tenure. *With Head and Heart*, p.149. His writings indicate his contact with the influential post-liberal responses of Albert Schweitzer, Paul Tillich, and Reinhold Niebuhr, among others. Mitchell, *Spiritual Dynamics*, pp. 27, 41.

33 Sidney Ahlstrom, *A Religious History of the American People* (New Haven: Yale University Press, 1972), p. 783.

34 William R. Hutchinson, *The Modernist Impulse in American Protestantism* (Cambridge: Harvard University Press, 1976), pp. 3-4.

35 Ibid., pp. 117, 121, 275; and Ahlstrom, *Religious History*, pp. 775-76.

36 Jean Burden, "Howard Thurman," *Atlantic*, October 1953, p. 39.

37 Thurman, *With Head and Heart*, p. 48.

38 On Jones see Elizabeth Gray Vining, *Friend of Life: The Biography of Rufus M. Jones* (Philadelphia: J.B. Lippincott, 1958); Hal Bridges, *American Mysticism: From William James to Zen* (New York: Harper & Row, 1973); Daniel Bassuk, "The Secularization of Mysticism — An Analysis and Critique of the Mystical in Rufus Jones and Martin Buber" (Ph.D. dissertation, Drew University, 1974); and Michael P. Decker, "A Hermeneutic Approach to the Problem of Mysticism" (Ph.D. dissertation, Emory University, 1978).

39 Howard Thurman, "Mysticism and Social Change," 15 - part lecture series presented at the Pacific School of Religion, Berkeley, Ca., July 5-28, 1978. Transcripts at the Howard Thurman Educational Trust. 25 July 1978, p. 17.

40 James Leuba and William Ralph Inge are also usually cited as contemporaneous authorities on mysticism. Leuba's passionately anti-religious stance and Inge's equally strident anti-catholic perspective tend, however, to limit the usefulness of their interpretations.

41 Jones privately corresponded and publicly exchanged ideas and criticisms in books and articles with James and Underhill. His first full length study of mysticism, *Studies in Mystical Religion* (1909), was published shortly after James' *Varieties of Religious Experience* (1902) and shortly before Underhill's encyclopedic *Mysticism: A Study in the Nature and Development of Man's Spiritual Consciousness* (1911).

42 Quoted by Jones in *The Trail of Life in the Middle Years* (New York: Macmillan Co., 1924), p. 202.

43 Rufus Jones, *Studies in Mystical Religion* (London: Macmillan & Co., 1909), p. xv.

44 Quoted in Bridges, *American Mysticism*, p. 33.

45 The "how" of this experience is never detailed by Jones. Thurman states that Jones "had a profound mistrust of the powers of the mind and an absolute devotion to the powers of the mind," "Mysticism and Social Change," July 1978.

46 Bridges, *American Mysticism*, p. 33.

47 Thurman, "Mysticism and Social Change," 25 July 1978, p.6.

48 Jenness, *Twelve Negro Americans*, p. 154.

49 Howard Thurman, *Mysticism and the Experience of Love* (Wallingford, Pa.: Pendle Hill Pamphlet 115, 1961), p. 3.

50 Thurman goes on to say "...I didn't ever feel that he [Jones] could ever get off the dime and deal — make the Quakers practice religion with Negroes. I just — I forgave him." "Mysticism and Social Change," 25 July 1978, p. 16; see also *With Head and Heart*, pp. 76-77.

51 Quaker schools, including Brynmawr College where Jones was Chairman of the Board of Trustees, were among the last private schools in the country to admit African Americans. On the other hand, Jones' biographer chronicles, he had no difficulty expressing his opposition to the Hitler regime, traveling to Germany where he held an unprecedented Quaker meeting at the Gestapo. See Thurman, "Mysticism and Social Change," 25 July 1978, p. 11; and Vining, *Friend of Life*, pp. 271-90.

52 Thurman notes that during the great Passaic N.J. strikes early in the century, "a great deal of pressure was put on the [pacifist] Fellowship of Reconciliation by mainline Philadelphia Quakers not to become involved in the economic labor struggle. And the same was true with reference to their witness about race." Thurman, "Mysticism and Social Change," 25 July 1978, p. 10.

53 See Yates' "Bibliography of Thurman's Oft-Used Books" in *Portrait of a Practical Dreamer*, pp. 243-44; and Mitchell, *Spiritual Dynamics*, pp. 27-28.

54 We are not in substantial disagreement with Luther Smith's omission of Schreiner and Gandhi as pivotal mentors of Thurman's. Hence, our analysis also views their contributions to Thurman's life work as somewhat less than direct. However, it is important to point out that in their active witnesses on the global stage, these two provided Thurman with an international point of reference that was catalytic and thus critical to the development of his inclusionary means to change. See Smith, *Mystic as Prophet*, p. 35, n. 1.

55 (New York: Harper & Row, 1973), p. xi.

56 Ibid., p. xvii.

57 Ibid., pp. xxvii-xxviii.

58 For a more recent perspective on Schreiner, see Ruth First and Ann Scott, *Olive Schreiner* (New York: Schocken, 1980).

59 Thurman, *Track to the Water's Edge*, p. xxix.

60 Ibid., p. xx. Schreiner was aware of her moral paradox, which she sought to exorcise in part through the writing of her novel *Trooper Peter Halket of Mashonaland* (Boston: Roberts Brothers, 1897).

61 Howard Thurman, "Thurman on Gandhi," *The Listening Ear* 17 (Summer 1986): 3. An excellent additional reference for Thurman and Gandhi is the reprint of their 1936 conversation found in *Non-Violence in Peace and War* by M.K. Gandhi, reprinted in Yates, *Portrait of a Practical Dreamer*, pp. 105-109.

62 Smith notes that "as early as 1928 in his article, 'Peace Tactics and a Racial Minority,' Thurman begins to outline how a 'philosophy of pacifism' can begin to eliminate whites' will to control and blacks' will to hate. Very little is said about techniques of interaction or confrontation; his primary concern is to call a truce to attitudes which promote separation." *Mystic as Prophet*, p. 114.

63 Thurman, "Thurman on Gandhi," p. 7. For a good brief exposition of Gandhi's non-violence see John J. Ansbro, *Martin Luther King, Jr.: The Making of a Mind* (Maryknoll, NY: Orbis Books, 1982), pp. 3-7, 129-46.

64 Thurman, *Jesus and the Disinherited*, p. 70.

65 Chapter 4 in *The Church and Organized Movements*, ed. Randolph C. Miller (New York: Harper & Bros., 1946), pp. 82-100. See also "Windbreak against Existence," *Bostonia* Fall 1960, pp. 7-9, and *Search for Common Ground*.

66 Isaiah Berlin, *The Hedgehog and the Fox*, quoted in Coser, *Masters of Sociological Thought*, p. 111.

67 Mozella Mitchell, "Howard Thurman and Olive Schreiner: Post-Modern Marriage Post-Mortem," *The Journal of Religious Thought* 38 (Spring-Summer 1981): 64.

68 The primary sources for this subchapter are several: Robert Allen and Pamela P. Allen, *Reluctant Reformers: Racism and Social Reform Movements in the United States*, rev. ed. (Washington, D.C.: Howard University Press, 1983); Robert H. Brisbane, *The Black Vanguard* (Valley Forge, Pa.: Judson Press, 1970); Florette Henri, *Black Migration: Movement North, 1900-1920* (Garden City, NY: Anchor Press/Doubleday, 1976); Martin E. Marty, *Righteous Empire: The Protestant Experience in America* (New York: Harper & Row, 1970); and Walter T.K. Nugent, *Modern America* (Boston: Houghton Mifflin Co., 1973).

69 It should be noted that this trend has dramatically reversed itself in the past decade, effecting important political and social changes in the modern South. See Daniel M. Johnson and Rex Campbell, *Black Migration in America: A Social Demographic History* (Durham, NC: Duke University Press, 1981), p. 170.

70 Thurman, *With Head and Heart*, p. 253.

71 Ibid., p. 113.

72 Smith, *Mystic as Prophet*, p. 40, n.40.

73 Thurman relates the following story concerning the kind of impact his grandmother had on his psyche: "When I was at Earlham College, one of the professors there, a counselor and a psychologist, heard me say that I had been reared without a father. So he said, 'Oh, then I have to revise my tests because none of the things that go with a male child reared in a home with women apply to you.' Well, now, that proves the indomitable quality in my grandmother." "Racial Roots and Religion," p. 533.

74 Howard Thurman, *Deep is the Hunger* (New York: Harper & Bros., 1951),and *With Head and Heart*, pp. 249-52; and Yates, *Portrait of a Practical Dreamer*, pp. 27-28.

75 Silber, "Remarks Commemorating Howard Thurman," p. 4.

76 Yates, *Portrait of a Practical Dreamer*, p. 25.

77 Thurman, *With Head and Heart*, p. 261. In *Footprints of a Dream*, pp. 17-18, Thurman states that his decision to enter the Christian ministry was imperiled

in part by "a vague feeling that somehow I was violating my father's memory by taking leadership in an institution that had done violence to his spirit."

78 "Fortunately for me," Thurman says, "the influence of my mother and grandmother tutored me in a kind of Christian experience that was less limiting than the teachings of our particular church.... Very early I distinguished between the demand to surrender my life to God and thus become a follower of Jesus, on the one hand, and the more prescribed demands of our local church, on the other hand." *Footprints of a Dream*, p. 16.

79 Thurman, *With Head and Heart*, p. 17. See also the excellent article by Cheryl Townsend Gilkes, "The Black Church as a Therapeutic Community," *The Journal of the Interdenominational Theological Center* 8 (Fall 1980): 29-44.

80 The name given the often overlooked period of African American struggle just prior to and inclusive of the World War II years. Roger Dalfiume, "The 'Forgotten Years' of the Negro Rebellion," *Journal of American History* 55 (June 1968): 90-106. Thurman also appraised the period between 1930-1943 in two unpublished essays, "The Negro in the City," (Howard University, n.d.) and an untitled piece written in 1943. Both are located in the Howard Thurman Archives, Boston University Mugar Memorial Library, Boston, Ma.

81 Charles Silberman, *Crisis in Black and White* (New York: Random House, 1964), pp. 60, 65.

82 During the war years discrimination remained the rule in numerous industries and especially in the armed forces. Added to this was the growing African American identification with dominated communities in Africa, South Asia, the Pacific, and elsewhere. Democracy was understood in increasingly sophisticated terms, leading to calls not only for social and political equality but *cultural* equality, i.e., the acceptance and affirmation of discrete non-white cultures and their individual members by the Euro-American community. See Vincent Harding, *The Other American Revolution* (Los Angeles and Atlanta: University of California and the Institute of the Black World, 1980); Dalfiume, "The 'Forgotten Years,'"; W.E.B. DuBois, "Race Relations in the United States: 1917-1947," *Phylon* 9 (1948): 234-47; and Ira De A. Reid, "Negro Movements and Messiahs: 1900-1949," *Phylon* 10 (1940): 362-69

83 Thurman's loyalty to democratic virtues is beyond dispute. However, his later writings indicate a subtle but persistent decrease in the employment of conventional democratic phraseology, confirming that his affinity lies with the ethos of democracy rather than its marred social and political expressions. See also Fluker, *They Looked for a City*.

84 Thurman, untitled 1943 article in the Howard Thurman Archives, pp. 2-3.

85 Smith, *Mystic as Prophet*, pp. 106-108.

86 Thurman, "Negro in the City," pp. 5-7. In addition, see "Fascist Masquerade," and "The Cultural and Spiritual Prospect for the Democratic Way of Life," (n.p., n.d.), Howard Thurman Archives, Boston University Mugar Memorial Library, Boston University, Boston, Ma.

87 Thurman, *Search for Common Ground*, pp. 87-88; and Smith, *Mystic as Prophet*, pp. 107-108.

88 Thurman, "Cultural and Spiritual Prospect," p. 1.

89 It should not be inferred, however, that Thurman dismissed the need for African American institutions with the advent of desegregation. In fact, the opposite was true. The critical determinant for him in this as in every involvement was that there exist the "freedom of alternative" with respect to one's affiliations.

90 Mitchell provides excellent exposition on this point. *Spiritual Dynamics*, p. 105.

91 Briefly, "role-set" is defined as "that complement of role relationships which persons have by virtue of occupying a particular social status," Robert K. Merton, *Social Theory and Social Structure*, p. 369, cited by Coser, *Masters of Sociological Thought*, p. 210, n. 63.

92 Samuel D. Proctor, "Finding Our Margin of Freedom: In Tribute to Howard Thurman," *1979 Consultation of Black Scholars* (Evanston: Garrett Evangelical Theological Seminary) pp. 55-56.

93 Howard Thurman, *Disciplines of the Spirit* (New York: Harper & Row, 1963), p. 48.

94 Thurman, *With Head and Heart*, pp. 168-69, 173-74.

95 Mitchell, *Spiritual Dynamics*, p. 97.

96 Ibid., p. 104.

97 See for example Marcus Bouware, *The Oratory of Negro Leaders: 1900-1968* (Westport, Ct.: Negro Universities Press, 1969), pp. 184-87; Kelly Miller Smith, *Social Crisis Preaching* (Macon, Ga.: Mercer University Press, 1984), pp. 17, 97; Gardner C. Taylor, *How Shall They Preach* (Elgin, Il.: Progressive Baptist Publishing House, 1977), p. 43; and Melvin Watson, "Howard Thurman, Teacher-Preacher," in *God and Human Freedom*, pp. 161-172, passim.

98 James Farmer, *Lay Bare the Heart: An Autobiography of the Civil Rights Movement* (New York: Arbor House, 1985), pp. 135-36.

99 Yates, *Portrait of a Practical Dreamer*, pp. 205-206.

Chapter Two

1 Robert S. Ellwood, Jr., *Mysticism and Religion* (Englewood Cliffs, NJ: Prentice-Hall, 1980), p. xi.

2 The phenomenological investigation of religion can refer to a variety of ways of understanding religion. In the narrower sense, it refers to the rigorous philosophical tradition which began with Edmund Husserl, and includes, among others, Maurice Merleau-Ponty, Paul Ricoeur and, in a somewhat different vein, Thomas Luckmann and Peter Berger. In its broader sense as a less explicit or general methodological orientation, it has been identified with the works of such thinkers as Rudolf Otto, Martin Buber, Mircea Eliade, and Gerhard van der Leeuw. In addition, we concur with Mozella Mitchell's inclusion of Howard Thurman among the phenomenologists.

Basic to any of the phenomenological approaches to religion is the description of the essence of religious experience, by which is meant conscious experiencing and its objective correlate. Stated somewhat differently, phenomenological religion takes as its point of departure the lived-experience of religion, attending to the full range of religious phenomena — ideas, activities, institutions, customs, and symbols. See the theoretical discussion in the introduction to this study as well as Joseph Dabney Bettis, ed. *Phenomenology of Religion* (New York: Harper & Row, 1969); William Earle, *Mystical Reason* (Chicago: Regnery Gateway, Inc., 1980); David Stewart and Algis Mickunas, *Exploring Phenomenology* (Chicago: American Library Association, 1974); and Daniel Guerriere, "Outline of a Phenomenology of the Religious," *Research in Phenomenology* 4 (1974):99-127. On Thurman and existentialist phenomenology, see Mitchell, *Spiritual Dynamics*, pp. 156-59.

3 Howard Thurman, "Mysticism and Social Change," 5 July 1978, pp. 4-5. See also Thurman, *The Growing Edge* (New York: Harper and Bros., 1956), p. 58; *With Head and Heart*, pp. 7-8; and *A Track to the Water's Edge*, pp. xxvii-xxviii.

4 Ibid., p. 4.

5 Thurman, *With Head and Heart*, p. 128.

6 Ibid., p. 127.

7 Thurman, *Footprints of a Dream*, p. 24.

8 Thurman, *With Head and Heart*, p. 129.

9 Ibid., pp. 246-47. See also "Spirit of Understanding Bridges Gap as Dr. Thurman Gets Message Across," *Boston Sunday Globe*, 4 November 1962.

10 Thurman, "Mysticism and Social Change," 5 July 1978, p. 4.

11 Howard Thurman, "Mysticism and Social Change," *Eden Theological Seminary Bulletin* 4 (Spring 1939):3. The interpretation of mysticism which

Thurman offers here is somewhat formal in comparison with later of his articulations. It is actually a series of four lectures given at the convocation of Eden Theological Seminary: "Mysticism — an Interpretation," "Mysticism and Symbolism," "Mysticism and Ethics," and "Mysticism and Social Change."

12 Among his presentations especially given to this theme are the aforementioned "Mysticism and the Experience of Love," and "Mysticism and Social Change," July 1978. Others include *The Creative Encounter* (originally lectures given as "Religious Experience and the Social Witness"); "Mysticism and Ethics," *The Journal of Religious Thought* 27 (Supplement 1970):23-30; "Mysticism and Social Change," lecture presented at the Pacific School of Religion, Berkeley, Ca., Summer 1959; and "Mysticism and Social Action," Lawrence Lecture on Religion and Society, First Unitarian Church of Berkeley, 13 October 1978.

13 Thurman's configuration of mysticism may be typified as an objectified disquisition based on first-hand experience; that is, he presents us with themes of general mysticism (but also themes often lacking) that mirror the inner movement of his own self-awareness. His thought clearly resonates with the symbolic language and structure of pilgrimage.

14 Thurman, "Mysticism and the Experience of Love," p. 6.

15 Thurman, *The Creative Encounter*, p. 20.

16 Ellwood, *Mysticism and Religion*, pp. 34-35.

17 Thurman gives Jones' definition of mysticism as "the type of religion which puts the emphasis on the immediate awareness of a relationship with God, on direct and intimate consciousness of the Divine Presence." Thurman, "Mysticism and the Experience of Love," p. 6.

18 Thurman, "Mysticism and Social Action," pp. 25-26. Similar statements are recorded in Jan Corbett, "Howard Thurman: A Theologian for Our Time," *The American Baptist* (December 1979), pp. 10-12; and Lerone Bennett, Jr., "Howard Thurman: 20th Century Holy Man," p. 85.

19 Thurman, "Mysticism and the Experience of Love," p. 10, and *The Creative Encounter*, pp. 19-55.

20 Thurman, *The Creative Encounter*, pp. 56-65.

21 What Thurman said of Rufus Jones may equally be true of himself: "He had a profound mistrust of the powers of the mind and an absolute devotion to the powers of the mind. He felt that always the role of the thinker was to put at the disposal of the motivations of his life, the best fruits of learning and the mastery of the external world. But this should be done best if the individuals who were seeking it would be inwardly motivated." "Mysticism and Social Change," 25 July 1978, pp. 13-14. Of related interest is Thurman's excellent

essay, "The Idea of God and Modern Thought," presented as the Garvin Lecture at the Church of Our Father, Lancaster, Pa., 23 November 1965.

22 Thurman, "Mysticism and the Experience of Love," p. 10.

23 John A. Taylor, "The Foundation of Moral Concern," in *Common Ground*, p. 80.

24 Thurman, *Disciplines of the Spirit*, p. 9.

25 Victor Turner describes "liminality" as one of the three stages of traditional initiatory procedure. As the middle stage of the process (separation and reincorporation or reaggregation being the others), liminality represents a temporary state of antistructure, in which the initiate undergoes the transition to new status. The significant parallels in mysticism are noted by Ellwood. Later in this study we will have occasion to explore the social correlate of liminality, "communitas." See Turner, *The Ritual Process: Structure and Anti-Structure* (Chicago: Aldine Pub., 1966; reprint ed., Ithaca, NY: Cornell University Press, 1969), and Ellwood, *Religion and Mysticism*, pp. 73-75.

26 Thurman, *Luminous Darkness*, p. x.

27 Thurman, *Deep River and the Negro Spiritual Speaks of Life and Death*, (Richmond, IN: Friends United Press, 1975), p. 111.

28 Ibid., p. 13.

29 "Mysticism and Ethics," p. 26.

30 Sam Keen, "Every Time I Feel the Spirit," *Toward Wholeness* (Spring 1983):33.

31 "Mysticism and Ethics," pp. 26-27.

32 For some examples see Thurman's detailed discussion of mysticism and symbolism in "Mysticism and Social Change," Eden Seminary Bulletin, pp. 10-19.

33 Ibid., p. 17. In addition, see *Deep River and the Negro Spiritual*, pp. 69-71.

34 S. Paul Schilling, "Howard Thurman as Theologian," *Toward Wholeness* (Spring 1983):22.

35 These themes are developed in many of Thurman's publications, such as *Meditations of the Heart* (New York: Harper & Row, 1953; *Deep is the Hunger* (New York: Harper & Row, 1951); *The Inward Journey* (Harper & Row, 1961); *The Growing Edge*; and *Disciplines of the Spirit*.

36 Thurman, *With Head and Heart*, p. 269.

37 Thurman, "Mysticism and Ethics," p. 28.

38 Thurman, "Mysticism and Social Change," Eden Seminary Bulletin, pp. 24, 27.

39 Ibid., p. 25.

40 Thurman, "Mysticism and the Experience of Love," p. 11.

41 A strong naturistic tendency is also clearly manifest of course in Thurman's mysticism. An illuminating discussion of this is found in Paul Chaffee, "Howard Thurman, Ecologist of the Spirit," unpublished paper, San Francisco, Ca., January 1979.

42 Thurman, "Mysticism and Social Change," 20 July 1978, p. 16.

43 Thurman, "Mysticism and the Experience of Love," p. 13.

44 Ibid., p. 15.

45 Thurman, "Mysticism and Social Action," p. 21.

Chapter Three

1 Thurman, *Search for Common Ground*, p. 104.

2 Ernst Troeltsch, *The Social Teachings of the Christian Churches* (New York: Macmillan, 1931) 2: 780.

3 Ibid., 777.

4 D. B. Robertson, *The Religious Foundations of Leveller Democracy* (New York: Columbia University Press, 1951), p. 19, cited by Alan L. Berger, "'Normal' Mysticism and the Social World: A Comparative Study of Quaker and Hasidic Communal Mysticism," (Ph.D. dissertation, Syracuse University, 1976), p. 45.

5 Robert C. Williams, "Worship and Anti-Structure in Thurman's Vision of the Sacred," *The Journal of the Interdenominational Theological Center* 14 (Fall 1986/Spring 1987): 164.

6 J. Randall Nicholls, "Worship as Anti-Structure: The Contribution of Victor Turner," *Theology Today* 41 (January 1985): 402. See also, Victor Turner, *The Ritual Process: Structure and Anti-Structure* (Ithaca, NY: Cornell University Press), p. 96.

7 Turner, *Ritual Process*, p. 96.

8 Victor Turner, "Passages, Margins, and Poverty: Religious Symbols of Communitas," *Worship* 46: 393.

9 Ellwood's comments in this regard are most instructive: "The antistructure of liminality and communitas is, as Turner emphasizes, not a negative term, but

implies certain primordial human yearnings for more than what structure gives." *Mysticism and Religion*, p. 75.

10 Turner, "Passages, Margins, and Poverty," p. 400.

11 Turner, *Ritual Process*, p. 129.

12 Turner, "Passages, Margins, and Poverty," pp. 409, 494.

13 Turner, *Ritual Process*, p. 129.

14 Howard Thurman, "The Commitment," a sermon preached at Fellowship Church and re-circulated in *The Growing Edge*, March 1949. Note: *The Growing Edge* was a journal of opinion written by members of The Church for the Fellowship of all Peoples. National in outreach, this overlooked publication attempted to characterize the genius of the church through printed sermons, literary pieces, reports on church activities, and other items of related interest. Publication ran from January 1949 until 1953, which also marked the end of Thurman's tenure as resident pastor. At present, the church sends out a slightly less ambitious newsletter by the same name.

15 Personal communication by Robert Bellah to Morris Augustine and Richard Kalish, cited by Ellwood in *Mysticism and Religion*, p. 121.

16 This is not to deny the important Durkheimian focus on the socially reinforcing tendencies of worship. Rather, it is to stress that worship paradoxically affords a means of transcendence of normative social structures. See Emile Durkheim, *The Elementary Forms of the Religious Life* (New York: Free Press, 1965); and Bobby C. Alexander, "Correcting Misinterpretations of Turner's Theory: An African-American Pentecostal Illustration," *Journal for the Social Scientific Study of Religion* 30 (March 1991): 26-44.

17 "... I Desire to Share," *The Growing Edge*, Fall 1951, pp. 2-3.

18 Thurman, *Footprints of a Dream*, p. 69.

19 Howard Thurman, "Building a Friendly World," *The Growing Edge*, Winter 1950, p. 12. See also Thurman, *With Head and Heart*, p. 160; and Nichols, "Worship as Anti-Structure," pp. 405-406.

20 Thurman's most exhaustive exposition on the meaning of community may be found in his *Search for Common Ground*.

21 Thurman, *Meditations of the Heart*, pp. 121-22.

22 "We Burn the Mortgage," *The Growing Edge*, Spring 1952, p. 4.

23 Peter Berger and Thomas Luckmann, *The Social Construction of Reality* (Garden City, NY: Doubleday & Co., 1966).

24 Ellwood, *Mysticism and Religion*, p. 142.

25 Howard Thurman, *The First Footprints: The Dawn of the Idea of the Church for the Fellowship of All Peoples: Letters Between Alfred Fisk and Howard Thurman, 1943-44* (San Francisco: Lawton and Alfred Kennedy, 1975), foreward, and *Footprints of a Dream*, prologue. An excellent background study correcting the traditional idyllic view of San Francisco's race relations is Alfred S. Broussard, "The New Racial Frontier: San Francisco's Black Community: 1900-1940," (Ph.D. dissertation, Duke University, 1977).

26 According to Thurman, the first contemporary effort toward establishing such a movement actually occurred in Philadelphia in 1936, where an interracial committee of the American Friends Service Committee undertook a Fellowship Church experiment, with Thurman participating in several of its services. The Philadelphia experiment differed from San Francisco, however, in two significant ways. First, it was conceived as a mobile testimony to group relations and not as a permanent full-time church, holding services from church to church. Also, it lacked an ongoing pastor, preferring to utilize the services of various clergy instead. See "The Fellowship Church of all Peoples," *Common Ground* 5 (Spring 1945): 29, and "The Church for the Fellowship of all Peoples," 1947, Howard Thurman Archives, Boston University Mugar Memorial Library, Boston University, Boston, Ma.

27 Thurman, *Footprints of a Dream*, pp. 55-56.

28 Ibid., pp. 56, 117; *The Growing Edge*, Fall 1952, p. 3.

29 Thurman, *Footprints of a Dream*, p. 116.

30 Interestingly enough, the ratio of white and black reversed when the ministerial leadership of the church changed, and has remained so to the present. Thurman, *Footprints of a Dream*, p. 109.

31 Personal interview, San Francisco, Ca., May 22, 1985; and Thurman, "Religion and Growth," *The Growing Edge*, Summer 1950, p. 7.

32 Dr. Fisk resigned as co-pastor shortly after the church elected to be an independent body rather than formally join the Presbyterian Church, U.S.A. or, for that matter, any other denomination. In an interview with Mrs. Eleanor Fisk (San Francisco, May 23, 1985) she reflected on her late husband's decision to leave Fellowship, and also on the foresight of Thurman: "Howard believed that it [Fellowship] should be an independent church, not connected with any denomination, so they would be free to include everybody. And my husband felt very indebted to the Presbyterian Church for all that it had done in breaking custom for us to begin in the first place, providing the building, financial provisions, etc. So I think this is where they came to a difference, but I think now he feels Howard did the right thing, because now we have come to the place where it [Fellowship] isn't only the inclusion of all churches, but other religions ..." The story is recounted in general in *Footprints of a Dream*, pp. 47-51.

33 It is interesting to note that one of the two student ministers who worked with the Fellowship group prior to Thurman's actual arrival was Albert Cleage,

well-known proponent of Black messianism. Recalls one member, "Cleage was sort of an Eastern radical. I think the thing that shocked everyone was his delivering himself on the subject of Abraham Lincoln as the archenemy of the Negro race, and that was just not bought by a lot of people.... Cleage was turning away more people than he was inviting in." Personal interview with Virginia Scardigli, San Francisco, May 26, 1985. Cleage's thoughts on the Fellowship Church, equally unflattering, are recorded in Hiley H. Ward, *Prophet of the Black Nation* (Philadelphia: Pilgrim Press, 1969), pp. 54-55. See also, *First Footprints*, pp. 16-23, 47-49.

34 Muriel Bullard remarked during our interview that, "in a sense Dr. Thurman didn't have good organizational skills. He had to have good organizational people around him, that just wasn't his field." May 22, 1985.

35 Thurman, *First Footprints*, p. 51.

36 Thurman, *Footprints of a Dream*, pp. 97, 130.

37 Thurman, *With Head and Heart*, p. 151.

38 Ellwood, *Mysticism and Religion*, p. 151.

39 Thurman, *Footprints of a Dream*, p. 52. The commitment has undergone slight revision over the years, including the incorporation of more non-Christian imagery and inclusive language.

40 Thurman, *With Head and Heart*, p. 147. Smith writes in this connection that "it is organic association ... which describes what Thurman means by 'fellowship.' In organic association possessing the same feelings, interest, thoughts, and purposes is *not* essential. Persons may differ significantly on issues, but through the fellowship, members develop an appreciation of other perspectives while finding their own nurtured by the contact. Service is not excluded from organic organization; its purpose is to create the environment which makes organic interaction possible." *Mystic as Prophet*, p. 104.

41 It has not been my intent to focus on the intercultural activities of the church. Careful attention to cross-cultural variables certainly constitutes one of the greatest prospects for establishing meaningful and sustained interaction among diverse peoples. At Fellowship such undertakings were commonplace as, for example, participation in UNESCO (the first independent church group to do so), and the development of an annual Children's International Workshop, where the children of the community and church were exposed to the culture of such peoples and nations as the Navajo Indians, India, Japan, Nigeria, and Mexico. See Thurman, *Footprints of a Dream*, and also issues of *The Growing Edge*.

42 Thurman, *Footprints of a Dream*, pp. 110-11.

43 Ibid., pp. 112-13.

44 Ibid., p. 114.

45 Victor Turner, "Metaphors of Anti-Structure in Religious Culture," in *Dramas, Fields, and Metaphors* (Ithaca, NY: Cornell University Press, 1974), pp. 46-47.

46 Thurman, *Footprints of a Dream*, p. 61.

47 Thurman, *With Head and Heart*, p. 144.

48 "Worship in Action," *The Growing Edge*, January 1949.

49 Thurman, *With Head and Heart*, p. 145.

50 See also the introduction.

51 Our definition gives strong credence to contemplation and the spiritual disciplines as modes of oppositional activity, a stance with which Thurman would obviously agree.

52 Thurman, "Mysticism and Social Action," p. 21.

53 Virginia Scardigli says in this connection that "Howard may have talked about society, but his message was to the individual it seems to me, and that society would be regenerated by individuals acting out of their best understandings." Interview, May 26, 1985.

54 "Worship in Action," *The Growing Edge*, April 1949.

55 "Worship in Action," *The Growing Edge*, January 1949.

56 Thurman, *Footprints of a Dream*, p. 114.

57 Thurman, *With Head and Heart*, pp. 160-61.

58 "The Church for the Fellowship of All Peoples," 1947, p. 11. Muriel Bullard noted that "Dr. Thurman was very careful that what we did in the way of social action or in the way of race relations, etc., was done as members or under the aegis of Fellowship Church, and not as representing this group or that." Interview, May 22, 1985.

59 The history behind the church's refusal to sign an oath signifying loyalty to the country is unclear. Surely, however, a contributing factor had to be Thurman's strong convictions about the sovereignty of God, even where the state as functional sovereign was concerned. For brief discussions, see *Search for Common Ground*, pp. 85-88, *Footprints*, p. 115, "Powers of this World," pp. 6-7. Also, "An Unorthodox 25 Years, *San Francisco Chronicle*, 6 October 1969, pp. 4-5.

60 Specific incidents are recorded in Thurman, *With Head and Heart*, p. 150; Burden, "Howard Thurman," p. 44.; and "Living Edges," *The Growing Edge*, Winter 1950, p. 16.

61 See especially Thurman, *Footprints of a Dream*, and the various issues of *The Growing Edge*.

62 Muriel Bullard interview, May 22, 1985.

63 Thurman, *Footprints of a Dream*, p. 125. See also *The Christian Century*, September 12, 1951.

64 "An Unorthodox 25 Years," *San Francisco Chronicle*, 6 October 1969, p. 4. For a fairly recent discussion see Barnett J.W. Grier, "Howard Thurman: An Examination and Analysis of Thurman's Idea of Community and the Viability of the Fellowship Church" (D. Min. Thesis, School of Theology at Claremont, 1983).

65 Ibid.

66 Specific examples may be found in the church's revived newsletter, "The Growing Edge."

Chapter Four

1 Among the other boards Thurman served on are the Congress of Racial Equality, the National Association for the Advancement of Colored People, the Fellowship of Reconciliation and the Mental Health Council. In addition to his voluminous literary output, Thurman was on occasion accompanist to orchestras and choirs, narrating music ranging from oratorios to spirituals. In terms of the media, he regularly delivered meditations on both radio and television. It is important to note that Sue Bailey Thurman, a respected author and historian, was immersed in her own distinctive social witness.

2 Thurman, *With Head and Heart*, pp. 181, 262. See also, *Footprints of a Dream*, p. 60.

3 Max Weber, *On Charisma and Institution Building*, ed. S.N. Eisenstadt (Chicago: University of Chicago Press, 1968), p. 48.

4 Talcott Parsons, *The Structure of Social Action* (New York: McGraw-Hill, 1937), p. 567, and ed., *The Sociology of Religion* (Boston: Beacon Press, 1963), pp. xxxiii-xxxiv.

5 Peter Worsley, *The Trumpet Shall Sound* (New York: Shocken Books, 1968), pp. ix-xxi.

6 Bryan Wilson, *The Noble Savages: The Primitive Origins of Charisma and Its Contemporary Survival* (Berkeley: University of California Press, 1975), p. 20.

7 Benjamin Zablocki, *Alienation and Charisma* (New York: Free Press, 1980), p. 10.

8 Aldon Morris, *The Origins of the Civil Rights Movement: Black Communities Organizing for Change* (New York: Free Press, 1984), p. 8.

9 Zablocki, *Alienation and Charisma*, p. 12.

10 Yates, *Portrait of a Practical Dreamer*, p. 222. See also Thurman, *Creative Encounter*, pp. 131-34.

11 Howard Thurman, address given at winter consultation of the Congress of National Black Churches, San Francisco, December 11, 1979.

12 Stewart, "Comparative Analysis of Theological-Ontology and Ethical Method in the Theologies of James H. Cone and Howard Thurman," (Ph.D. dissertation, Northwestern University, 1982), pp. 362-75. Thurman himself refers to an "epistemology of intuition" in *Mysticism and the Experience of Love*, p. 6, and "Mysticism and Social Action," p. 18.

13 Smith, *Mystic as Prophet*, p. 117.

14 Thurman, address given at the 1979 Congress of National Black Churches.

15 Thurman, *Creative Encounter*, pp. 40, 85-87, 119.

16 Ellwood, *Mysticism and Religion*, p. 144.

17 Francis Hall, *Practical Spirituality: Selected Writings of Francis B. Hall*, eds. Howard Alexander, Wilmer A. Cooper, and James Newley (Dublin, IN: Prinit Press, 1984), p. 13.

18 Joseph Glaser tribute in *Debate and Understanding*, p. 77.

19 E. Pauline Myers, "Howard Thurman: An Appreciation in Retrospect," *The AME Zion Quarterly Review* 96 (October 1984): 35-37.

20 Related examples are recorded in *Debate and Understanding*; and Makechnie, "Howard Thurman, 1900-1981: Mentor to the Great, the Humble, and the Disinherited."

21 This is not to deny that in all probability there were persons who venerated Thurman (or the next closest thing), the very idea of which horrified him. Says Thurman, "I was constantly harassed by the reference to Thurman followers while, with all of my heart, I wanted them to have a sense of God rather than a sense of Thurman." *Footprints of a Dream*, p. 130.

22 Joachim Wach, *The Comparative Study of Religion* (New York: Columbia University press, 1958), p. 40.

23 Thurman, address given at the 1979 Congress of National Black Churches.

24 Thurman, "Mysticism and Social Action," p. 35.

25 Barnett Grier notes that Thurman used an interesting illustration to describe vital community, contrasting the canal, reservoir, and swamp. In Thurman's opinion, the canal most properly exemplifies the life of the spiritually transformed person, conducting and not inhibiting the flow of love and community to the various strata and layers of society. Thurman likens this energy moving out and away from the center of mass to a "centrifugal force." The resultant pattern of communal relatedness could in turn be defined, it seems, as "concentric." "Howard Thurman: An Examination and Analysis of Thurman's Idea of Community," pp. 69-70.

26 Thurman, *Creative Encounter*, pp. 90, 152.

27 Reinhold Niebuhr, *Moral Man and Immoral Society* (New York: Charles Scribner's Sons, 1932), pp. xxii-xxiii. On the liberalists, see chapter one of this study.

28 Smith, *Mystic as Prophet*, p. 122.

29 Thurman, *Mysticism and Social Change*, Eden lectures, p. 29.

30 Thurman, *With Head and Heart*, p. 250.

31 Thurman, "Mysticism and Social Action," pp. 22-23.

32 Ibid., p. 22.

33 Thurman, *Deep is the Hunger*, p. 98.

34 Ibid., p. 36.

35 Howard Thurman, "The Power of the Spirit and the Powers of this World" (Washington, D.C.: The School of Religion, Howard University, 1950), p. 7.

36 Thurman, *Creative Encounter*, p. 133.

37 Smith collaborates this view in *Mystic as Prophet*, pp. 121-133.

38 At times Thurman's position sounds similar to that of sociologist Georg Simmel, who also images of a further, less conflictual stage of relationship between individual and objective culture. See Georg Simmel, *The Sociology of Georg Simmel*, ed. and trans. Kurt H. Wolfe (New York: Free Press, 1950); and Lewis Coser, ed. *Georg Simmel* (Englewood Cliffs, NJ: Prentice-Hall, 1965).

39 Numerous references may be found in his *Meditations of the Heart*.

40 Roland Robertson, *Meaning and Change* (New York: New York University Press, 1978), p. 150.

41 Howard Thurman, "Community and the Prophet's Dream." This sermon is one of an eight part series entitled "Community and the Will of God," Howard Thurman Educational Trust.

42 Ellwood, *Mysticism and Religion*, p. xii.

43 In this connection, it is interesting to note that sociologist Andrew Greeley concludes from his research on mysticism that Blacks are "substantially more likely to be mystics than white." Curiously enough, he offers no further elaboration on the subject. See *The Sociology of the Paranormal: A Reconnaissance* (Beverly Hills, Ca: Sage Publications, 1975), p. 59.

44 Thurman, "Mysticism and Social Action," p. 34. Of related interest is Thurman's comment that even "at the center of my experiences [of mysticism] I feel that I must fight for my life because I do not want to be absorbed in the Creator of existence because I cannot trust what the Creator will do with me, yet — yet." "Mysticism and Social Change," 26 July 1978, p. 15.

45 See the excellent works by Morris, *Origins of the Civil Rights Movement*; David Garrow, *Bearing the Cross* (New York: William Morrow and Co., 1986); Vincent Harding, *The Other American Revolution* (Los Angeles and Atlanta: Center for Afro-America Studies and Institute of the Black World, 1980); Clayborne Carson, In Struggle: SNCC and the Awakening of the 1960's (Cambridge: Harvard University Press, 1981), and with David Garrow, Vincent Harding, and Darlene Clark Hines, eds., *Eyes on the Prize: America's Civil Rights Years* (New York: Penguin Books, 1987); as well as the various personal reconnaissances.

46 Bennett, "20th Century Holy Man," p. 70. See also David M. Tuelser, *Black Pastors and Leaders: Memphis, 1819-1972* (Memphis: Memphis State University Press, 1975), pp. 146-48; and Smith, Mystic as Prophet, pp. 166-67.

47 Thurman, "Mysticism and Social Action," p. 26.

48 Bennett, "20th Century Holy Man," p. 70.

49 Gerald Horne, *Black & Red: W.E.B. DuBois and the Afro-American Response to the Cold War, 1944-1963* (New York: State University of New York Press, 1986), p. 250. Ethel Ray Nance, former secretary to DuBois (and Charles S. Johnson) and long-time member of the Fellowship Church, confirmed in a private interview that DuBois and Thurman interacted on occasion. The only written evidence I have located is a brief memorandum from Thurman to DuBois on March 24, 1934, in which Thurman expresses interest in a Negro youth movement. Howard Thurman Archives.

50 Thurman, "Mysticism and Social Change," 18 July 1978, p. 5.

51 Thurman, *Search for Common Ground*, pp. 89-103, and "Mysticism and Social Change," 25 July 1978, p. 14.

52 Thurman, *Luminous Darkness*, p. 21.

53 Thurman, unpublished notes on Black spirituality and identity, March 23, 1972, Howard Thurman Archives.

54 Thurman, *Search for Common Ground*, pp. 97-101.

55 Thurman, *Disciplines of the Spirit*, pp. 111-22, and "Mysticism and Social Action," p. 22. A number of scholars have identified Thurman as the creative mind behind the development of a philosophy of nonviolence in the African American context. See Hanes Walton, *The Political Philosophy of Martin Luther King, Jr.* (Westport, Ct.: Greenwood Publishing Corp., 1971), pp. 24-25, 28-29; Fullinwider, *Mind and Mood of Black America*, p. 239; and Smith, *Mystic as Prophet*, pp. 113-18.

56 Thurman, "Mysticism and Social Change," 19 July 1978, p. 5.

57 Morris, *Origins of the Civil Rights Movement*, pp. 158, 161.

58 Thurman letter to K.H. Beach, September 4, 1942, Howard Thurman Archives.

59 Howard Thurman, "Violence and Non-Violence," sermon preached July 14, 1963. Howard Thurman Educational Trust.

60 Thurman, *Luminous Darkness*, p. 55.

61 Thurman, "Mysticism and Social Change," 19 July 1978, p. 8.

62 Thurman, *With Head and Heart*, pp. 160-61.

63 Bennett, "20th Century Holy Man," p. 70.

64 For further tributes, see *Toward Wholeness* and *Debate and Understanding*, pp. 71-88, passim.

65 Lerone Bennett, dedicatory address of the Howard Thurman Chapel, Howard University School of Divinity, Washington, D.C., April 23, 1987.

66 The debate over the degree of Thurman's influence on King is longstanding, the resolution of which is not our primary interest. Contextually speaking, however, it is helpful to note that Lerone Bennett, ethicists John Cartwright and Walter Fluker and Urban League head Vernon Jordan believe that Thurman had a profound impact on King, philosophically, theologically and spiritually. "Dr. King Mentor Remembered," Boston Globe, 15 January 1973. On the other side, most of the major studies on King don't even mention Thurman. The evidence from King himself is scarcely better. The only evidence that we came across was a letter in which King advises a Boston student interested in participating in the civil rights struggle, to speak to "my good friend Howard Thurman" concerning "movements started in universities devoted to a great cause." Communication from King to Lafayette Dudley, September 15, 1956, Martin Luther King Papers, Mugar Memorial Library, Boston University. The most provocative assessment comes from long-time Thurman friend and colleague George Makechnie: "Mahatma Gandhi became the world's great symbol of non-violence. Martin carried Howard's interpretation of that, Jesus and the Disinherited, in terms of the

Western and Christian tradition ... I have a feeling that this younger man [King] was thinking of identifying with the internationally recognized authority on non-violence.... In my own mind it is the psychology of it, that the interpretive insight probably came in the book that [Lerone Bennett] saw Martin carrying, ... and the big figure was the one with which to identify. Identifying with the top dog, if you please, world recognized, would have been something that with maturity he [King] might have put in the kind of perspective that Lerone put him in." Personal interview, Boston, Ma., April 29, 1986. For further commentary, see Lewis V. Baldwin, *There is a Balm in Gilead: The Cultural Roots of Martin Luther King, Jr.* (Minneapolis: Fortress Press, 1991), pp. 146, 300-301; and Fluker, *They Looked for a City.*

67 Elizabeth O. Colton, *The Jackson Phenomenon: The Man, The Power, The Message* (New York: Doubleday, 1989), p. 32.

68 Thurman, "What Can We Believe In?" reprinted from *Journal of Religion and Health* (April 1973): 117, quoted in Luther Smith, "Community: Partnership of Freedom and Responsibility" in *God and Human Freedom*, p. 23.

69 Specific incidents are recounted in Thurman, *Footprints of a Dream*, and *With Head and Heart*. See also Larry Murphy, "Howard Thurman and Social Activism" in *God and Human Freedom*, pp. 150-60; and letters and memoranda in the Howard Thurman archives.

70 Thurman supported the F.O.R., the outstanding pacifist organization in America in its opposition to racism, the proliferation of atomic weapons, and the Vietnam War. Howard Thurman archives.

71 See the 1949 issues of *The Growing Edge.*

72 Activities of the Howard Thurman Educational Trust are published in its quarterly newsletter, *The Listening Ear.*

Chapter Five

1 Thurman, *Jesus and the Disinherited*, pp. 111-12.

2 Martin E. Marty, "Mysticism and the Religious Quest for Freedom," in *God and Human Freedom*, p. 8.

3 Werner Stark, *The Sociology of Knowledge* (Glencoe, Il: Free Press, 1958), p. 209.

4 Roger Bastide, *The African Religions of Brazil* (Baltimore: Johns Hopkins University Press, 1978), p. 381.

5 *Wilmington* (Delaware) *News* 12 December 1959. Fellowship Church was not the only integrated effort prior to mid-century. In addition to the Philadelphia Fellowship Church (see chapter three), Egbert Ethelred Brown unsuccessfully sought to accomplish the same at Harlem's Community

Church (Unitarian). Mark Morrison-Reed writes, "the barriers of race were so overwhelming that only someone with the spiritual depth and national stature of a Howard Thurman could have succeeded." *Black Pioneers in a White Denomination* (Boston: Beacon Press, 1980), pp. 102, 105, 164-65. On the other side, now retired United Methodist Bishop Roy Nichols successfully established the integrated Downes Memorial Methodist Church in Oakland in 1949. All of the above churches differed from Thurman-led Fellowship, however, in retaining their respective denominational postures. "Prophetic Mysticism Symposium," the San Anselmo Lectures, Pacific School of Religion, Berkeley, Ca., 1985.

6 This comment in isolation certainly does not do full justice to Smith's excellent presentation on the merit of Fellowship Church in *Mystic as Prophet*, pp. 16, 133-34.

7 See Thurman, *Footprints of a Dream*, p. 59, and *With Head and Heart*, p. 169.

8 Letter from Howard Thurman to Bob Cantrell, Knoxville, Tn., September 16, 1967. Howard Thurman Archives.

9 Untitled 1956 communique from Howard Thurman concerning the Fellowship Church and Boston University ministries. Howard Thurman Archives.

10 Robertson, *Meaning and Change*, p. 158.

11 Untitled 1943 essay, p. 10, Howard Thurman Archives.

12 Thurman, *Footprints of a Dream*, p. 136.

13 Smith, *Mystic as Prophet*, p. 135.

14 Thurman, *Luminous Darkness*, p. 48-54. Similar comments may be found in *Search for Common Ground*, p. 99, and *Footprints of a Dream*, p. 126.

15 Howard Thurman, "Journey in Understanding," address given at Freedom House, Boston, Ma., June 8, 1964. Transcript at Howard Thurman Educational Trust, pp. 16-17.

16 Thurman, *Luminous Darkness*, p. 55.

17 The literature in this field is of course considerable. See the introduction to this study for some representative works.

18 Thurman, "Aspects of Freedom," address given in Toronto, Canada, May 6, 1964. Transcript at Howard Thurman Educational Trust, pp. 13-14.

19 J. Needham, *Science and Civilization in China*, vol. 2, pp. 97-98, quoted in Sal Restivo, *The Social Relations of Physics, Mysticism, and Mathematics* (Dordrecht, Holland: D. Reidel, 1983), p. 78.

20 Personal communication by Vincent Harding to Larry Murphy in "Howard Thurman and Social Activism," pp. 158-59. See also Harding, Introduction

to *For the Inward Journey: The Writings of Howard Thurman*, selected by Anne Spencer Thurman (New York: Harcourt Brace Jovanovich, 1984), pp. ix-xv.

21 Thurman, *With Head and Heart*, p. 270.

Appendix

1 It is fair to say that the majority of studies in the sociology of religion offer no more than passing references to contemporary Western mysticism, and few view it as a viable social fact or independent strategy. Representative of works which support mysticism's asocial or anti-social stance are Howard Becker, *Systematic Sociology* (New York: Wiley, 1932); J. Milton Yinger, *Religion and the Struggle for Power* (Durham, NC: Duke University Press, 1946), and *The Scientific Study of Religion* (New York: Macmillan, 1970); and David Martin, *The Religious and the Secular: Studies in Secularization* (New York: Schocken, 1969).

2 Edward Shils and Henry Finch, eds., *Max Weber on the Methodology of the Social Sciences* (New York: Free Press, 1949), p. 93.

3 Ibid., p. 90.

4 Benjamin A. Reist, *Toward a Theology of Involvement: The Thought of Ernst Troeltsch* (Philadelphia: Westminster Press, 1966), p. 109. See also Shils and Finch, *Max Weber on the Methodology of the Social Sciences*, pp. 89-90.

5 Shils and Finch, *Max Weber on the Methodology of the Social Sciences*, pp. 91-92.

6 Allan W. Eister, "Toward a Radical Critique of Church-Sect Typology," *Journal for the Scientific Study of Religion* 6 (Spring 1967): 87.

7 Shils and Finch, *Max Weber on the Methodology of the Social Sciences*, p. 104. Note also William H. Swatos, Jr., "Weber or Troeltsch? Methodology, Syndrome, and the Development of Church-Sect Theory," *Journal for the Scientific Study of Religion* 15 (June 1976): 131-32.

8 It seems timely to reiterate Weber's recognition of a certain real distance between empirical data and the concepts used both to discover and analyze them. So, too, he cautioned against improper deployment of the ideal type, which misapplication leads to erroneous and prejudicial interpretations. Weber's own failure to consistently follow his injunction (see later in this essay) emphasizes the difficulty of attaining objective empirical certainty in social research.

9 Julian Freund, *The Sociology of Max Weber* (New York: Pantheon, 1968), p. 69.

10 Gerth and Mills note, for example, in their introduction to *From Max Weber*, p. 11, that "[Weber's] circle of friends included Georg Jellinek, Paul Hensel,

Karl Neumann, the art historian, and Ernst Troeltsch, the religionist, who was
to become one of Weber's greatest friends and intellectual companions, and
who for a long time lived in the Weber household." Ronald Bainton indicates
further that Troeltsch resided in Weber's home during the time in which he
produced *Social Teachings*. "Ernst Troeltsch — Thirty Years Later," *Theology Today*, April 1951, p. 70. Notwithstanding, the degree of actual or unilat-
eral influence by Weber remains a matter of considerable speculation.

11 Shils and Finch, *Max Weber on the Methodology of the Social Sciences*, pp. 93-
    94.

12 Max Weber, *The Protestant Ethic and the Spirit of Capitalism*, trans. Talcott
    Parsons (New York: Charles Scribners Sons, 1958).

13 Reprinted in Ernst Troeltsch, *Aufsatze zur Geistesgeschicte und Religionssozi-
    ologie* (Tubingen: J.C.B. Mohr, 1925), pp. 166-91. Moreover, "this essay was
    only one among several where Troeltsch was still polishing up his typology
    that would inform the *Social Teachings* study." See William Garrett,
    "Maligned Mysticism: The Maledicted Career of Troeltsch's Third Type,"
    Sociological Analysis 36 (Fall 1975): 207, n. 2. Other conference participants
    included such pioneering figures in the discipline as Ferdinand Toennies,
    Georg Jellinek, Georg Simmel, and Max Weber.

14 Max Weber, "'Kuchen' und 'Sekten' im Nordamerika," *Christliche Welt* 20
    (1906): 558-62, 577-83.

15 Ernst Troeltsch, *Gesammelte Schuften, I: Die Soziallehren der Christlichen
    Kirchen and Gruppen* (Tubingen: Verlag von J.C.B. Moha, 1912), excerpt
    trans. Reist, *Theology of Involvement*, p. 116. See also, *Social Teachings*, 2:
    993.

16 Troeltsch, *Social Teachings*, 1: 377.

17 Ibid., 2: 730-31.

18 Ibid., p. 734.

19 Ibid., pp. 734, 737.

20 Troeltsch used various terms to describe these most elusive groupings, such
    as "the association of mystics," "intimate circles for edification," and
    "parallelism of spontaneous religious personalities." Ibid., pp. 744, 746.

21 Ibid., p. 735.

22 Ibid., p. 377.

23 Ibid., p. 991.

24 Garrett, "Maligned Mysticism," p. 216.

25 Reist, *Theology of Involvement*, p. 147; and Troeltsch, *Social Teachings*, p. 381.

26 Troeltsch, *Social Teachings*, p. 381.

27 Ibid., pp. 798-99.

28 Ibid., p. 1009.

29 Obvious shortcomings in Troeltsch's work include his too narrow focus on Protestant mysticism prior to 1800, and inattentiveness to the highly institutionalized forms of mysticism in non-Christian traditions, such as Hinduism and Buddhism. Whereas his typology helped him to understand the history of Christianity, it could not unravel the complexities of his own day, let alone the future.

30 For the translated portion of this meeting, see "Max Weber on Church, Sect, and Mysticism," trans. Jerome L. Gittleman, ed. Benjamin Nelson, *Sociological Analysis* 34 (Summer 1973): 140-49.

31 Arthur Mitzman, *The Iron Cage: An Historical Interpretation of Max Weber* (New York: Alfred A. Knopf, 1970), pp. 195, 253-96. It should also be noted in this connection that Weber was closely acquainted with the mystical notions of Stefan George, Georg Lukacs, and Ernst Bloch, as well as a number of East European students. See Richard Bendix and Guenther Roth, *Scholarship and Partisanship: Essays on Max Weber*, (Berkeley: University of California Press, 1971), pp. 6-33.

32 I am in substantial agreement with Garrett's inference, "that Weber may have learned a good deal more than was previously suspected from Troeltsch's penetrating analysis of mysticism." "Maligned Mysticism," p. 219.

33 Weber, "Max Weber on Church, Sect, and Mysticism," p. 144.

34 Weber, *Sociology of Religion*, p. 176. Garrett states that aside from the discussion before the Sociological Society, Weber never included mysticism as a third type in church-sect analyses, not even when he was specifically referring to the schema undergirding the Troeltschian formulation in *Social Teachings*. "Maligned Mysticism," p. 208.

35 Weber, "Max Weber on Church, Sect, and Mysticism," p. 148.

36 Roland Robertson, "On the Analysis of Mysticism: Pre-Weberian and Post-Weberian Perspectives," *Sociological Analysis* 36 (Fall 1975), p. 249.

37 Weber, *From Max Weber*, pp. 267-301, 322-59, and *Sociology of Religion*, pp. 164-83, 207-45.

38 Garrett, "Maligned Mysticism," p. 208.

39 Weber, *Sociology of Religion*, pp. 166-71.

40 See Robertson's treatment of this subject in "On the Analysis of Mysticism," pp. 248-53.

41 Troeltsch's notion of mysticism and Weber's concept of charisma may also be compatible. Garrett makes a case for this in "Maligned Mysticism," pp. 217-219.

42 This observation is made by Swatos in "Weber or Troeltsch," pp. 133-35. See also N.J. Demerath, III, *Social Class in American Protestantism* (Chicago: Rand McNally, 1965), p. 38.

43 See Garrett, "Maligned Mysticism," pp. 210-213.

44 Several factors figure into Troeltsch's ascendency in Anglo-American church-sect theorizing and Weber's dominance in mysticism studies. With reference to Troeltsch, the vicissitudes of translation played a major role — his *Social Teachings* was translated into English 18 years earlier (1931) than Weber's methodological offering, *Methodology of the Social Sciences* (1949). H. Richard Niebuhr's work laid the groundwork for virtually all subsequent developments; his *Social Sources of Denominationalism*, a Troeltschian application of church-sect typology in the American context, ignored mysticism as a credible type. Thus in one fell swoop Niebuhr unwittingly gave credence to Weber's asocial/antisocial model of mysticism. On a more general level, the tendency in American scholarship to bifurcate sacred/secular and church/state motifs has encouraged the differentiation of individualistic and social-structural studies and, conversely, too often denied their interactive possibilities. See articles by Swatos, "Weber or Troeltsch"; Garrett, "Maligned Mysticism"; and Robertson, "On the Analysis of Mysticism." In addition, see the excellent article by Allan Eister, "H. Richard Niebuhr and the Paradox of Religious Organization," in *Beyond the Classics*, eds. Charles Glock and Phillip Hammond (New York: Harper & Row, 1973), pp. 355-408.

45 The recent trend in sociological studies seems to point to less of a concern for exploring mysticism's social-cultural contingencies than elucidating the degree and nature of intensity of mystical experience *per se*. We need only point to such examples as N. Adler, *The Underground Stream: New Life Styles and the Antinomian Personality* (New York: Harper & Row, 1972); L. Eugene Thomas and Pamela E. Cooper, "Measurement and Incidence of Mystical Experiences: An Exploratory Study," *Journal for the Scientific Study of Religion* 17 (December 1978): 433-37; and David Hay and Ann Morisy, "Reports of Escatic, Paranormal, or Religious Experience in Great Britain and the United States — A Comparison of Trends," *Journal for the Scientific Study of Religion* 17 (September 1978): 255-68. Variations on the same theme but with a stronger social component are Andrew Greeley, *The Sociology of the Paranormal: A Reconnaissance* (Beverly Hills: Sage Publications, 1975), and *Ecstasy: A Way of Knowing*; and Robert Ruthnow, "Political Aspects of the Quietistic Revival," in *In Gods We Trust*, eds. Thomas Robbins and Dick Anthony (New Brunswick, NJ: Transaction, Inc., 1981), pp. 229-43.

46 Staal, *Exploring Mysticism*, pp. 99-100.

47 Swatos, "Weber or Troeltsch," pp. 133.

48 Weber, *Max Weber on the Methodology of the Social Sciences*, p. 93.

49 Benjamin Nelson, "Max Weber, Ernst Troeltsch, Georg Jellinek as Compara-
    tive Historical Sociologists," *Sociological Analysis*, p. 236.

50 The same is true, of course, in reference to his unwillingness to address the
    complexities of Roman Catholicism.

51 Talcott Parsons writes, "...Weber's atomism of types introduces into his anal-
    ysis a rigidity which tends to suppress notice of the ranges of variation
    between the components included in the types." Introduction to Weber,
    Sociology of Religion, p. lxvi.

52 The works of several of these researchers have already been identified in this
    chapter. Excepted are Benjamin Nelson, "Self-Images and Systems of Spiri-
    tual Direction in the History of European Civilization," in *The Quest for Self-
    Control*, ed. Samuel Z. Klausner (New York: Free Press, 1965), pp. 49-103;
    Gert H. Mueller, "Asceticism and Mysticism," in *International Yearbook for
    the Sociology of Religion*, 8: 68-132; and David McCloskey, "Anomie,
    Egoisme, and the Modern World: Suicide, Durkheim and Weber, Modern
    Cultural Traditions, and the First and Second Protestant Ethos" (Ph.D.
    dissertation, University of Oregon, 1978).

53 *Meaning and Change* (New York: New York Universities Press, 1978);
    "Religious Movements and Modern Societies: Toward a Progressive Prob-
    lemshift," *Sociological Analysis* 40 (Winter 1979): 297-314; "On the Analysis
    of Mysticism"; "Aspects of Identity and Authority in Sociological Theory," in
    Identity and Authority: Explorations in the Theory of Society, eds. Roland
    Robertson and Burkart Holzner (New York: St. Martins Press, 1979), pp.
    232-33.

54 Robertson, *Meaning and Change*, p. 239.

55 Ibid., p. 133.

56 Weber, *Sociology of Religion*, p. xlix, cited by Robertson, *Meaning and
    Change*, p. 132.

57 Robertson, *Meaning and Change*, p. 128.

58 Ibid.

59 Ibid., p. 131. Robertson also makes a statement about other-worldly asceti-
    cism. It is clear from the body of his argument however that his main concern
    is with inner-worldly mysticism.

60 At this point, Robertson's treatment justifiably highlights Weber's unwilling-
    ness to address in any significant way the impact of Lutheranism in the Occi-
    dent. Ibid., pp. 108-109, 119-22, 130, 134-35.

61 Ibid., p. 131.

62 Ibid., p. 139.

63 Nelson, "Max Weber, Ernst Troeltsch, Georg Jellinek," p. 237.

64 Troeltsch and Weber did express knowledge of and interest in the Quakers. Unfortunately, neither went to any lengths to assess the meaning and importance of this collectivity. Troeltsch attests that "the Quakers overcame the natural anti-social, or rather individualistic, tendency of mysticism..." *Social Teachings* 2: 780. For Weber, see the scattered references in *Sociology of Religion*; and Mitzman, *Iron Cage*, p. 291.

65 Joachim Wach, *The Sociology of Religion* (Chicago: University of Chicago Press, 1944), p. 164, cited by Robertson, *Meaning and Change*, p. 135.

66 Robertson, *Meaning and Change*, p. 125.

67 This is not to deny the existence of other gaps in Robertson's work. For one, he neglects discussion of Catholic mysticism. In addition, his preoccupation with the modern West results in non-Western mystic traditions either being interpreted as passive (Eastern types) or not interpreted at all (Africa, Latin America, etc.).

68 Robertson, *Meaning and Change*, p. 140.

Selected Bibliography

1. Works by Howard Thurman

A. Books and Pamphlets

Apostles of Sensitiveness. Boston: American Unitarian Association, 1956.

The Centering Moment. New York: Harper & Row, 1969.

The Creative Encounter: An Interpretation of Religion and the Social Witness. New York: Harper & Bros., 1954.

Deep is the Hunger. New York: Harper & Bros., 1951.

Deep River: An Interpretation of Negro Spirituals. Mills College, CA: Eucalyptus Press, 1945.

Deep River and the Negro Spiritual Speaks of Life and Death. Single volume. Richmond, IN: Friends United Press, 1975.

Disciplines of the Spirit. New York: Harper & Row, 1963.

Footprints of a Dream: The Story of the Church for the Fellowship of All Peoples. New York: Harper & Row, 1959.

For the Inward Journey. Selected by Anne Spencer Thurman. New York: Harcourt Brace Jovanovich, 1984.

The Greatest of These. Mills College, CA: Eucalyptus Press, 1944.

The Growing Edge. New York: Harper & Row, 1956.

The Inward Journey. New York: Harper & Row, 1961.

Jesus and the Disinherited. Nashville: Abingdon-Cokesbury Press, 1949; reprinted in the Apex edition paperbacks, 1969.

The Luminous Darkness: A Personal Interpretation of the Anatomy of Segregation and the Ground of Hope. New York: Harper & Row, 1965.

Meditations for Apostles of Sensitiveness. Mills College, CA: Eucalyptus Press, 1947.

Meditations of the Heart. New York: Harper & Row, 1973.

The Mood of Christmas. New York: Harper & Row, 1973.

Mysticism and the Experience of Love. Wallingford, PA: Pendle Hill Pamphlet 115, 1961.

The Negro Spiritual Speaks of Life and Death. New York: Harper & Bros., 1947.

The Search for Common Ground: An Inquiry into the Basis of Man's Experience of Community. New York: Harper & Row, 1971.

Temptations of Jesus: Five Sermons. San Francisco: Lawton Kennedy, Printer, 1962; reprint ed., Richmond, IN: Friends United Press, 1978.

With Head and Heart: The Autobiography of Howard Thurman. New York: Harcourt Brace Jovanovich, 1975.

Ed., *The First Footprints: The Dawn of the Idea of the Church for the Fellowship of All Peoples: Letters Between Alfred Fisk and Howard Thurman, 1943-1944.* San Francisco: Lawton and Alfred Kennedy, 1975.

Editor and Introduction to *A Track to the Water's Edge: The Olive Schreiner Reader,* by Olive Schreiner. New York: Harper & Row, 1973.

B. Contributions to Books and Journals

"And When Thou Prayest..." Chapter 9 in *Sermons From an Ecumenical Pulpit*, pp. 86-90. Edited by Max F. Daskam. Boston: Starr King Press, 1956.

"The Christian Minister and the Desegregation Decision." *Pulpit Digest* 37 (May 1957): 13-19.

"Christ's Message to the Disinherited." *Ebony*, September 1963, pp. 58-62.

"Critic's Corner: An Interview with Howard Thurman and Ronald Eyre." *Theology Today* 38 (July 1981), pp. 208-13.

"Exposition to the Book of Habakkuk." *The Interpreter's Bible*. Vol. 6. Nashville: Abingdon Press, 1956, pp. 979-1002.

"Exposition to the Book of Zephaniah." *The Interpreter's Bible*. Vol. 6 Nashville: Abingdon Press, 1956, pp. 1013-1034.

"The Fascist Masquerade." Chapter 4 in *The Church and Organized Movements*, pp. 82-100. Edited by Randolph C. Miller. New York: Harper & Bros., 1946.

"The Fellowship Church of All Peoples." *Common Ground* 5 (Spring 1945): 29-31.

"Finding God." Chapter V in *Religion on the Campus*, pp. 48-52. Edited by Francis P. Miller. New York: Association Press, 1927.

"God and the Race Question." Chapter 12 in *Together*, pp. 118-125. Compiled by Glenn Clark. Nashville: Abingdon-Cokesbury Press, 1946.

"Good News for the Underprivileged." In *The Negro Caravan*, pp. 685-92. Edited by Sterling Brown. New York: The Citadel Press, 1940; reprinted from the 1935 article in *Religion in Life*.

"Human Freedom and the Emancipation Proclamation." *Pulpit Digest* 42 (December 1962): 13-16, 66.

"Interracial Church in San Francisco." *Social Action*, 15 February 1945, pp. 27-28.

Introduction to *Why I Believe There is a God: Sixteen Essays by Negro Clergymen.* Chicago: Johnson Publishing, 1965.

"Judgment and Hope in the Christian Message." Chapter 12 in *The Christian Way in Race Relations*, pp. 229-35. Edited by William Stuart Nelson. New York: Harper & Bros., 1948.

"The Meaning of Purpose in Religious Experience." Chapter 15 in *Religion Ponders Science*, pp. 266-78. Edited by Edwin P. Booth. New York: Meredith Pub. Co., 1964.

"Mysticism and Ethics." *The Journal of Religious Thought* 27 (Supplement 1970): 23-30.

"Mysticism and Social Change." *Eden Theological Seminary Bulletin* 4 (Spring 1939): 3-34.

"The New Heaven and the New Earth." *The Journal of Negro Education* 28 (1958): 115-19.

"Peace Tactics and a Racial Minority." *The World Tomorrow*, December 1928, pp. 505-507.

"The Power of the Spirit and the Powers of This World." Mimeographed address given at The School of Religion, Howard University, Thirty-Fourth Annual Convocation, November 14, 1950.

"Putting Yourself in Another's Place." *Childhood Education* 38 (February 1962): 259-60.

"The Quest for Stability." *The Woman's Press*, April 1949.

"Racial Roots and Religion." An interview with Mary E. Goodwin. *Christian Century* 9 May 1973, pp. 533-35.

"The Religion of Jesus and the Disinherited." In *In Defense of Democracy*, pp. 125-35. Edited by Thomas H. Johnson. New York: G.P. Putnam's Sons, 1949.

"Religious Ideas in Negro Spirituals." *Christendom* 4 (Autumn 1939): 515-28.

"Religion in a Time of Crisis." *The Garrett Tower* 18 (August 1943): 1-3.

"The Responsibility of the Professional Person to Society." *Nursing Outlook* 5 (June 1957): 334-335.

Review of *Liberation and Reconciliation: A Black Theology*, by J. Deotis Roberts. *Religious Education* 66 (November December 1971): 464, 466.

Review of *The Manner of Prayer*, by William D. Chamberlain. *The Journal of Religious Thought* 1 (Spring-Summer 1944): 179.

Review of *On Beginning from Within*, by Douglas V. Steere. *The Journal of Religion* 24 (October 1944): 284-85.

Review of *Religion in Higher Education Among Negroes*, by Richard I. McKinney. *Religion in Life* 15 (Autumn 1946): 619-20.

"The Search for Common Ground." *Perspective: A Journal of Pittsburgh Theological Seminary* 13 (Spring 1972): 127-37.

"The Search for God in Religion." *The Laymen's Movement Review* 5 (November - December 1962): 3-8.

"Sermon Preached by the Reverend Dr. Howard Thurman at the American Embassy, Lagos, Nigeria, on Sunday, November 24, 1963 in Memory of the Late President John F. Kennedy." In *That Day With God*, pp. 143-47. Edited by William M. Fine. New York: McGraw-Hill Co., 1965.

"Why We Belong to the Fellowship of Reconciliation." A folder of testimonials by eight American ministers. May 1958.

"Windbreak ... Against Existence." *Bostonia*, Fall 1960, pp. 7-9.

C. Taped Sermons, Lectures and Interviews. These tapes are in the library of the Howard Thurman Educational Trust. The dates and location of each are given where indicated.

"A Faith to Live By — Democracy." Fellowship Church, San Francisco, CA. 19 October 1952.

"A Faith to Live By — Democracy and the Individual II." Fellowship Church, San Francisco, CA. 26 October 1952.

"Aspects of Freedom." Toronto, Canada. 6 May 1964.

"Community and the Will of God." 8 - part series.

"Declaration of Independence - I." Fellowship Church, San Francisco, CA. 29 July 1951.

"Declaration of Independence - III." Fellowship Church, San Francisco, CA. 12 August 1951.

"Declaration of Independence - IV." Fellowship Church, San Francisco, CA. 19 August 1951.

"The Dilemma of the Religious Professional." 3 - part Earl Lecture series, Pacific School of Religion.

"The Divine Encounter." 3 - part series.

"Footprints of the Disinherited." Eliot Congregational Church, Roxbury, MA. 31 May 1972.

"Growing in Love." 3 - part series.

"Journey in Understanding." Freedom House, Boston, MA. 8 June 1964.

"The Life and Thought of Howard Thurman." Conversations with Landrum Bolling. Audio of the documentary film produced by the British Broadcasting Corporation, 1976.

"Man and Social Change — Violence and Non-Violence." 21 March 1969.

"Mysticism and Social Change." 15 - part series. Pacific School of Religion. 5-28 July 1978.

"Mysticism and Social Change." Pacific School of Religion. Summer 1959.

"Reflections on the Black Experience and the Experience of the Spirit." Interview conducted in Roxbury, MA. 30 May 1972.

"The Sources of Tradition - III." 11 October 1959.

"Violence and Non-Violence." 14 July 1963.

D. Unpublished Essays, Lectures, and Memoranda. These items are located in the Howard Thurman Archives, Mugar Memorial Library, Boston University, Boston, MA. The dates and location of each are given where indicated.

"Black Spirituality — Black Religious Experience."

"The Cultural and Spiritual Prospect for the Democratic Way of Life."

"The Dilemma of the Religious Professional." 3 - part Burkhart Lecture series, April 1971.

"The Idea of God and Modern Thought." Address delivered as the 25th annual Garvin Lecture on the Idea of God as Affected by Modern Knowledge at the Church of Our Father (Unitarian), Lancaster. PA., November 23, 1965.

"Man and the Moral Struggle — Paul." 9 January 1959.

"The Negro in the City." Howard University.

"The Significance of Jesus." A series of addresses given at the 1937 Central Area Conference of the Student Christian Movement of Canada.

Untitled discussion on the state of relations between American blacks and whites in 1943.

II. Works About Howard Thurman

A. Monographs and Articles

Lerone Bennett. "Howard Thurman: 20th Century Holy Man." *Ebony*, February 1978, pp. 68-85.

Boulware, Marcus. *The Oratory of Negro Leaders: 1900-1968.* Westport, CT: Negro Universities Press, 1969.

Bridges, Hal. *American Mysticism: From William James to Zen.* New York: Harper & Row, 1973.

Burden, Jean. "Howard Thurman." *Atlantic Monthly*, October 1953, pp. 39-44.

Cannon, Katie G. *Black Womanist Ethics.* Atlanta: Scholar's Press, 1988.

Cartwright, John H. "The Religious Ethics of Howard Thurman." *The Journal of the Interdenominational Theological Center* 12 (Fall 1984/Spring 1985): 22-34.

Chaffe, Paul. "Howard Thurman, Ecologist of the Spirit." San Francisco, 1979. (Mimeographed)

Corbett, Jan. "Howard Thurman: A Theologian for Our Time." *The American Baptist* (December 1979), pp. 10-12.

Eisler, Benita. "Keeping the Faith." Review of *With Head and Heart*, by Howard Thurman. *The Nation*, 5-12 January 1980, pp. 22-25.

Fluker, Walter E. *They Looked for a City: A Comparative Analysis of the Ideal of Community in the Thought of Howard Thurman and Martin Luther King, Jr.* Landham, MD: University Press of America, 1989.

Franklin, James L. "Dr. King Mentor Remembered." *The Boston Globe*, 15 January 1983.

Gandy, Samuel L., ed. *Common Ground: Essays in Honor of Howard Thurman on the Occasion of His Seventy-Fifth Birthday, November 18, 1975.* Washington, D.C.: Hoffman Press, 1976.

Gredler, David. "Spirit of Understanding Bridges Gap as Dr. Thurman Gets Message Across." *Boston Globe*, 4 November 1962.

"Great Preachers." *Life*, 6 April 1953, pp. 127-30.

Grier, Barnett J.W. "Howard Thurman: An Examination and Analysis of Thurman's Idea of Community and the Viability of the Fellowship Church." D.Min. Thesis, School of Theology at Claremont, 1983.

Henderson, Dorothy. *Biographical Sketches of Six Humanitarians.* New York: Exposition Press, 1958.

"Howard Washington Thurman: Campus Minister of the Century," a special edition. *Toward Wholeness* (Spring 1983).

Jenness, Mary. Chapter 9 in *Twelve Negro Americans.* New York: Friendship Press, 1956.

McNeil, Pearl. "Baptist Black Americans and the Ecumenical Movement." *Journal of Ecumenical Studies* 17 (Spring 1980): 103-117.

Makechnie, George K. "Howard Thurman - Mentor to the Great, the Humble, and the Disinherited." *President's Idea Journal* 19 (September/October 1985): 1-12.

_____. *Howard Thurman: His Enduring Dream*. Boston: Boston University, 1988.

Massey, James Earl. "Bibliographical Essay: Howard Thurman and Rufus M. Jones, Two Mystics." *Journal of Negro History* 57 (April 1972): 190-95.

_____. "Howard Thurman and Olive Schreiner on the Unity of All Life: A Bibliographical Essay." *The Journal of Religious Thought* 34 (Fall-Winter 1977): 29-33.

Mitchell, Mozella G. "Howard Thurman: Literary/Humanist Theologian." *The Journal of the Interdenominational Theological Center* 11 (Fall 1983/Spring 1984): 31-56.

_____. "Howard Thurman and Olive Schreiner: Post-Modern Marriage Post-Mortem." *The Journal of Religious Thought* 38 (Spring-Summer 1981): 62-72.

_____. *Spiritual Dynamics of Howard Thurman's Theology*. Bristol, IN: Wyndham Hall Press, 1985.

Moxley, Irvin S. "An Examination of the Mysticism of Howard Thurman and its Relevance to Black Liberation." D.Min. Thesis, Louisville Presbyterian Theological Seminary, 1974.

Myers, E. Pauline. "Howard Thurman: An Appreciation in Retrospect." *The A.M.E. Zion Quarterly Review* 96 (October 1984): 35-37.

Owens, Irene. "Dr. Benjamin Elijah Mays and Dr. Howard Thurman: A Bibliography." Prepared for the dedication of the Benjamin E. Mays Hall and the Howard Thurman Chapel, April 22-24, 1987. Howard University School of Divinity, Washington, D.C.

"Simmering on the Calm Presence and Profound Wisdom of Howard Thurman," a special edition. *Debate and Understanding* (Spring 1982).

Smith, Luther E., Jr. "Black Theology and Religious Experience." *The Journal of the Interdenominational Theological Center* 8 (Fall 1980): 59-72.

_____. *Howard Thurman: The Mystic as Prophet.* Lanham, MD: University Press of America, 1981.

_____. "Intimate Mystery: Howard Thurman's Search for Ultimate Meaning (1900-1981)" *Ultimate Reality and Meaning* 11 (1988): 85-101.

Stewart, Carlyle F. "A Comparative Analysis of Theological Ontology and Ethical Method in the Theologies of James H. Cone and Howard Thurman." Ph.D. dissertation, Northwestern University, 1982.

Wiley, Dennis W. "The Concept of the Church in the Works of Howard Thurman." Ph.D. dissertation, Union Theological Seminary, 1988.

Williams, Robert C. "Worship and Anti-Structure in Thurman's Vision of the Sacred." *The Journal of the Interdenominational Theological Center* 14 (Fall 1986/Spring 1987): 161-174.

Yates, Elizabeth. *Howard Thurman: Portrait of a Practical Dreamer.* New York: The John Day Co., 1964.

Young, Henry J., ed. *God and Human Freedom.* Richmond, IN: Friends United Press, 1983.

B. Interviews

Bullard, Muriel. Fellowship Church, San Francisco, CA. Interview, 16 May 1985.

Carter, Woody. Howard Thurman Educational Trust, San Francisco, CA. Interview, May 1985.

Chaffee, Jan and Paul. Fellowship Church, San Francisco, CA. Interview, 22 May 1985.

Chandler, Marvin. Fellowship Church, San Francisco, CA. Interview, 21 May 1985.

Fisk, Eleanor. Fellowship of Reconciliation, San Francisco, CA. Interview, 23 May 1985.

Makechnie, George. Boston University Howard Thurman Center and Fellowship, Boston, MA. Interview, 29 April 1986.

Nance, Ethel Ray. Fellowship Church, San Francisco, CA. Interview, 24 May 1985.

Scardiglia, Virginia. Fellowship Church, San Francisco, CA. Interview, 26 May 1985.

Weaver, Andrew. Fellowship Church, San Francisco, CA. Interview, 16 May 1985.

C. Symposiums

Bennett, Lerone, Jr. Dedicatory address of the Howard Thurman Chapel, Howard University School of Divinity, Washington, D.C., April 23, 1987.

Bennett, Lerone, and Silber, John R. "A Day of Commemoration of the Life and Thought of Howard Thurman." Memorial messages given at Boston University, April 10, 1983.

Carter, Woody. "Howard Thurman's Vision of Mysticism and Social Action." The second Howard Thurman Consultation. Garrett-Evangelical Theological Seminary, Evanston, IL. 22 April 1985.

Geddes, Frances. "Howard Thurman: Man and Mission." Moderator of 1985 symposium on prophetic mysticism. Pacific School of Religion, Berkeley, CA.

Keen, Sam. "Myth and Mysticism." 1985 San Anselmo Lectures, Pacific School of Religion, Berkeley CA.

Martin, B. Herbert. "The Place of Spirituality and Social Transformation in the Life of the Church." The second Howard Thurman Consultation. Garrett-Evangelical Theological Seminary, Evanston, IL. 23 April 1985.

Proctor, Samuel D. "Finding Our Margin of Freedom: In Tribute to Howard Thurman." 1979 Consultation of Black Theological Scholars, Garrett-Evangelical Theological Seminary, Evanston, IL.

Smith, Earnest A. "Howard Thurman: The Prophet and Poet of Spiritual Unity and Personal Wholeness." 1979 Consultation of Black Theological Scholars, Garrett-Evangelical Theological Seminary, Evanston, IL.

Steere, Douglas V. "Thou Hast Enlarged My Boundaries." 1985 San Anselm Lectures, Pacific School of Religion, Berkeley, CA.

Thurman, Howard. Address given at the winter consultation, Congress of National Black Churches, San Francisco, CA. 11 December 1979.

————. "Identity Grounded in Faith and Heritage: A Sermonic Address." 1979 Consultation of Black Theological Scholars, Garrett-Evangelical Theological Seminary, Evanston, IL.

Williams, Robert S. "Existence and Ritual in Howard Thurman's Vision of Spirituality." The second Howard Thurman Consultation. Garrett-Evangelical Theological Seminary, Evanston, IL. 23 April 1985.

Wilmore, Gayraud. "Spirituality and Transformation in the Context of the Black Church Tradition." The second Howard Thurman Consultation. Garrett-Evangelical Theological Seminary, Evanston, IL. 22 April 1985.

III. Related Articles

A. Fellowship Church

"The Church for the Fellowship of All Peoples: A Brief History." San Francisco, CA. Mimeographed copy, August 1979.

"The Church for the Fellowship of All Peoples." Church publication, 1947.

"Constitution and Bylaws of The Church for the Fellowship of All Peoples." San Francisco, CA. Mimeographed copy.

"Fellowship Church's Anniversary: An Unorthodox 25 Years." *San Francisco Chronicle*, 6 October 1969, sec. 1, pp. 4-5.

The Growing Edge. The Publication of the Church for the Fellowship of All Peoples. January 1949 - Fall 1952. Reinstituted at present as bimonthly newsletter.

"Howard Thurman Appointed to Boston University Faculty." *San Francisco Sun Reporter*, 28 March 1958.

"Race Relations Improving in San Francisco and Bay Cities." *Amsterdam News* (New York), March 1949.

"S.F. -- The City of Churches." *San Francisco News*, 24 March 1949, sec. 3, p. 25.

San Francisco Chronicle, March 1949 - 22 March 1953.

"San Francisco's Interracial Church Represented at 'Economic, Social and Cultural' Meeting by Members of Many Races." *Shreveport Sun* (Louisiana), 17 May 1949.

"Thurman Church Leads the Way." *Colgate Rochester Divinity School Bulletin*, October 1957.

"Trumpet Ready in the West." *The Christian Century*, 12 September 1951.

"What Color Are Your Eyes?" A pamphlet produced by The Church for the Fellowship of All Peoples during the 1950's.

B. The Howard Thurman Educational Trust

"A Matter of Human Concern." A statement of purpose by the trustees of the Howard Thurman Educational Trust, San Francisco, CA.

The Listening Ear. A Newsletter of the Howard Thurman Educational Trust. Spring 1980 - Spring 1991.

C. The Boston University Howard Thurman Center

"Progress Report on the Founding of the Boston University Howard Thurman Center." Boston, MA., 1986.

IV. Perspectives on Mysticism/Religion and the Social World

Alexander, Bobby C. "Correcting Misinterpretations of Turner's Theory: An African-American Pentecostal Illustration." *Journal for the Scientific Study of Religion* 30 (March 1991): 26-44.

Bassuk, Daniel E. "The Secularization of Mysticism — An Analysis and Critique of the Mystical in Rufus Jones and Martin Buber." Ph.D. dissertation, Drew University, 1974.

Berger, Alan L. "'Normal' Mysticism and the Social World: A Comparative Study of Quaker and Hasidic Communal Mysticism." Ph.D. dissertation, Syracuse University, 1976.

Decker, Michael P. "A Hermeneutic Approach to the Problem of Mysticism." Ph.D. dissertation, Emory University, 1978.

Eister, Alan W. "Comment on 'Max Weber on Church, Sect and Mysticism.'" *Sociological Analysis* 36 (Fall 1975): 227-28.

_____. "H. Richard Niebuhr and the Paradox of Religious Organization: A Radical Critique." In *Beyond the Classics*, pp. 355-402. Edited by Charles Y. Glock and Phillip E. Hammonds. New York: Harper & Row, 1973.

_____. "Toward a Radical Critique of Church-Sect Typologizing: Comment on 'Some Critical Observations on the Church-Sect Dimension.'" *Journal for the Scientific Study of Religion* 6 (Spring 1967): 85-90.

Eliade, Mircea. *The Two and the One*. Chicago: University of Chicago Press, 1979.

Ellwood, Robert. *Mysticism and Religion*. Englewood Cliffs, NJ: Prentice-Hall, 1980.

Fenton, John Y. "Mystical Experience as a Bridge for Cross-Cultural Philosophy of Religion: A Critique." *The Journal of the American Academy of Religion* 49 (Spring 1981): 51-76.

Garrett, William R. "Maligned Mysticism: The Maledicted Career of Troeltsch's Third Type." *Sociological Analysis* 36 (Fall 1975): 205-223.

Gerth, H.H., and Mills, C. Wright. *From Max Weber: Essays in Sociology*. New York: Oxford University Press, 1946.

Greeley, Andrew M. *Ecstasy: A Way of Knowing*. Englewood Cliffs, NJ: Prentice-Hall, 1974.

_____. *The Sociology of the Paranormal: A Reconnaissance*. Sage Research Papers in the Social Sciences, series no. 90-023. Beverly Hills: Sage Publications, 1975.

Gustafson, Paul M. "The Missing Member of Troeltsch's Trinity: Thoughts Generated by Weber's Comments." *Sociological Analysis* 36 (Fall 1975): 224-26.

Hay, David, and Morisy, Ann. "Reports of Esctatic, Paranormal, or Religious Experience in Great Britain and the United States — A Comparison of Trends." *Journal for the Scientific Study of Religion* 17 (Fall 1978): 255-68.

Kolakowski, Leszek. *Religion*. New York: Oxford University Press, 1982.

McCloskey, David D. "Anomie, Egoisme, and the Modern World: Suicide, Durkheim and Weber, Modern Cultural Traditions, and the First and Second Protestant Ethos." Ph.D. dissertation, University of Oregon, 1978.

Moore, Peter G. "Recent Studies of Mysticism: A Critical Survey." *Religion* (Fall 1973): 146-56.

Mueller Gert H. "Asceticism and Mysticism: A Contribution Towards the Sociology of Faith." In *International Yearbook for the Sociology of Religion*. Vol. 8, pp. 68-132. Germany: Westdeutscher Verlag Opladen, 1973.

Nelson, Benjamin. "Max Weber, Ernst Troeltsch, Georg Jellinek as Comparative Historical Sociologists." *Sociological Analysis* 36 (Fall 1975): 229-240.

_____. "Self-Images and Systems of Spiritual Direction in the History of European Civilization." In *The Quest for Self-Control*, pp. 49-103. Edited by Samuel Z. Klausner. New York: Free Press, 1965.

Otto, Rudolf. *The Idea of the Holy*. Translated by John W. Harvey. Oxford: Oxford University Press, 1923, 1958.

_____. *Mysticism East and West*. Translated by Bertha L. Bracey and Richenda C. Payne. New York: Macmillan, 1932.

Restivo, Sal. *The Social Relations of Physics, Mysticism, and Mathematics.* Dordrecht, Holland: D. Reidel, 1983.

Robertson, Roland. *Meaning and Change.* New York: New York University Press, 1978.

_____. "Aspects of Identity and Authority in Sociological Theory." In *Identity and Authority: Explorations in the Theory of Society.* Edited by Roland Robertson and Burkart Holzner. New York: St. Martins Press, 1979.

_____. "On the Analysis of Mysticism: Pre-Weberian, Weberian and Post-Weberian Perspectives." *Sociological Analysis* 36 (Fall 1975): 241-66.

_____. "Religious Movements and Modern Societies: Toward a Progressive Problemshift." *Sociological Analysis* 40 (Winter 1979): 297-314.

Scholem, Gershom. "Mysticism and Society." *Diogenes* 58 (1967): 1-24.

Sharot, Stephen. *Messianism, Mysticism, and Magic.* Chapel Hill: The University of North Carolina Press, 1982.

Smart, Ninian. "Interpretation and Mystical Experience." *Religious Studies* 1 (Spring 1965): 75-87.

_____. *The Phenomenon of Religion.* New York: Seabury Press, 1973.

Staal, Frits. *Exploring Mysticism: A Methodological Essay.* Berkeley: University of California Press, 1975.

Steedman, Theodore M. "Church, Sect, Mysticism, Denomination: Periodological Aspects of Troeltsch's Types." *Sociological Analysis* 36 (Fall 1975): 181-204.

Swatos, William H. "Church-Sect and Cult: Bringing Mysticism Back In." *Sociological Analysis* 42 (Spring 1982): 17-26.

_____. "The Disenchantment of Charisma: A Weberian Assessment of Revolution in a Rationalized World." *Sociological Analysis* 42 (Summer 1982): 119-36.

_____. "Enchantment and Disenchantment in Modernity: The Significance of 'Religion' as a Sociological Category." *Sociological Analysis* 44 (Winter 1983): 321-37.

_____. "Weber or Troeltsch?: Methodology, Syndrome, and the Development of Church-Sect Theory." *Journal for the Scientific Study of Religion* 15 (Summer 1976): 129-144.

Thomas, L. Eugene, and Cooper, Pamela E. "Measurement and Incidence of Mystical Experiences: An Exploratory Study." *Journal for the Scientific Study of Religion* 17 (Winter 1978): 433-37.

Troeltsch, Ernst. *The Social Teaching of the Christian Churches.* 2 vols. Translated by Olive Wyon. New York: Macmillan, 1931.

Turner, Victor. *Dramas, Fields, and Metaphors.* Ithaca, NY: Cornell University Press, 1974.

_____. "Passages, Margins, and Poverty: Religious Symbols of Communitas." *Worship* 46.

_____. *The Ritual Process: Structure and Anti-Structure.* Ithaca, NY: Cornell University Press, 1969.

Weber, Max. "Max Weber on Church, Sect, and Mysticism." Translated by Jerome L. Gittleman, ed. Benjamin Nelson. *Sociological Analysis* 34 (Summer 1973): 140-49.

_____. *On Charisma and Institution Building.* Edited by S.N. Eisenstadt. Chicago: University of Chicago Press, 1968.

_____. *The Sociology of Religion.* Translated with an introduction by Ephraim Fischoff. Boston: Beacon Press, 1963.

Wisdom, William A. "A Phenomenological Review of Mysticism and Childhood Experience." *Philosophy and Phenomenological Research* 21 (March 1961): 397-401.

Wuthnow, Robert. "Political Aspects of the Quietistic Revival." In *In Gods We trust*, pp. 229-43. Edited by Thomas Robbins and Dick Anthony. New Brunswick, NJ: Transaction Books, 1981.

Zablocki, Benjamin. *Alienation and Charisma.* New York: Free Press, 1980.

V. Works of General Background and Criticism

Ahlstrom, Sydney E. *A Religious History of the American People.* New Haven: Yale University Press, 1972.

Allen, Robert in collaboration with Allen, Pamela P. *Reluctant Reformers: Racism and Social Reform Movements in the United States.* Revised ed. Washington, D.C.: Howard University Press, 1983.

Ansbro, John J. *Martin Luther King, Jr.: The Making of a Mind.* Maryknoll, NY: Orbis, 1982.

Baham, Venita M. "Mysticism and the Afro-American Religious Experience." *The Journal of Religious Thought* 34 (Spring-Summer 1978): 68-77.

Baldwin, Lewis V. *There is a Balm in Gilead: The Cultural Roots of Martin Luther King, Jr.* Minneapolis: Fortress Press, 1991.

Bastide, Roger. *The African Religions of Brazil.* Translated by Helen Sebba. Baltimore: The Johns Hopkins University Press, 1978.

Bennett, Lerone. *What Manner of Man.* 4th ed. Chicago: Johnson Pub. Co., 1976.

Berger, Peter. *The Sacred Canopy*. Garden City, NY: Doubleday & Co., 1967.

Berger, Peter, and Luckmann, Thomas. *The Social Construction of Reality: A Treatise in the Sociology of Knowledge*. Garden City, NY: Doubleday & Co., 1966.

Bettis, Joseph D., ed. *Phenomenology of Religion*. New York: Harper & Row, 1969.

Bloom, Jack M. *Class, Race, & the Civil Rights Movement*. Bloomington, IN: Indiana University Press, 1987.

Bracey, John H.; Meier, August; and Rudwick, Elliott, eds. *Black Nationalism in America*. Indianapolis: Bobbs-Merrill Co., 1970.

Brisbane, Robert. *The Black Vanguard*. Valley Forge, PA: Judson Press, 1970.

Broussard, Alfred S. "The New Racial Frontier: San Francisco's Black Community: 1900-1940." Ph.D. dissertation, Duke University, 1977.

Burridge, Kenelm. *New Heaven, New Earth*. Oxford: Basil Blackwell, 1969, 1980.

Carson, Clayborne; Garrow, David J.; Harding, Vincent; and Hine, Darlene Clark. *Eyes on the Prize: America's Civil Rights Years*. New York: Viking Penguin, 1987.

Clark, Elmer T. *The Small Sects in America*. Nashville: Abingdon-Cokesbury Press, 1965.

Colton, Elizabeth O. *The Jackson Phenomenon: The Man, The Power, The Message*. New York: Doubleday, 1989.

Coser, Lewis A. *Masters of Sociological Thought*, 2nd ed. New York: Harcourt Brace Jovanovich, 1977.

Coser, Lewis, ed. *Georg Simmel.* Englewood Cliffs, NJ: Prentice-Hall, 1965.

Cruse, Harold. *The Crisis of the Negro Intellectual.* New York: William Morrow and Co., 1967.

Dalfiume, Roger. "The 'Forgotten Years' of the Negro Rebellion." *Journal of American History* 55 (June 1968): 90-106.

de Vries, Jan. *Perspectives in the History of Religions.* Translated with an introduction by Kees W. Bolle. Berkeley and Los Angeles: University of California Press, 1977.

Drake, St. Clair, and Cayton, Horace. *Black Metropolis.* New York: Harper & Row, 1945.

Du Bois, W.E.B. "Race Relations in the United States: 1917-1947." *Phylon* 9 (1948): 234-47.

_____. *The Souls of Black Folk.* Greenwich, CT: Fawcett Publications, 1961.

Dunbar, Anthony P. *Against the Grain: Southern Radicals and Prophets, 1929-1959.* Charlottesville: University Press of Virginia, 1981.

Durkheim, Emile. *The Elementary Forms of the Religious Life.* George Allen & Unwin, 1915; reprint ed., New York: Free Press, 1965.

Eck, Diana L., and Jain, Devaki, eds. *Speaking of Faith: Global Perspectives on Women, Religion & Social Change.* Philadelphia: New Society Publishers, 1987.

Edwards, G. Franklin. "E. Franklin Frazier." In *Black Sociologists: Historical and Contemporary Perspectives.* Edited by James E. Blackwell and Morris Janowitz. Chicago: University of Chicago Press, 1974.

Eliade, Mircea. *The Sacred and the Profane.* Translated by Willard R. Trask. New York: Harcourt Brace Jovanovich, 1959.

Farmer, James. *Lay Bare the Heart.* New York: Arbor House, 1985.

Fauset, Arthur Huff. *Black Gods of the Metropolis.* University Park, PA: University of Pennsylvania Press, 1971.

Fichter, Joseph H. "The Concept of Man in Social Science: Freedom, Values and Second Nature." *Journal for the Scientific Study of Religion* 11 (1972): 109-21.

Franklin, John Hope. "The Dilemma of the American Negro Scholar." In *Soon, One Morning: New Writing by American Negroes, 1940-1962,* pp. 62-76. Edited by Herbert Hill (New York: Alfred A. Knopf, 1963).

Frazier, E. Franklin. *The Negro Church in America.* New York: Schocken, 1964.

_____. "A Note on Negro Education." *Opportunity,* March 1924, p. 76.

Frazier, Thomas R. *An Analysis of Social Scientific Writing on American Negro Religion.* Ann Arbor, MI: University Microfilms International, 1967.

_____. "Changing Perspectives in the Study of Afro-American Religion." *The Journal of the Interdenominational Theological Center* 6 (Fall 1978): 51-68.

Fullinwider, S.P. *The Mind and Mood of Black America: 20th Century Thought.* Homewood, IL: Dorsey Press, 1969.

Gaustad, Edwin S. *Dissent in American Religion,* Chicago History of American Religion series edited by Martin E. Marty. Chicago: University of Chicago Press, 1973.

Gerson, Elihu M. "On 'Quality of Life'." *American Sociological Review* 41 (1976): 793-806.

Gilkes, Cheryl Townsend. "The Black Church as a Therapeutic Community." *The Journal of the Interdenominational Theological Center* 8 (Fall 1980): 29-44.

Green, Vera M. "The Confrontation of Diversity within the Black Community." *Human Organization* 29 (Winter 1970): 267-72.

Greisman, H.C., and Mayes, Sharon S. Mayes. "The Social Construction of Unreality: The Real American Dilemma." *Dialectical Anthropology* 2 (February 1977): 57-67.

Guerriere, Daniel. "Outline of a Phenomenology of the Religious." *Research in Phenomenology* 4 (1974): 99-127.

Hall, Francis B. *Practical Spirituality: Selected Writings of Francis B. Hall.* Edited by Howard Alexander with Wilmer A. Cooper and James Newley. Dublin, IN: Prinit Press, 1984.

Harding, Vincent. *Beyond Chaos: Black History and the Search for the New Land.* Atlanta: Institute of the Black World, 1970.

_____. "Black Power and the American Christ." In *The Black Power Revolt*, pp. 85-93. Edited by Floyd B. Barbour. Boston: Porter Sargent Publisher, 1968.

_____. *The Other American Revolution.* Volume 4 of the Center for Afro-American Studies monograph series. University of California, Los Angeles and the Institute of the Black World, Atlanta, 1980.

_____. "Out of the Cauldron of Struggle: Black Religion and the Search for a New America." In *Religion: North American Style*, 2nd ed., pp. 256-64. Edited by Patrick H. McNamara.

_____. *There is a River.* New York: Harcourt Brace Jovanovich, 1981.

Henri, Florette. *Black Migration: Movement North, 1900-1920.* Garden City, NY: Anchor Press/Doubleday, 1976.

Herskovits, Melville. *The Myth of the Negro Past.* Boston: Beacon Press, 1958.

Hollenweger, Walter J. *Pentecost Between Black and White.* Belfast: Christian Journals Limited, 1974.

Holloway, Joseph E. *Africanisms in American Culture.* Bloomington: Indiana University Press, 1990.

Horne, Gerald. *Black & Red: W.E.B. DuBois and the Afro-American Response to the Cold War, 1944-1963.* New York: State University of New York Press, 1986.

Hurston, Zora Neale. *The Sanctified Church.* Berkeley: Turtle Island, 1981.

Hutchinson, William R. *The Modernist Impulse in American Protestantism.* Cambridge: Harvard University Press, 1976.

Isichei, Elizabeth. "Organization and Power in the Society of Friends, 1852-59." In *Patterns of Sectarianism*, pp. 182-211. Edited by Bryan R. Wilson. London: Heinemann Educational Books Ltd., 1967.

James, William. *The Varieties of Religious Experience.* New York: Random House, 1929.

Jarvie, I.C. *The Revolution in Anthropology.* Chicago: Henry Regnery Co., 1967.

Johnson, Charles S. *Shadow of the Plantation.* Chicago: University of Chicago Press, 1934.

Johnson, Daniel M., and Campbell, Rex. *Black Migration in America: A Social Demographic History.* Durham, NC: Duke University Press, 1981.

Jones, Mary Hoxie. *Rufus M. Jones.* London: Friends Home Service Committee, 1955.

Jones, Raymond. *A Comparative Study of Religious Cult Behavior Among Negroes with Special Reference to Emotional Conditioning Factors.* Howard University Studies in the Social Sciences, 1939.

Jones, Rufus. *Finding the Trail of Life.* New York: Macmillan Co., 1931.

Katz, Steven T., ed. *Mysticism and Philosophical Analysis.* London: Sheldon press, 1978.

Kolb, William L. "Images of Man and the Sociology of Religion." *Journal for the Scientific Study of Religion* 1 (Fall 1961): 5-22.

Kelsey, George D. *Racism and the Christian Understanding of Man.* New York: Charles Scribner's Sons, 1965.

Kierkegaard, Soren. *Either/Or.* Translated by David F. Swenson and Lillian Marvin Swenson. Princeton: Princeton University Press, 1959.

_____. *Fear and Trembling and The Sickness Unto Death.* Translated by Walter Lowrie. Princeton: Princeton University Press, 1949.

King, Martin Luther, Jr. *Stride Toward Freedom.* New York: Harper & Row, 1958.

_____. *Where Do We Go From Here: Chaos or Community?* New York: Harper & Row, 1967.

_____. *Why We Can't Wait.* New York: New American Library, 1964.

Ladner, Joyce A., ed. *The Death of White Sociology.* New York: Random House, 1973.

Lee, Carlton L. "Religious Roots of the Negro Protest." In *Assuring Freedom to the Free: A Century of Emancipation in the U.S.A.*, pp. 45-71. Edited by Arnold M. Rose. Detroit: Wayne State University, 1964.

_____. "Toward a Sociology of the Black Religious Experience." *The Journal of Religious Thought* 29 (Autumn-Winter 1972): 5-18.

Lincoln, C. Eric. "Aspects of American Pluralism." *The Journal of the Interdenominational Theological Center* 1 (Spring 1974): 17-26.

_____. *The Black Church Since Frazier.* New York: Schocken, 1974.

_____. "Contemporary Black Religion: In Search of a Sociology." *The Journal of the Interdenominational Theological Center* 5 (Spring 1978): 91-104.

_____. *Race, Religion, and the Continuing American Dilemma.* New York: Hill and Wang, 1984.

_____. "The Social Cosmos of Ecumenism." *The Journal of the Interdenominational Theological Center* 7 (Fall 1979): 11-21.

_____, ed. *The Black Experience in Religion.* New York: Anchor press, 1974.

_____ and Lawrence Mamiya. *The Black Church in the African American Experience.* Durham, NC: Duke University Press, 1990.

Long, Charles. "Assessment and New Departures for a Study of Black Religion in the United States of America." Address at the tenth annual meeting, *The Society for the Study of Black Religion.* New York: n.p., 1982.

_____. "The Meaning of Religion in the Contemporary Study of the History of Religions." *Criterion* (Spring 1963).

_____. *Significations: Signs, Symbols, and Images in the Interpretation of Religion*. Philadelphia: Fortress Press, 1986.

Luckmann, Thomas. *The Invisible Religion*. New York: Macmillan, 1967.

Lukas, J. Anthony. *Common Ground*. New York: Alfred A. Knopf, 1985.

McAdam, Doug. *Political Process and the Development of Black Insurgency, 1930-1970*. Chicago: University of Chicago Press, 1982.

McGuire, Meredith B. *Religion: The Social Context*. Belmont, CA: Wadsworth Pub. Co., 1981.

Marable, Manning. *Black American Politics: From the Washington Marches to Jesse Jackson*. London: Verso, 1985.

Marty, Martin E. *Righteous Empire*. New York: Harper & Row, 1970.

Mays, Benjamin. *Born to Rebel*. New York: Charles Scribners Sons, 1971.

_____. *The Negro's God*. Boston: Chapman & Grimes, 1938.

Mays, Benjamin, and Nicholson, Joseph. *The Negro's Church*. New York: Russell & Russell, 1969.

Meier, August; Rudwick, Elliott; and Broderick, Francis L., eds. *Black Protest Thought in the Twentieth Century*. Indianapolis: Bobbs-Merrill Co., 1971.

Meier, August, and Rudwick, Elliott. *From Plantation to Ghetto*. Revised ed. New York: Hill and Wang, 1970.

Mitzman, Arthur. *The Iron Cage: An Historical Interpretation of Max Weber*. New York: Alfred A. Knopf, 1970.

Moberg, David O., ed. *Spiritual Well-Being: Sociological Perspectives*. Washington, D.C.: University Press of America, 1979.

Mol, Hans. *Meaning and Place*. New York: The Pilgrim Press, 1983.

Morris, Aldon D. *The Origins of the Civil Rights Movement: Black Communities Organizing for Change*. New York: Free Press, 1984.

Morrison-Reed, Mark D. *Black Pioneers in a White Denomination*. Boston: Beacon Press, 1980.

Myrdal, Gunnar. *An American Dilemma*. Vol. 1. New York: Harper & Bros., 1944.

Nelsen, Hart M.; Yokley, Ratha L.; and Nelsen, Anne K., eds. *The Black Church in America*. New York: Basic Books, 1971.

Nelsen, Hart, and Nelsen, Anne K. *Black Church in the Sixties*. Lexington, KY: University of Kentucky Press, 1975.

Nichols, J. Randall. "Worship as Anti-Structure: The Contribution of Victor Turner." *Theology Today* 41 (January 1985): 401-409.

Niebuhr, H. Richard. *The Social Sources of Denominationalism*; reprint ed., New York: New American Library, 1975.

Niebuhr, Reinhold. *Moral Man and Immoral Society*. New York: Charles Scribner's Sons, 1937.

O'Dea, Thomas F. *The Sociology of Religion*. Englewood Cliffs, NJ: Prentice-Hall, 1966.

Oates, Stephen B. *Let the Trumpet Sound*. New York: Harper & Row, 1982.

Paris, Peter. *The Social Teaching of the Black Churches*. Philadelphia: Fortress Press, 1985.

Parsons, Talcott. *The Structure of Social Action.* New York: McGraw-Hill, 1937.

Peck, Gary R. "Black Radical Consciousness and the Black Christian Experience: Toward a Critical Sociology of Afro-American Religion." *Sociological Analysis* 43 (1982): 155-69.

Psathas, George, ed. *Phenomenological Sociology.* New York: John Wiley & Sons, 1973.

Reid, Ira De A. *The Negro Immigrant.* Number 449 in the Columbia University studies in history, economics and public law. New York: Columbia University Press, 1939.

_____. "Negro Movements and Messiahs: 1900-1949." *Phylon* 10 (1949): 362-69.

Reist, Benjamin A. *Toward a Theology of Involvement: The Thought of Ernst Troeltsch.* Philadelphia: Westminster Press, 1966.

Roberts, J. Deotis. *Liberation and Reconciliation: A Black Theology.* Philadelphia: The Westminster Press, 1971.

Rooks, Shelby . "The Minister as Change Agent." *The Journal of the Interdenominational Theological Center* 4 (Fall 1977): 12-24.

Shaw, Talbert. "Afro-Americans and Religion: A Propadeutic." *The Journal of Religious Thought* 32 (Spring-Summer 1975): 65-73.

Shils, Edward, and Finch, Henry, eds. *Max Weber on the Methodology of the Social Sciences.* New York: Free Press, 1949.

Shopshire, James M. "A Socio-Historical Characterization of the Black Pentecostal Movement in America." Ph.D. dissertation, Northwestern University, 1975.

Sitkoff, Harvard. *The Struggle for Black Equality: 1954-1980.* New York: Hill and Wang, 1981.

Smart, Ninian. *The Science of Religion and the Sociology of Knowledge.* Princeton: Princeton University Press, 1973.

Smith, F. J. *Phenomenology in Perspective.* The Hague, Netherlands: Martinus Nijhoff, 1970.

Smith, Kelly Miller. *Social Crisis Preaching.* Macon, GA: Mercer University Press, 1984.

Spilka, Bernard; Hood, Ralph W., Jr.; and Gorsuch, Richard l. *The Psychology of Religion: An Empirical Approach.* Englewood Cliffs, NJ: Prentice-Hall, 1985.

Stace, W.T. *Mysticism and Philosophy.* London: Macmillan, 1960.

Staples, Robert. *Introduction to Black Sociology.* New York: McGraw-Hill, 1976.

Stark, Werner. *The Sociology of Knowledge.* Glencoe, IL: Free Press, 1958.

Stewart, David, and Mickunas, Algis. *Exploring Phenomenology.* Chicago: American Library Association, 1974.

Swatos, William H. "The Comparative Method and the Special Vocation of the Sociology of Religion." *Sociological Analysis* 38 (Summer 1977): 106-14.

Taylor, Gardner C. *How Shall They Preach.* Elgin, IL: Progressive Baptist Publishing House, 1977.

Tiryakian, Edward A. "Sociology and Existential Phenomenology." In *Phenomenology & the Social Sciences,* pp. 187-222. Edited by Maurice Nathanson. Evanston: Northwestern University Press, 1973.

Troetsch, Ernst. *Protestantism and Progress: A Historical Study of the Relation of Protestantism to the Modern World.* Translated by W. Montgomery. Boston: Beacon Press, 1958.

Trulear, Harold. "A Critique of Functionalism: Toward a More Holistic Sociology of Afro-American Religion." *The Journal of Religious Thought* 42 (Spring-Summer 1985): 38-50.

_____. *An Analysis of the Formative Roles of Ideational and Social Structures in the Development of Afro-American Religion.* Ann Arbor, MI: University Microfilms International, 1983.

Tuelser, David M. *Black Pastors and Leaders: Memphis, 1819-1972.* Memphis: Memphis State University Press, 1975.

Vining, Elizabeth Gray. *Friend of Life: The Biography of Rufus M. Jones.* New York: J.B. Lippincott Co., 1958.

Wach, Joachim. *The Comparative Study of Religions.* Edited and with an introduction by Joseph M. Kitagawa. New York: Columbia University Press, 1958.

_____. *Sociology of Religion.* Chicago: University of Chicago Press, 1944.

Walker, Alice. *In Search of Our Mothers' Gardens.* New York: Harcourt Brace Jovanovich, 1983.

Wallace, Anthony F.C. "Revitalization Movements." *American Anthropologist* 58 (1956): 264-81.

Walton, Hanes. *The Political Philosophy of Martin Luther King, Jr.* Westport, CT: Greenwood, 1971.

Ward, Hiley H. *Prophet of the Black Nation.* Philadelphia: Pilgrim Press, 1969.

Washington, Joseph. *Black Religion.* Boston: Beacon Press, 1964.

_____. *Black Sects and Cults.* C. Eric Lincoln Series on Black Religion. New York: Anchor Press, 1972.

Weber, Max. *The Protestant Ethic and the Spirit of Capitalism.* Translated by Talcott Parsons. New York: Charles Scribners Sons, 1958.

West, Cornel. *Prophecy Deliverance!: An Afro-American Revolutionary Christianity.* Philadelphia: Westminster Press, 1982.

Williams, Preston N. "Toward a Sociological Understanding of the Black Religious Community." *Soundings* 54 (Fall 1971): 260-70.

Wilmore, Gayraud S. *Black Religion and Black Radicalism.* Revised ed. Maryknoll, NY: Orbis Books, 1983.

_____. "Spirituality and Social Transformation as the Vocation of the Black Church." In *Churches in Struggle: Liberation Theologies and Social Change in North America*, pp. 240-53. Edited by William K. Tabb. New York: Monthly Review Press, 1986.

Wilmore, Gayraud, and James H. Cone. *Black Theology: A Documentary History, 1966-1979.* Maryknoll, NY: Orbis, 1979.

Wilson, Bryan R. *The Noble Savages: The Primitive Origins of Charisma and Its Contemporary Survival.* Berkeley: University of California Press, 1975.

Wilson, John. *Religion in American Society: The Effective Presence.* Englewood Cliffs, NJ: Prentice-Hall, 1978.

Worsley, Peter. *The Trumpet Shall Sound.* New York: Schocken, 1968.

Yinger, J. Milton. *The Scientific Study of Religion.* New York: Macmillan, 1970.

_____. "The Sociology of Religion of Ernst Troeltsch." In *An Introduction to the History of Sociology*, pp. 309-15. Edited by Harry Elmer Barnes. Chicago: University of Chicago Press, 1948.

Zaehner, R.C. *Mysticism: Sacred and Profane*. London: Oxford University Press, 1961.

Index

Martin Luther King, Jr. Memorial Studies
in Religion, Culture and Social Development

This series is named for Martin Luther King, Jr., because of his superb scholarship and eminence in Religion and Society, and is designed to promote excellence in scholarly research and writing in areas that reflect the inter-relatedness of religion and social/cultural/political development both in the American society and in the world. Examination of and elaboration on religion and socio-cultural components such as race relations, economic development, marital and sexual relations, inter-ethnic cooperation, contemporary political problems, women, Black American, Native American, and Third-World issues, and the like are welcomed. Manuscripts submitted must be equal in size to a 200 to 425 page book. Two copies must be submitted.

Mozella G. Mitchell
Religious Studies Department 310 CPR
University of South Florida
Tampa, Florida 33620